What Christian Leaders are Saying about
The Cinderella Challenge

Valson Abraham's leadership in church planting and training pastors is legendary in India. His global influence is increasing daily. It deserves to! I know of no world ministry, strategist, or wise and proven pastor anywhere whose leadership I respect or trust more. I want to affirm the practical and penetrating content of his book *The Cinderella Challenge*. It is a remarkable tool and a dynamic resource—effective to spark vision and target the global passion and pursuits of any sensitive church leader.

—**Jack W. Hayford**
Founding Pastor | The Church on the Way
Chancellor | The King's University

Combining intellect, compassion, and experience—Valson Abraham clearly exposes the serious dangers facing the modern church, the unbelievable suffering of unreached people, and what we must do if we are going to fulfill the Great Commission. This is a must-read for anyone who is serious about evangelism and missions.

—**Jimmy Evans**
Senior Pastor | Trinity Church, Amarillo, Texas
Author and Television Host | Marriage Today

Reading *The Cinderella Challenge* was like being given the privilege of monitoring a graduate class on world missions taught by an articulate, well-informed, and impassioned instructor.

—**Dr. David R. Mains**
Director | Mainstay Ministries

Through his life and testimony, Valson Abraham invites every believer to participate in the joy and responsibility of renewed personal commitment in fulfilling the Great Commission. *The Cinderella Challenge* is a beautiful love story. God is wooing you into action to get involved in the harvest. This book provides powerful insight, answers, and hope.

—John Dawson
President | Youth with a Mission International

The Cinderella Challenge takes a unique approach to worldwide issues. This inspiring and engaging book is a helpful addition to Christian literature.

—Dr. Mark Rutland
President | Oral Roberts University, Tulsa, Oklahoma

Valson Abraham deserves to be heard and read by all who have room in their hearts for a lost world. The ingenious drama of *Cinderella* is brilliantly used to challenge our hearts for the greatest—and perhaps the last—great offensive against darkness and the millions lost in its grip in India and around the world. May this vital word be mightily used to break through that darkness with the light of the gospel of Jesus Christ. This work is strategically thought out and presented simply, directly, and attractively. May the reader experience new fires of compassion and commitment in the reading of this splendid and God-anointed book.

—Jack Taylor
President | Dimensions Ministries, Melbourne, Florida

In his book, *The Cinderella Challenge*, Valson Abraham gives new insights into the church's role to proclaim the gospel of Jesus Christ with global purpose. He takes a familiar fairytale and uses it like a parable to unfold biblical truths for the individual believer and the church to embrace.

—**Pastor Robert Morris**
Senior Pastor | Gateway Church, Southlake, Texas

The Cinderella Challenge, written by Dr. Valson Abraham, is an insightful and inspiring book on the urgency of global Christian missions in the twenty-first century. As a third generation minister, Dr. Abraham is a strategic leader and innovative practitioner of contemporary missionary work. He is comfortable in diverse cultures and understands well the multiple challenges facing today's missions from both eastern and western perspectives. Written for general readers, the curiously named book contains very important biblical, theological, and missiological information useful for pastors and academics. It also contains many practical ideas that can be implemented by individuals, families, and churches. *The Cinderella Challenge* is inspiring reading. A careful reader will agree that its subtitle is aptly worded: Discover God's Beauty and Urgency in Life's Ashes.

—**Thomson K. Mathew, D.Min., Ed.D.**
Dean, School of Theology and Missions | Oral Roberts University, Tulsa, Oklahoma

This book will connect you to the heart, vision, and passion of one of the world's greatest leaders, Valson Abraham. While reading this book you will get acquainted with Valson and his rich heritage of global evangelism, which is a reward in itself; you'll also connect to his global vision, incredible insight into the state of the church, and, most importantly, be motivated to do something about it. Plan on having your world shaken.

—Larry Titus
President | Kingdom Global Ministries

There are but a few books that prompt me to read with a highlighter in hand. There are even fewer that are apt to become a "reference manual" for second or third readings. And then there are those that have so changed or expanded my thinking that I must share copies with friends and fellow Christians. Such is the case with *The Cinderella Challenge* by the Rev. Dr. T. Valson Abraham, a choice and gifted servant of our Lord Jesus Christ who I count as a dear friend, and who has been a frequent radio guest on The Don Kroah Show. I recommend it highly as a must-read for every pastor, Christian leader, and follower of Jesus Christ, as well as a superb resource for any serious study of global missiology.

—**Don Kroah** | Broadcaster, WAVA105.1, Washington, DC
Founder/President | Reach Africa Now, Inc.

As a third-generation Indian evangelist, Valson Abraham is committed to sharing the good news and fulfilling the Great Commission. I appreciate his heart to reach out to the lost through *The Cinderella Challenge*.

—**Frank Pastore**
Radio Host & Author | KKLA 99.5, Glendale, California

Valson Abraham has captured the heart of outreach ministry in his book *The Cinderella Challenge*. He has taken the many years of experience he and his family have touching the world, together with his heart for people, and created a wonderfully crafted message on reaching the world. His approach is very thorough but easily digested. This book is a must-read for every pastor who hungers to touch and change the world. It will be required reading for all of the pastors on my staff.

—Pastor Dan Carroll
Senior Pastor | Water of Life Community Church,
Fontana, California

Valson Abraham takes the well-known story of Cinderella and uses insightful analogies to address every area of missions for the local church. His more than forty years of experience as a missionary, pastor, strategist, and church planter provide a proven roadmap to mobilize people from the pew to taking part in the Great Commission. I highly recommend *The Cinderella Challenge* for every church as a resource and guide for their mission planning.

—Garvin McCarrell
Executive Pastor | New Life Church,
Colorado Springs, Colorado

*The Cinderella Challeng*e is not a fairytale! It is a prophetic call of the Holy Spirit through one of today's most passionate, innovative, and effective mission leaders, calling the church and church leaders to actually *do* the Great Commission. Your questions about the Great Commission, world missions, and the church's responsibility in the world will be answered, and you will find rising in your heart a growing passion to *do* Matthew 28:19–20.

—Pastor Amos Dodge
Senior Pastor | Capital Church, Washington, DC

Dr. Valson Abraham, along with his father and grandfather before him, has devised a marvelous church-planting strategy aimed at establishing a church in every zip code in India. Their highly successful efforts have demanded unusual motivation. Dr. Abraham shows how every Christian can also be motivated by the Great Commission of Jesus Christ. He does so using a novel literary approach that is highly readable and memorable. This volume is well worth your time. Read it.

—**Olan Hendrix**
President | Leadership Resource Group
Co-Founder | Evangelical Council for
Financial Accountability (ECFA)

Dr. Valson Abraham challenges and inspires us as believers to reach this end-time harvest of souls. He helps us to see that the Great Commission is not a suggestion, but a command and a responsibility based upon our love for God and our love for others. God blesses us to be a blessing to this world. God wants to raise every available Christian to move in His compassion and sensitivity and bring others into His truth that can save them and set them free. Time is running out for many. It is time for the body of Christ to reach this world for Jesus!

—**Sharon Daugherty**
Pastor | Victory Christian Center,
Tulsa, Oklahoma

If the final commission of the Lord Jesus Christ is the primary purpose of His Church and the essential responsibility of every Christian, then the index of our faithfulness to Him is rather easily discernible. We answer a simple question: how are we coming in personal and corporate obedience to the Resurrected Commissioner? Except each person and church must answer that question for himself, each congregation for herself. The Cinderella Challenge helps us in the process of self-examination and church-evaluation. Beyond explaining the importance and urgency of obeying the Risen King's Commission by principles, Scriptures, fable, and illustrations, Rev. Dr. Valson Abraham leads us to personal application and practical obedience in both reflection and prayer. I encourage you to visit a subject that refuses to be dismissed from spiritual and eternal considerations, as joyfully serious members of the highly sought, deeply valued, and chosen Bride of the Prince of Heaven.

—**Ramesh Richard ThD, PhD,**
President | Ramesh Richard Evangelism and Church Health (RREACH)
Professor of Global Theological Engagement and
Pastoral Ministries | Dallas Theological Seminary
Founder & Chair | Trainers of Pastors International Coalition (TOPIC)

The
CINDERELLA
CHALLENGE

The
CINDERELLA
CHALLENGE

Discover God's Beauty & Urgency in Life's Ashes

VALSON ABRAHAM

TATE PUBLISHING
AND ENTERPRISES, LLC

This book is designed to provide accurate and authoritative information with regard to the subject matter covered. This information is given with the understanding that neither the author nor Tate Publishing, LLC is engaged in rendering legal, professional advice. Since the details of your situation are fact dependent, you should additionally seek the services of a competent professional.

The opinions expressed by the author are not necessarily those of Tate Publishing, LLC.

Published by Tate Publishing & Enterprises, LLC
127 E. Trade Center Terrace | Mustang, Oklahoma 73064 USA
1.888.361.9473 | www.tatepublishing.com

Tate Publishing is committed to excellence in the publishing industry. The company reflects the philosophy established by the founders, based on Psalm 68:11,
"The Lord gave the word and great was the company of those who published it."

Book design copyright © 2011 by Tate Publishing, LLC. All rights reserved.
Cover design by April Marciszewski
Interior design by Christina Hicks

Published in the United States of America
ISBN: 978-1-61346-103-7
1. Religion / Christian Ministry / Missions
2. Religion / Christian Life / Inspirational
11.09.26

To:

Laly, my wife, co-laborer, and encourager for more than thirty-five years;

and our four children: Sneha, Ann, Asha, and Santosh, who love and serve the Lord;

above all, I thank Jesus Christ, my Lord and Savior, the Lord of glory.

ACKNOWLEDGMENTS

Every author is dependent upon all who are instrumental in molding and shaping his character. In this regard, I thank my parents, Stephen and Mary Abraham; my paternal grandparents, K.E. and Annamma Abraham; my maternal grandparents, P.T. and Annamma Chacko, each of whom modeled a life of strong reliance upon the Word of God and the Holy Spirit. All of their accumulated wisdom has provided for my own growth. The list of others who formed my character in earlier years would grow quite long, and I cannot acknowledge all of them here. I thank God for their influence and rich contribution.

I especially thank my wife, Laly, for her many years of invaluable support. Her unending sacrifice, patience, and encouragement have enabled me to devote myself to ministry, including the development of this book. She has lovingly and faithfully maintained our home and guided our children's development during my long and frequent absences. Our four children, Sneha, Ann, Asha, and Santosh, have also been of great encouragement while they were growing into a maturity of commitment to the Lord's service.

This book began as lectures given several years ago to a graduate class at Biola University in southern California. Afterward,

I used those lectures at many different times, in whole or in part. When I was repeatedly asked for my lecture notes, I gradually conceived the idea of putting those lectures into book form. I realized that the average person in the pew had a need and gravitated to the message. I did not so much want to write a scholarly treatise, but a book to motivate both pastors and laypeople to become involved in Christ's work.

Presenting ideas in oral and written form require very different structures of communication. I want to thank my staff and special friends who helped in my early manuscript development by transcribing tapes, deciphering my handwritten notes, and making several edits. Their service was extremely helpful.

Another key person who greatly helped the book's development is Robert Martin, our staff writer for India Gospel Outreach. Robert has been part of my life and ministry for over thirty years. Our journey together began in a small group while we both were students at Fuller Theological Seminary. I was looking for a story line for the book, and Robert suggested the Cinderella analogy. The more we reviewed the chapters, the more I realized that this would provide many apt analogies. I thank God for the way we have served in ministry together down through the years as friends and co-laborers.

I thank Connie Wise, my office manager for more than twenty years, for helping in more ways I can count. She has tied up so many loose ends as I have traveled, always reminding me of what I need to do so our work does not lose focus.

I am deeply grateful to those who read the manuscript at different stages and offered valuable suggestions and insights: my two older daughters, Sneha and Ann; Dean Owen; Ron Widman; Dr. Mary Ann Lind; Kaj Martin; Michelle Dalton; and Holmes Bryan. Ron Widman also provided invaluable editorial services and designed the book and the cover for our pre-publication copy of this book.

I thank my faithful staff in India and the United States for doing the daily and unseen tasks that are necessary to sustain the ministry and make possible the writing of this book.

The Board of India Gospel Outreach has been a constant support to me in this effort: Mark Mitchell, David Pruitt, David Pletcher, Bill Oostra, and Curtis Nestegard. I have had a close relationship with these faithful men for many years.

Nothing would have been possible apart from the dear friends and faithful prayer warriors who have interceded for us and sustained us through their friendship and support.

Above all, I thank Jesus Christ, my Lord and Savior, the Lord of glory, the name above all other names.

TABLE OF CONTENTS

Foreword..21

The Cinderella Story 25

1. The Cinderella Challenge 31

2. Cinderella, the Prince, and the Glass Slipper 43

3. The Challenge of the Glass Slipper................................ 63

4. Confronting Wickedness 87

5. Between the Cellar and "Happily Ever After"............... 113

6. Three Great Needs, Three Exciting Opportunities!....... 161

7. More Powerful than the Fairy Godmother!.................. 195

8. Divine Connections 223

9. What It's All About.. 245

10. Becoming Part of the Story.. 259

11. What's Keeping You in the Cellar?............................ 281

12. The Urgency of the Night 291

For Further Reading/Bibliography................................ 299

About India Gospel Outreach...................................... 305

This Day, I Commit Myself To:.................................... 309

About the Author Rev. Dr. T. Valson Abraham............... 311

FOREWORD

I met Valson Abraham when he was a student at Fuller Theological Seminary. I learned much about the history of evangelism and missions in India by reading several of Valson Abraham's papers and articles. I also learned much about his own grandfather, K.E. Abraham, who founded the India Pentecostal Church in 1924, with a strong emphasis upon reaching all of India with the gospel.

With the strong Christian heritage of his two grandfathers and his father, Valson Abraham has been used of God to recruit, train, and send thousands of evangelists and pastors who have planted more than twelve thousand churches throughout India. No other Indian Christian leader has a greater and richer heritage on which to build than Valson Abraham.

Through Valson, I was invited to visit the annual conference, which convened in Kumbanad in the state of Kerala. It was astonishing to speak to over thirty thousand people who gathered under the vast tree arbor for the services. On that trip and three others to India, I also visited and spoke at several Bible colleges and institutes, which were founded or supported by Valson Abraham's ministry, India Gospel Outreach.

Over the years, I have kept up with the phenomenal ministry of Valson Abraham and India Gospel Outreach. In every sense, he is a missionary statesman who has contributed to the explosive growth of the church in all parts of India. His vision to plant a church in every one of the twenty-seven thousand zip codes of India is a creative goal that I have every reason to believe will be successful. For many years, it was difficult to build churches in India with more than one hundred members. But today, with vast healing crusades drawing hundreds of thousands of people, great mega-churches have begun to emerge like the great Assembly of God congregation in Madras, with forty thousand members and a church that seats all forty thousand persons.

In his new book, *The Cinderella Challenge*, Valson writes out of over forty years of experience in ministry of preaching and teaching the Word of God, sending and supporting missionaries, founding and supporting Bible colleges, and leading in vast church-planting efforts. Valson's missiological training from Fuller Seminary gave him an unparalleled grasp of the challenges to church growth in India. Out of his forty years of significant leadership have come the wisdom and experience that enlivens every page. Although he is writing from an Indian context, the principles he enunciates so forcefully can be applied to almost all of the mission fields in the world.

The Cinderella Challenge is both simple and profound. Using an allegorical method of teaching, Abraham weaves his missionary principles around the famous story of Cinderella, who was mistreated by her sisters but miraculously chosen by the prince to become his bride. In *The Cinderella Challenge* the Indian outcasts, known as "untouchables" in the West and as Dalits in India, are represented by Cinderella, while the prince is Jesus Christ who chooses his beautiful bride from the neglected and outcasts of society. Though the setting is in India, the story is much the same in the rest of the world. From the stone that the builders rejected, the Lord is putting into place the chief cornerstone, who is Jesus Christ. His bride will be made up of other stones that were also rejected.

I cannot say too much in recommending this book to all Christians, pastors, students, and missiologists who want to know how the Spirit-filled Christians of India are rising up to change that ancient nation.

—**Vinson Synan**
Regent University School of Divinity
September 23, 2010

The Cinderella Story

Once upon a time there was a great king who had an only son, the prince and heir who was about to come of age. So the king summoned all maidens of noble birth to a royal ball, where his highness the prince would select a lady to be his bride and the future queen.

Now, there was among the nobles of the king's court one who had married twice, and by the first marriage he had but one daughter. When his first wife died, the father married again, a lady with two daughters. His new wife, instead of caring for his daughter, thought only of her own and favored them in every way. The noble's daughter was set to do all the drudgery of the house, to attend the kitchen fire, and had naught to sleep on but the heap of cinder raked in the scullery; and that is why they called her Cinder Maid, or Cinderella. No one took pity on her and she would go often to weep at her mother's grave.

One could imagine how excited they all were when they heard about the royal ball, where the prince would choose his bride and future queen.

"What shall we wear, Mother; what shall we wear?" cried out the two daughters, and they all began talking about which dress should suit the one and which dress should suit the other.

But when the father suggested that Cinderella should also have a dress they cried out, "What, Cinderella going to the king's ball? Why, look at her, she would only disgrace us all."

When the night came for the royal ball Cinderella had to help the two sisters dress in their fine gowns and saw them drive off in the carriage with her father and their mother. But she went to her own mother's grave and wept. A fairy godmother saw Cinderella's sorrow and suddenly appeared to her. "Why are you weeping?" she asked.

"Because my two stepsisters have gone to the royal ball, dressed in beautiful gowns and riding in a carriage with my father and stepmother," she replied. "And I cannot go to the ball because I would disgrace them with my shabby dress."

At that, the fairy godmother touched Cinderella's tattered dress with her wand, and it became a beautiful silk gown, blue as the heavens, all embroidered with stars, and two lovely little slippers made of the finest crystal glass.

Then the fairy godmother spied a pumpkin on the ground nearby, and when she touched it with her wand it became a coach with golden trappings. Six tiny mice then caught her eye, and she turned them into four milk-white horses to draw the chariot, and a coachman and footman wearing splendid uniforms all trimmed in gold.

As Cinderella drove away to the royal ball, the fairy godmother called to her: "Be home, be home ere midnight, else again you'll be affright."

When Cinderella entered the ballroom she was the loveliest of all the ladies, and the prince, who had been dancing with her stepsisters, would dance only with her. But as it came toward midnight, Cinderella remembered what the fairy godmother had told her, and slipped away to her carriage. When the prince missed her he went to the guards at the palace door and told them to follow the carriage.

When the prince's soldiers tried to follow Cinderella there came such a mist that they couldn't find which way Cinderella went.

When her father and stepmother and two sisters came home after the ball they could talk of nothing but the lovely lady: "Ah, would not you have liked to have been there?" said the sisters to Cinderella as she helped them to take off their fine dresses. "There was a most lovely lady with a dress like the heavens and slippers of glass, and the prince would dance with none but her. But when midnight came she disappeared and the prince could not find her."

Twice more the prince gave a royal ball, hoping his ladylove would appear. Each time the fairy godmother dressed Cinderella in a fine gown and turned a pumpkin into a chariot and mice into magnificent horses and a coachman and footman.

When Cinderella came to the third ball, she wanted to dance only with the prince and he with her. And so, when midnight came 'round she forgot to leave 'til the clock began to strike: one … two … three … four … five … six … and then she began to run away down the stairs as the clock struck eight … nine … ten. But as she ran, one of her glass slippers slipped from her foot, and just then the clock struck twelve, and the golden coach with its horses and footmen disappeared, and the beautiful dress of Cinderella changed again into her ragged clothes, and she had to run home wearing only one glass slipper.

Now, when the prince learned that his guards could not trace where his ladylove had gone, he showed his father the glass slipper, and told him that he would never marry anyone but the maiden who could wear it. So the king, his father, ordered that whatsoever lady of noble birth could fit the shoe upon her foot shall become the bride of his highness the prince and the future queen. And so the king's herald, accompanied by the prince himself, took the glass slipper to every noble house in the kingdom, searching for the lady whose foot should fit the slipper.

When the herald and the prince came to the house of Cinderella's father, the prince waited outside in his chariot while the herald carried the glass slipper inside. The eldest of Cinderella's two stepsisters tried on the glass slipper, but it was much too small for her, as it was for every other lady who had tried it up to that time.

Then the second sister tried her chance; but her foot was too large for the slipper, too.

The herald asked, "Have you no other daughter?" and the sisters cried out, "No, sir."

But the father said, "Yes, I have another daughter."

And the sisters cried out, "Cinderella, Cinderella, she could not wear that slipper."

But the herald said, "As she is of noble birth she has a right to try the slipper." So the herald went down to the kitchen and found Cinderella.

When she saw her glass slipper she took it from him and put it on her foot, which it fitted exactly; and then she took the other slipper from underneath the cinders where she had hidden it and put that on, too.

Then the herald knew that she was the true bride of his master; and he called for the prince to come inside. And when the prince saw Cinderella's face, he knew that she was the lady of his love. So he took her in his chariot to the palace.

And so they were married and lived happily ever afterward.

Adapted from *The Cinder Maid* by Joseph Jacobs.

Your God is present among you,
A strong Warrior there to save you;
Happy to have you back,
He will calm you with His love,
And delight you with His songs.

Zephaniah 3:17b (The Message)

THE CINDERELLA CHALLENGE

Fiction often has more truth than your daily newspaper. You know the story of Cinderella— the tale of a beautiful young woman consigned by a wicked stepmother to a drab and ugly life. Even so, the young woman experiences an "unveiling," and an entire kingdom discovers her wholesome beauty and value. Overnight she is transformed from pauper to princess. This wonderful story is a favorite of people around the world. Many cultures either know the fairy tale or have their own version of it.

Much of the focus of the story is on Cinderella and the fantastic powers of her fairy godmother, but there would be no story apart from an ardent prince. Except for the prince, Cinderella would have returned to her drab life as a servant in her stepmother's home. When Cinderella leaves her glass slipper at the palace ball, the prince launches an all-out campaign to search the kingdom and find the girl who can wear it. A single person becomes his all-consuming passion. He possesses an urgency he has never had before. He does not stop until he finds her and makes her his own.

When the prince finds Cinderella, he changes her destiny. In a heartbeat, she becomes a member of the royal family. The story of Cinderella has all the elements that make for a great drama: romance, inner beauty and outer ugliness, the conflict between good and evil, the contrast between rich and poor, the triumph of justice, and the overcoming of impossible odds. It has been the plot line for countless movies and novels.

This is a book about fulfilling Jesus' Great Commission. You may ask why I chose the story of Cinderella to convey biblical truths about missions. The reason is very simple. Most of the Bible is written, not in platitudes or as ideas, but in narrative form. It is filled with biography, stories, graphic images, and metaphors. The great majority of Jesus's teachings and the gospels themselves come as narratives. Jesus's favorite form of teaching is parables. Most of the Sermon on the Mount is filled with images, metaphors, and stories. Whether we are young or old, we gravitate toward stories even as Jesus's stories attracted people of all ages.

Too often, the Great Commission has been promoted in obscure, abstract language. That was never Jesus's intent. Jesus encapsulates the gospel in such parables as the Prodigal Son, the Lost Coin, and the Lost Sheep. Shouldn't this become our example as we try to understand the Great Commission with new eyes?

As we shall see, the story of Cinderella has many facets analogous to the Great Commission of Jesus Christ: "Go into all the world and preach the gospel to every creature" (Mark 16:15). The story presents a wonderful analogy of what has happened to the cause of missions in our lifetimes and what *might* happen. The story of Cinderella is being played out before our eyes in many ways. We all have a part in the drama, for good or for evil. That drama will ultimately impact everything we know and do.

While Cinderella is not a real-life story, *it does reflect real life because its values are largely Christian in nature. How you perceive the story's values determines your response to it.*

———◆◆◆———

I think you would agree that there are some very dysfunctional people in the story of Cinderella. Specifically, I speak of the wicked stepmother and her perverse daughters who did everything they could to slander Cinderella and reduce her to the role of a slave in spite of her good birth and character. Overcoming their selfish ways presents a challenge to Cinderella that she could not do on her own.

Today, a sickness in missions affects most churches in the West and many churches beyond. It is more pernicious and far-reaching than anything Cinderella had to endure. It is a clever "syndrome," if you will, of lies from the enemy, Satan, blighting the minds and hearts even of God's people. For the most part, God's people are unaware and asleep as Satan quietly and craftily tries to rob us of our heritage and mandate.

Satan is the wicked stepmother we all face. He will use every trick in his mighty arsenal of tricks to keep us in the cellar and separate us from our birthright as children of the heavenly King. Satan intends to obscure, limit, and slander Jesus Christ and His Great Commission. He wants to turn Christians everywhere into lukewarm believers afflicted with spiritual myopia and confused priorities. He wants to rob us of the joy of working alongside our loving heavenly Father. He wants to turn the Great Commission into a caricature and a laughingstock because its success means the end of his illegitimate rule and that of his "wicked step-daughters" and partners, the fallen angels and demons.

Wherever they live, few believers fully escape the effects of this syndrome of lies from the enemy. *We must bring the truth out of the cellar so that we can live free in Christ and His Great Commission.* As we shall see, Jesus gave us the Great Commission, not to burden us but to free us and help us live in good spiritual health, joy, and celebration.

I had the rare privilege of being born into a strong Christian family in India, a nation that few people would regard as Christian. My parents, maternal and paternal grandparents, and I have devoted our lives to fulfilling the Great Commission in India. Today, missions are booming in our fellowship in India as young men and women gladly respond to God's call upon their lives. Some come from Christian backgrounds, but many others came to Christ out of Hinduism, Islam, Buddhism, and Sikhism. They have come out of the cellar of Satan's deception. They have put on the glass slipper and found their divinely ordained place in the kingdom. They rejoice in the gospel. They expect—and see—great victories from the hand of God. As a result, they are experiencing great joy and celebration as they experience king-dom life as their King's rightful heirs. So I write this book not as a book of theory but as a work based upon my own family experience and the experiences of a growing number of Indian evangelists and church planters whom we have trained and sent.

I mention my own experience because our perceptions of missions are often based upon emotions and unconscious cultural assumptions, inadequate experience, and lack of biblical considerations. This can be true, even if a person is a Christian. It happens in the West and in mainstream churches outside the West. Spiritual myopia is a universal problem. Most people do not realize that Satan is covering their eyes. Tragically, most people live in the cellar and don't even know it.

I bring up the story of Cinderella because it includes many analogies that can help us see the sickness that prevails in so many churches and in so many places. I use this familiar children's story to visualize biblical truth and to do something to restore the beauty and joy of the Great Commission that our Savior always intended.

Numerous emotions and experiences have unconsciously affected the response that many people have to missions:

- *I can't handle a culture or customs other than my own.* If Cinderella had felt this way, she would never have gone to the ball.

- *I don't want to get involved with backward people.* If the fairy godmother had looked only at Cinderella's outward appearance, Cinderella would never have received the help she needed.

- *Pursuit of the Great Commission will interrupt or ruin my life. I am afraid of God's "call" on my life.* If Cinderella had felt this way, she would never have tried on the slipper when it arrived at her doorstep.

- *Missionary life seems boring, and missionaries don't seem to have much charisma. They definitely are out of touch with today's society and fashions: misfits, narrow-minded, and provincial in their thinking.* If the prince had felt this way, he never would have allowed a servant girl who cleaned the cinders from a fireplace to try on a glass slipper.

- *Being a missionary is totally irrelevant to my life. Mission work just isn't "my thing," so why bother with it?* When people are relegated to the cellars of life for time and eternity, it should become the "thing" of every believing Christian. Otherwise, we unwittingly collaborate in their imprisonment even as Cinderella's stepmother and stepsisters collaborated in her imprisonment.

- *I see too many problems in my own life, my own family, and my own society to get involved in anything else.* When we are hurting deeply from emotional dysfunctions in our personal lives, families, and society, we don't care about Cinderella's problems or anyone else's.

Cinderella was a treasure. But as long as she was kept in the cellar, out of sight and out of mind, she didn't have a chance to show her beauty and worth as a person, and to better her conditions.

All these common responses to missions are strong indications that the full beauty of the Great Commission remains out of sight and out of mind for most people in our churches. This is the challenge we face here: to bring the Great Commission "out of the cellar" for all to see and to become renewed in amazement at God's wondrous ways. When we see the truth, we will gladly get involved. It will not be a burden, but a joy.

Misperception and Misplaced Priority. Consider Cinderella's position. She was under the domination of a wicked stepmother who made sure she was kept out of sight, burdened with mundane chores. The wicked stepmother promoted her own daughters, who could never match Cinderella's beauty or goodness. Ultimately, the wicked stepmother feared that if Cinderella was discovered to be the rightful heir of her father's estate, the step-mother and her daughters would be undone and thrown aside. In truth, had the stepmother promoted Cinderella and loved her dearly instead of relegating her to the cellar, she and her stepsisters would likely have played roles of greater importance in the kingdom after Cinderella became princess and later, queen. The stepmother was undermining the very person she should have been promoting.

Who has lied in a similar way to the church about the role of missions? Satan. For Satan, the fulfillment of missions is the fulfillment of the kingdom of God. The fulfillment of the kingdom of God means the end of Satan's kingdom.

To protect his interests, Satan has done a fairly good job of hiding the true beauty and goodness of the Great Commission, portraying missions as a drab and uninviting task. Missions are often relegated to the bottom of the giving heap—a position that cries, "We will gladly support missions … if we have anything left over after all other bills have been paid." Missions are often regarded as unimportant, without enough marketing appeal, and are therefore kept out of the lineup of sermon topics and special meetings. Satan has done his best to keep the church from acting on countless missions opportunities, while allowing more mundane programs to be dolled up and promoted.

In truth, a church that is not in pursuit of full promotion of missions is a church that has set aside the number-one priority established by Jesus for His church! It is a church that has promoted secondary "stepchildren" programs into a top position, where they drain the majority of a church's time, talent, and treasure.

Some churches claim, "Missions are important—there are just other things more important right now." According to whom? As we shall soon see, Jesus doesn't think this way. Is Jesus wrong? Or are we, like the stepmother, keeping Jesus's priorities "in the cellar" to fulfill our own agendas? If we allow Jesus's priorities to come "out of the cellar" to have their due (like Cinderella at the ball), we may be more pleasantly surprised than we imagine at the stunning beauty that Christ invites us to meet in His Great Commission. Satan's lies will be put to flight, because lies cannot stand against the revealed truth of God.

A Loving Prince and an Intervening Rescuer. Just as

Cinderella was subject to the will of the prince, so the church and missions are subject to a divine prince, the Lord Jesus Christ. And just as Cinderella relied on a fairy godmother with powers greater than hers, so missions relies on the power of the Holy Spirit for its ultimate presentation and promotion.

The prince is relentless in his search for Cinderella. Jesus Christ is relentless in His efforts to seek out those who are lost.

The prince has a single glass slipper as a clue to help him identify his beloved and make her a part of his family. In similar fashion, Jesus has an established means to identify those who will enter His royal family—belief in His life, death and resurrection, and acknowledgment of Jesus as the Son of God.

The prince is aided by a faithful servant who traverses every corner of the kingdom to find the young woman whose foot can wear the glass slipper. Jesus also has His servants who take the good news to every person, giving all a chance to accept what Jesus offers to gain release from the curse of sin. The difference is that any person who chooses to accept Jesus as the prince is automatically capable of wearing the glass slipper He offers.

The Holy Spirit actively works throughout the process—with powers far greater than those of a fairy godmother. He pre-

The Urgent Call

1. What are the most common statements you hear regarding missions? How would Jesus respond to these statements?

2. Does your church have any higher priority than reaching lost souls? If so, what is it? What Scriptural justification do you have for that priority?

3. Have you ever considered the possibility of missions work for your own life?

pares the hearts and lives of those who will accept Christ. He allows for them to encounter the prince, even arranging all of the details so that the person will hear the gospel and respond to it. The Holy Spirit provides opportunity to accept Jesus as Savior, and to become part of the bride of Christ. What we as human beings are incapable of doing for ourselves, the Holy Spirit does on our behalf as we humbly yield our lives to His greater plans and purposes.

The Relentless Search. The prince saw something very beautiful and special in Cinderella that led him to search so relentlessly for her throughout his kingdom.

What eternally beautiful and special qualities does Jesus see that leads Him to search so relentlessly for us and for others in every place on the globe? What makes each person so precious in His sight that He asks each of us to get involved in seeking them out as His princess, His bride? Ultimately, this is our challenge: to see the Great Commission as Jesus Christ sees it. Therein lies our hope—and the hope of an entire world.

What Might One Person Do?

Re-evaluate your opinions about missions and missionaries. Are missionaries obsolete, irrelevant, or unnecessary? Do your opinions line up with God's Word?

Heavenly Father, I confess that I am more deceived by Satan's ways than I can possibly know, and that he is keeping me in the cellar by ways I cannot imagine at this point. Open my eyes to the truth that sets me free to live the life you have intended for me from before the beginning of time. Open my eyes to the loving and compassionate way You see the world and the way You take the initiative to save lost souls from Satan's cellar as you have saved us. Apart from Your glory

and love, missions would not even exist. Help me to love and worship You as I ought so that I may experience every good thing You have for me. Open my mind to the possibilities that You have for my life. Help me to see missions as You see missions! I ask this in Your name and for Your glory, Amen.

Jesus said, "The Son of Man has come to seek and to save that which was lost."

Luke 19:10

CINDERELLA, THE PRINCE, AND THE GLASS SLIPPER

After Cinderella runs from the ball, the prince of the land seeks her. He loves her for her unique beauty and character. He decides to comb his entire kingdom to find her. He will do anything—pay any price—to make her his own. He has a sense of urgency about the opportunity before him, surging feelings of joy and love, and a deep and abiding confidence that he will ultimately find her. He longs for her with mixed feelings of desperation, expectation, and hope. He must find her. For him, every moment counts, and he begins his search without delay.

This search resembles Jesus and His desire and urgency toward us, and toward all people. In fact, we see this sense of urgency and desire all through the Gospels in Jesus's miracles and in His words to His followers. The Great Commission has become a statement of "last words" from Jesus; but in truth, the spirit of the Great Commission is found throughout the Gospels. In Matthew, Mark, Luke, and John we see an urgency in Jesus's words and actions—a seizing of every opportunity, a joy and a love, a deep confidence, a longing for the lost that is coupled with great hope and expectation. For Jesus, every moment counts.

The Urgency of Opportunity

A number of Jesus's parables are marked by a sense of deep urgency at finding His lost loved ones. Consider, for example, Jesus's parable about the harvest from the vineyard.

> [Jesus said to them,] But what do you think? A man had two sons, and he came to the first and said, "Son, go, work today in my vineyard.'" He answered and said, "I will not," but afterward he regretted it and went. Then he came to the second and said likewise. And he answered and said, "I'll go, sir," but he did not go. "Which of the two did the will of his father?"
>
> They said to Him, "The first."
>
> Jesus said to them, "Assuredly, I say to you that tax collectors and harlots enter the kingdom of God before you. For John came to you in the way of righteousness, and you did not believe him; but tax collectors and harlots believed him; and when you saw it, you did not afterward relent and believe him."
>
> (Matthew 21:28–32).

During Jesus's day, the harvest provided:

- food and provisions;
- Income for the family—meeting of material necessities of life, including payment for or improvements on a home, clothing, items for the home, entertainment, travel, and comfort. The bigger the harvest, the bigger the income and the more good things a family might enjoy;
- Pleasure—aesthetic enjoyment of grapes on the table, wine, grape juice, good fellowship, and prosperity for the family;
- Income for the workers of the harvest;
- Gleanings for the poor;
- Blessings for the fabric of society. The whole community benefited from a good harvest. In this amazing passage, Jesus even sees beauty in the tax collector and harlot, two despised people of that day. Even society's lowest are included in the blessings of the harvest. The harvest does not excuse the sin but redeems the sinner. This resembles our Cinderella analogy in the fact that although we wear the cinders of sin, that does not exclude us from God's intent to lavish us with the dress of the heavens and the glass slippers of blessings beyond our power to imagine.

All good benefits for the vineyard owner depended upon a prompt picking of the grapes. If the vineyard owner waited too long, he could lose the entire harvest. He had to act immediately when the grapes became ripe. They possessed urgency for the task.

In Kerala, India, one of the main agricultural crops is coconuts from palm trees. Coconuts do not require the same urgency as grapes. Grapes must be harvested immediately upon ripening; otherwise, they will drop from the vine and rot or develop mildew on the vine.

The people to whom Jesus told this parable would have known from experience the urgency of harvesting grapes, as well as other tree and vine harvests in the region. Much of their lives likely depended upon a successful harvest of Israel's vineyards and orchards.

Throughout the Bible, an abundant crop is considered a sign of God's favor. The principle is very direct: harvest the massive crop that God has provided, and experience the favor of God. A harvest is hard work, but it has the built-in motivator of tremendous reward. Those motivated by the benefits of the harvest are willing to put in long hours of backbreaking labor under a hot sun. Such temporary discomforts pale in comparison to the great joy of the rewards. To the farmer willing to put up with temporary discomfort, those rewards are like the prince's royal ball in their effects of providing plenty and prosperity. Those who failed to accommodate the temporary discomforts, or who refused to participate in the harvest, risked missing out on the harvest's rewards, and possibly becoming beggars, subject to the whims of fate and the generosity of others.

The planting of vineyards and their harvests were considered so important that the planter and owner of a vineyard were exempt from military service (see Deuteronomy 20:6).

The harvest that Jesus has in mind is a harvest of souls. As in the case of grape harvests, timing is critical. The rewards of the harvest are easily seen: our nourishment, well-being, pleasure and enjoyment of life, provision for others, care for the poor, and fellowship with other people. Jesus urgently calls us to engage in the harvest so we might enjoy the blessings of the harvest. A harvest of souls benefits all who participate in that harvest, in all areas of life. A harvest of souls leads many out of the cellar to experience their birthright as children of the King.

Consider a place like India, with the largest concentration of unreached people groups in the world—the biggest harvest field of all. India has more Hindus than any other nation. If you want to reach the Muslim world, come to India, the world's third largest Muslim nation after Indonesia and Pakistan. Indians make up the world's second largest concentration of immigrant population: about thirty million. Millions of Indians live and work in the Middle East. The concentration of Indian Sikhs in Canada is becoming so great that Punjabi is about to become the fourth largest language group in the country. We must constantly export evangelists to keep up with this growing overseas Indian population. My point is this—the bigger the harvest field, the greater the potential for harvest. Think of the celebration that can take place in the presence of our King and heavenly Father.

Urgency of Reaching the Young. The prince knew that such an eligible and beautiful young woman like Cinderella would not likely remain open to marrying him forever. He knew he must find her immediately, before she became committed to someone else.

Eighty-five percent of those who come to know Jesus make that decision by age eighteen. Ninety percent of those who come to Christ before age eighteen actually come to Christ before age twelve. If we don't win children and teenagers to Christ, their minds and hearts have a strong tendency to harden to the point that they will not accept Christ later. We must, as my mentor and professor at Fuller Theological Seminary, the late Donald McGavran, has said, "Win the winnable while they are winnable."

If we neglect to win this generation to Christ, who will win the generation that follows them? We must go to work in the vineyard now!

Many times, that vineyard arrives at our own doorstep. Did you know that India has sent more university students to the United States than any other country since 2004? Each year, the United States trains one hundred and fifty thousand Indians and Chinese to lead companies in their homelands. What are we doing to reach them?

First, the ripeness of the vineyard determines the urgency of the harvest, not the "ripeness" of our emotions or desires. We are not to go "when it pleases us," but rather, today.

Second, the harvest begins in response to a command from the vineyard owner—in the case of the parable and in our case today, God the Father. God's vineyard includes the entire world. In every area of the globe, we find some form of harvest that is ripe and in need of reaping.

Third, delayed obedience is still disobedience. The harvest of vineyards and of people requires strict adherence to the vineyard owner's timing to maximize the harvest's good quality. Delayed obedience to the vineyard owner may still result in a harvest but an inferior one that unnecessarily fails to match the vineyard owner's intent.

Fourth, full care of a vineyard and preparation for a harvest require a sequence of prescribed tasks. They begin with the preparation of the ground. This included moving away rocks and cultivating the soil close to the vines. It required seasons of planting, pruning, and supporting the growing branches. A hedge or wall is usually constructed around vineyards to protect the vines and harvest from wild animals. Additionally, a watchtower was erected in the past to protect against thieves.

Our involvement in a harvest can come at any point in that harvest, from initial ground clearing, to planting, to cultivating, to reaping. All aspects of a harvest must come in place, and in proper order, for the harvest to reach maximum level. Harvesting is the end phase of a long process.

Fifth, harvest time is marked by great joy. In another teaching moment, Jesus spoke of a harvest field "white unto harvest." He not only noted the urgency of this harvest, described in John 4:35, but He said, "Both he who sows, and he who reaps may rejoice together." All who participate in an eventual harvest will experience the rewards of that harvest.

We are not to be urgent out of desperation, but as a joyful, heart-leaping response to opportunities. Think of the prince. He was so smitten with Cinderella, he did not waste a moment to seek her out. He could not imagine living life without her. He knew that she was utterly unique in her beauty and character. He anticipated the great joy he would experience once he found her. He valued her as much as his own flesh and blood. These are things that motivated him to immediate action.

Sixth, harvests come with different levels of reward. As much as a "hundredfold" return was promised by Jesus in Matthew 19:27–29.

Seventh, harvests often are "ripe" in unexpected places. In speaking to a Samaritan woman by a well, Jesus told His disciples, "Lift up your eyes and look at the fields, for they are already white for harvest" (John 4:35b). Jesus was likely referring to the white-robed people who were coming out of the nearby gates of the Samaritan city of Sychar. He likened them to a glistening white-for-harvest grain field. The Samaritans, however, were not at all a "likely" harvest for Jesus's Jewish disciples. The disciples and all other Jews tended to regard the Samaritans as inferiors. Jesus was saying that to hold this negative attitude was to miss out on a blessing!

We have to think "outside the box" like the prince. Ordinary thinking would not place a future princess and queen of the realm in the scullery. Fortunately, the prince left no stone unturned, knowing that life is complex, and that there is much that is not as it appears on the surface. In God's sight, this is even truer. Every day, we pass hundreds of potential princes and princesses for God's kingdom, and we don't give them a thought. Sometimes we even forget our own birthright and get caught up in thoughts far below our calling as members of God's royal family.

Think about those who get even lesser attention than those we pass on the street—people unknown to us but beloved of God from before time began. He has given them their birthright no less than He has given us ours. We have many unexpected opportunities in our world to make a difference in these people's lives, several being in the so-called 10/40 window: the area of Africa and Asia between the tenth and fortieth-parallels north of the equator. More than three billion people live there—almost half the world's population. In the 10/40 window live 82 percent of the world's poorest people; twenty-three countries with an annual per capita gross national product of less than $500; twenty-nine countries with the lowest quality of life. Forgotten and lowly people by the world's standards, yet people, precious in God's sight, who receive only 3 percent of the church's global efforts.

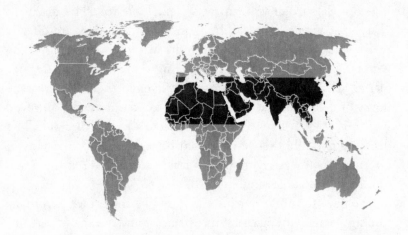

The 10/40 Window

Throughout His ministry, Jesus taught His followers to *expect the unexpected*. Jesus gave attention to the prostitutes, tax collectors, and political zealots—the troublemakers and sinners of His day. These were "in the cellar" people whom God had eternally loved as His children and wanted them back home where they belonged. Many of these disfranchised, overlooked people became His followers and disciples. In speaking to us today, Jesus most likely would say, "Don't exclude anyone from consideration—gang members, drug dealers, terrorists, or thieves."

For example, one of our effective evangelists in the state of Gujarat, India, was a thief and gang leader before he accepted Jesus as his Savior. Two of my friends were once drug dealers and criminals, whose lives Jesus Christ completely changed. With God all things truly are possible (Luke 18:27).

The Quality of the Harvest

Jesus is interested not only in the souls and lives of others; as He brings them out of the cellar and into His palace, He also wants to give us excitement and joy as we participate with Him in the process of transforming lives. Our participation in the harvest is a sign of God's love for the world and for us as well. It is a way of bringing us out of the drabness of our own lives, even as searching for Cinderella would bring the prince out of his lonely state. What will be accomplished by the harvest? What will the harvest be?

A harvest is measured by two things: quantity and quality. Jesus desires that all people become part of His kingdom. He also speaks of a "quality factor" for the harvest.

The "people harvest" to whom Jesus calls us is first and foremost a harvest of "saved souls" (John 3:16). It is a harvest of people who experience forgiveness, freedom from guilt and shame, and the assurance of eternal life, not condemnation.

Jesus also promises many other benefits to those who follow Him. Those who turn to Jesus become people who will reflect a very high quality of new life. They are people who:

- Live by the Word of God, and experience all the promises of God (Matthew 4:4)
- Live in light (Matthew 4:16)
- Live blessed lives (Matthew 5:3–12)
- Live as salt and light in a decaying and dark world (Matthew 5:13–16)

- Experience heaven on earth (Matthew 6:10)
- Have fruitful lives (Matthew 7:15–20)
- Manifest wisdom in the way they live (Matthew 7:24–25)
- Experience God's healing, cleansing, resurrection, and deliverance (Matthew 10:5–10)
- See greatness in serving (Mark 10:35–44)
- Experience healing of broken hearts, liberty, sight, freedom from oppression, and the deep joy of God's rule and blessing (Luke 4:18–19)
- Extend mercy to those in need (Luke 10:37)
- Are fully restored to God their Father (Luke 15)
- Experience a transformed life, rising above their circumstances (John 4)
- Do great things even as Jesus did (John 14:12)

Think of a society filled with these kinds of people. Think of them living in and changing their communities. The Welsh revival of 1905 was marked by a change in the character and activities of entire communities. This was also true of the revival that swept across the "Bible belt" states of the United States in the first few decades of the twentieth century. Similarly, we are seeing dramatic changes in entire communities in various areas of India today.

Think of an entire world made up of people who reflect these "harvest qualities." What a joyful place this world would become!

The Holy Spirit is already working in the lives of millions around the world. They are just waiting to be harvested. The fruit is already ripe. What are *you* waiting for? Today is the day to get out there and begin to experience the tremendous joy that comes from being a participant in the harvest! Think of how you will feel when you know that you have participated in this, in the power of God Himself! Cinderella's dance with the prince has no comparison to it.

Becoming part of Christ's harvest team is a way of experiencing heaven on earth, and helping others to have the same experience. In Christ, we really can wear glass slippers and the dress of the heavens of God's transforming power and enable others to do the same!

> When love and skill work together, expect a masterpiece.
>
> —John Ruskin

Urgency as a Matter of Confidence

Cinderella must have experienced a sense of urgency as she discovered the prince's interest in her. She had full confidence that life with him would transform her drab existence, and she knew she had to win his heart quickly before some other young woman succeeded in doing so.

We sometimes hear of people voting "no confidence" in a particular leader. Some governments are structured so that a no-confidence vote signals the need for elections to select new leadership.

What is your vote regarding "confidence" in Jesus as the prince, the Lord of the harvest?

Throughout the Gospels, Jesus makes certain claims about Himself. He has no doubts about who He is, or the capabilities He has. He refers to Himself as the Good Shepherd, the Bread of Life, Light of the World, the Door, the Resurrection and Life. Jesus said that He is the Way, the Truth, and the Life. He called Himself the True Vine. All of these are metaphors for the work of Jesus in the life of each person who turns to Him.

The question is not whether Jesus is capable of transforming lives, but whether you have full confidence that He can and does transform lives, and that He can use what you do as part of His process.

Do we really believe that people are worth loving as Jesus says they are? If so, we will have a sense of urgency to reach them in Jesus's name.

Do we really believe Jesus can do what He said He would do? Do we really believe the world—right now—is ripe unto harvest for the gospel? If so, then what are we waiting for?

The prince also had full confidence that once he found Cinderella, his life and the life of the kingdom would change for the better. He had the guarantee of his father, the king. That moved the prince to spare no effort in finding her and to make that effort immediately. Cinderella had full confidence that wearing the glass slipper would make her a princess.

Do we have full confidence in God to change our earthly lives and eternal destinies? Do we have confidence that God's power to change other people's earthly lives and eternal destinies will also change our own lives for the better?

The great missionary to India, William Carey, once said, "Expect great things from God. Attempt great things for God." Like the prince, our ability to attempt great things depends upon our ability to expect great things, to demonstrate our confidence in our King's faithfulness.

There is the belief of the lips—of giving attitudinal assent and even verbal assent to what Jesus commands us to do. There is also the belief of action—of "putting our money where our mouth is" and getting busy in our sharing of the gospel. *Acting* in faith counts.

In the Bible, the word "belief" means "to put one's trust in another." It refers to acting on the basis of where and in whom we put our trust. The word "belief" is never merely a conceptual principle or intellectual idea. The word is used ninety times in the Gospel of John alone as a word of action.

Remember the urgency of the four friends who had enough confidence in Jesus that they were willing to risk the ire of a house owner and the highest religious leaders to remove a roof and lower their paralyzed friend into their midst so Jesus could heal him. Their belief led to action and to healing for their friend.

Do you really trust Jesus's words to the point where you are willing to *act* in your sacrificial giving to those who go, or to use your own talents and abilities in the way that God directs *you* to participate personally in the harvest?

For you truly to have maximum belief—born of trust and with full confidence in Christ Jesus—you must have a sense that Jesus is the only way to the Father. Jesus was convinced only He alone could accomplish the task. He said, "No one comes to the Father except through me" (John 14:6b). Do you believe that? Do you believe it to the point of acting on it?

Imminent Danger

There was another reason why the prince could have felt urgency in finding Cinderella: he had no guarantee that Cinderella would be there tomorrow. For all he knew, he might be in danger of actually losing her altogether.

Do you really believe that being lost for eternity is life's ultimate danger?

The urgency of Jesus is expressed at times in His teachings as an urgency born out of awareness that people are in grave danger. More than anyone who has ever lived, Jesus knew the power of Satan and the designs of Satan on human beings. He loved people with a desperate desire that they be rescued from the snares of the enemy—that they be delivered from the devil who sought to steal, kill, and destroy them (John 10:10).

Jesus saw that people were like sheep without a shepherd (Mark 6:34). They had no shelter, no protection, and no guidance. They were subject to attack by wolves, following each other over cliffs, getting lost or getting caught in brambles. He saw that if their wool grew and was not cut—they would not be part of a process of prosperity, but rather, their unharvested wool would lead to their downfall. Unshorn wool can make a sheep heavy to the point that if it topples over, it cannot get up, and if it falls into water, it will drown. Jesus saw that people were in immediate danger of being injured and dying.

What urgency do you feel over your child lost in a store? Like all people who have lost their children, you become desperate. Your child is alone, helpless, unprotected, and possibly in danger from unknown predators. What is worse, your child may not even know he or she is in danger.

Do you feel what Jesus felt for the lost? Do you have the same sense of desperation that people are in grave danger apart from the saving, protecting, and providing power of Christ?

Urgency and Hope of Christ's Coming

The prince urgently looked for Cinderella because of his deep hope that finding her would give him more happiness than he had ever known in his life from any other human being.

There is also an urgency born out of the hope that Christ Jesus is coming again soon! Jesus spoke of this urgency in Matthew 24–25, Mark 13, and Luke 17, 21.

Many Christians need to recapture the truth of Jesus's second coming. There are more references and prophecies regarding His second coming than of His first coming. Just as assuredly as He came the first time in fulfillment of the prophecies about His birth, He will *come again* in fulfillment of the prophecies about His return. True followers of Jesus Christ see Christ's second coming as the hope of the world and long for it.

Many of those prophecies of His second coming have already been fulfilled, especially regarding Israel. Most of the prophecies about the church and the world have been fulfilled. The major prophecy yet remaining to be fulfilled is the proclamation of the gospel.

Jesus has given us the key to His second coming—the proclamation of the gospel. Will we use that key? Will we join Christ in His work?

Be aware of the signs of His coming (Luke 12:54–56). Know that it will take place whether we get involved or not.

The one thing we know about the timing of Christ's return is that we do not know when it will take place. Expectant people get busy and get to work sharing the gospel, sensing they are working against an unknown but very real deadline. Expectant people act in ways that indicate their expectancy, gathering in the harvest from every tongue, tribe, and nation. When that gathering is complete from God's perspective—not man's—Jesus will come again.

The Urgent Call

1. Have you ever participated in a harvest of some type? What was that experience like? What were the results?

2. Are you more motivated by rewards and opportunities, or by threats and avoidance of danger?

3. Do you believe Jesus is coming soon? Why or why not? How does this impact your concern for lost souls?

At that time, Jesus will judge the nations and separate the sheep from the goats—that is, those who have believed from those who haven't. He will reward those who treated others as if they were treating Jesus Himself. He will reward those who offered the salvation and love that Jesus offered. He will reward those who acted in Jesus's name to accomplish what Jesus wanted done. The reward will be eternal life. Eternal life is a *quality* of life, not only unending but infinitely better. Eternal life is perfection. It is the culmination of the harvest, the enjoyment of its fruits.

When Jesus talked of judgment, He did not prejudge, nor did He threaten hellfire and brimstone. The Gospels tell us clearly that the Son of God did not come to destroy lives but to save them (Luke 9:55–56). He did not come to condemn, but rather that the world through Him might be saved (John 3:17). Jesus stated very clearly that there was great opportunity for many to be saved, from every culture and nation of the world. Jesus's prayer in John 17 is a great prayer of anticipation: Jesus is looking forward to coming generations that would follow Him and become part of the great harvest, though they never saw Him or personally witnessed His miracles. In Matthew 24, we read that Jesus envisioned a vast multitude of peoples from every tongue, tribe, and nation in the kingdom of God.

With certainty we can know at the close of each day that we are one day closer to the coming of Christ. The question we must ask ourselves is: what did I do today to prepare myself and to reach others with the gospel, so that I and others can be at a state of "maximum readiness" for Jesus's return?

To obey Jesus is to have Jesus's urgency to reach souls before the deadline that only God the Father knows.

Certainly that day is coming. Jesus was very clear on that point. He said, "I must work the works of Him who sent me while it is day; the night is coming when no one can work" (John 9:4).

There is a limited time in which we can accomplish all the work that God requires. God gives each of us a task to do. We are to discover it and do it!

Let me assure you of two things.

First, there is still plenty for you to do. In His earthly ministry, Jesus by Himself did much, but He did not heal everybody or save everybody all at once. He had His bodily limitations just as we do. Just as God had work for Jesus, God has work for you. He knows your limitations and He knows the length of your days. He can maximize all of your talents and all of your times. Jesus lived only thirty-three years, but look what He did!

Just as Jesus had limited time to accomplish His task, we have limited time to accomplish ours. We are limited by our mortality. But when we rely upon Him, our mortality need not be a burden. Whether our lives are long or short, we can accomplish exactly what God intends for us to accomplish as long as we trust Him.

Second, God will help you do whatever He calls you to do. Jesus's great accomplishments came from reliance upon His heavenly Father to work through Him. Jesus invites us to take His yoke upon us, but

He also says that His yoke is easy and His burden light (Matthew 11:25–30). Do not let the size of any task discourage you.

Focus upon this day before you and seek out the opportunities that God puts in your path. These are your opportunities to trust Him and work in partnership with Him to accomplish great and mighty things.

What If the Harvest Isn't Harvested?

As he looked for Cinderella, the prince must have had a deep, underlying fear: what if he never found her? What if, after his painstaking search, he missed her completely?

Consider the grim possibilities if we do not gather the harvest. Individual souls go into eternity without a Savior. Families and entire communities lose out. Lifestyles are constricted. People become victims of their circumstances. Many become beggars, dependent upon others who do not have their best interests at heart. The poor go hungry. People suffer widespread lack of joy, lack of purpose, and lack of hope. There is also widespread lack of food and energy. Every society of the world becomes even more troubled.

If we fail to win the lost, we lose a generation of young people. Time and again Israel fell into dire straits because the people lost their sense of God's presence and power. As a people and a nation, we also can lose God's protection and provision if we lose our focus upon God.

Jesus also spoke of a spiritual "loss" to the person who does not do everything possible to extend the kingdom of God. In what is often called the "parable of the talents," Jesus told of a man who called his servants and delivered his goods to them before traveling to a far country. To one of his servants he gave five talents, to another, two talents, and to a third, one talent. When he returned, he found that the five-talent and two-talent servants had both doubled what had been left in their stewardship. The one-talent servant, however, had done nothing. In fear, he had hidden the talent in the ground. The master of these servants said to this one-talent man, "You wicked and lazy servant," and then he ordered that the talent be taken from him and that he be cast into "the outer darkness" where there is "weeping and gnashing of teeth" (Matthew 25:14–30).

When a person fails to enter the harvest field and use his God-given talents and abilities to win souls, judgment comes upon that person. This is not a threat from God; it is a simple statement of consequences.

A friend once said to me, "We're having a great party next weekend. If you don't come, you will really miss something wonderful." I believe that's the attitude that Jesus had about those who participate in the harvest; there's tremendous joy and reward for participating. Those who don't participate will really miss out!

There is a loss to any church that does not participate actively in missions. A lack of urgency about winning the lost quickly turns into complacency in Christian living and an indifference regarding God's Word. Such churches become more like the world, seeing less reason to change the world. Prayer for the lost begins to disappear from such churches. In many cases, congregations that do not seek to win the lost diminish in size and in numbers of young people. What is happening? Those who are not challenged to share their faith become lukewarm in their faith. Their lukewarm nature repels rather than attracts.

The urgency to share the gospel is, in the end, an urgency that we must ask the Holy Spirit to plant into our hearts so that we will want to act—and to act quickly, boldly, and with maximum effectiveness. Now is the appointed time! Today is the day!

Whatever our personal problems, is there a worse problem than suffering an eternal destiny without Christ?

If you do not have a sense of urgency in your heart, ask the Holy Spirit to implant a sense of urgency in you.

What Might One Person Do?

Evaluate your own heart. Do you have urgency about winning the lost to Christ Jesus? Instead of asking the Lord with a sense of despair, "What can I *possibly* do?" ask the Lord with sincere desire, "What *can* I possibly do?" Then, listen for His answer. Jesus will show you. He will always turn it into an exciting adventure of faith, hope, and love. The question in your life will then become, Will you do what He says?

When the world sees the transforming power of Jesus Christ in the lives of people around them, they cannot help but notice and talk about it. Some, like the wicked stepmother, may try to cover it up and keep it from spreading. But others, covered in cinders and ashes of sin and locked in the dark cellars of Satan's lies, will see hope for themselves and their children after generations of living in darkness. We cannot let them down—or ourselves.

Heavenly Father, help me to approach missions with the princely urgency and vision for transformation with which Jesus approached His ministry. Make me aware of the time in which I live, and the season of my life. Show me how to engage more fully in the harvest to which You are calling me. I want to follow You not only as my Savior, but also as my Lord. Help me to obey You, Lord Jesus. I may be inadequate for the task, but I put my trust in Your great adequacy to equip me for whatever You have me to do. In Your great name, Amen.

Jesus came and spoke to them, saying, "All authority is given unto me in heaven and on earth. Go therefore and make disciples of all the nations, baptizing them in the Name of the Father, and of the Son, and of the Holy Spirit, teaching them to observe all things that I have commanded you, And lo, I am with you always, even to the end of the age."

Matthew 28:18–20

THE CHALLENGE OF THE GLASS SLIPPER

In the story of Cinderella, the prince had a clear concept of what the glass slipper meant for him, for his future, and for the future of the kingdom. He knew that the slipper also held the potential to change Cinderella's life, transforming her into a princess. He enlisted others to help him find his beloved.

Likewise, Jesus enlists us to join Him in helping others to become the people God meant them to become. He enlists us to take the good news to all people. He expects us to share His urgency, and to pursue the full scope of His challenge to us. Everyone is involved in the harvest, whatever his or her personal problems. For the good of all, the individual must give up his own inclinations; otherwise, the entire community suffers.

To what mission does Christ Jesus call us? How large is this mission? We are looking for many people from all cultures and ranks of society, created in His image. Jesus has an urgency to reach each of them with the good news that will release them to new lives.

The word *mission* means "to send." "Mission" comes from the Greek word, *apostolos*, "one who is sent on a mission." The Father sends His Son on a mission to earth; Jesus sends us on a mission to proclaim the gospel. "Mission" comes from a context in which Jesus sends us out to complete a mission. The missionary is one who is sent. God the Father sent Jesus to the world, making Jesus God's own missionary from heaven—the fulfillment of all that was foretold and proclaimed by the prophets who prepared His way. Before Jesus ascended to heaven, He commissioned His followers to proclaim the good news. They believed His Word and did their job. Since that time, Jesus's command has not changed.

As good followers of Jesus Christ, we must also become missionaries. *Missionary work is about going to people.* Just as Jesus was sent to people, so are we. The great salvation we have in Christ compels us to share the good news with others. If you know Jesus, you cannot remain silent. You have to live as a missionary every day.

For us to have a real sense of urgency about the task we face, we must clarify these key points:

- The command;
- The need;
- The message;
- The nature of our witness.

If we are clear on these matters, and we open our hearts to the truth of Christ's claim on our lives, we come to the core conclusion of this book: *every* Christian can and must become involved in the task of missions.

The Command

Those who helped the prince look for Cinderella had to have complete clarity about what they needed to find: the girl who could wear the glass slipper.

Jesus clearly stated His mission challenge:

- Go and proclaim the good news of redemption (Mark 16:15)
- Go and preach repentance and remission of sin (Luke 24:47)
- Go and disciple the nations (Matthew 28:19)
- Go to the uttermost parts of the earth (Acts 1:8)

Jesus commanded His followers to do these things. His final words on this earth do not comprise the "Great Suggestion." Commands are not options but obligations. This is a *command* motivated by the love of the Father.

The Need

For all they knew, those who helped the prince had a potentially huge task that might take them to the farthest corners of the kingdom before they found the prince's true love. But they knew the effort was worth it for the sake of the prince and the kingdom's future.

There is much good news. The small band of Christ-followers huddled in an upper room in Jerusalem more than two thousand years ago became the earth's largest faith—with more than two billion adherents. Praise God for each of those souls!

The number of Christians in the world is certainly impressive until we realize that the earth has almost seven billion inhabitants.

That means more than two-thirds of the world is *not* Christian.

Of almost four billion who do not know Jesus as Savior, approximately 1.7 billion are completely unevangelized—they have never heard the gospel of Jesus Christ. The remaining 2.3 billion people adhere to religions that deny Jesus as the Savior.

"Missiologists have researched and determined that there are approximately twenty-four thousand people groups in the world. Roughly half of the world's population live in twelve thousand "reached" people groups. This does not mean all these individuals are Christians; it simply means they live in people groups where it is possible to respond to a clear presentation of the Gospel from within their own culture in their own language." (Neal Pirolo, *Serving as Senders*, pg. 171)

Even with massive media efforts to spread the gospel around the world, missiologists such as David Barrett are predicting that in the year 2025, some 26 percent of the world's population will still be unevangelized. Most of those people will live in South Asia, Africa, and China—in what the late Ralph Winter [missionary, missions professor, founder of U.S. Center for World Mission (and my professor at Fuller Theological Seminary)], and others, have dubbed the "10/40 Window"—an imaginary band across Africa and Asia located between ten and forty degrees north of the equator. Many of the world's poorest people live in this band.

The 10/40 window concept is the result of complicated research combining the work of David Barrett and Ralph Winter. Before he became a missionary, Dr. Ralph Winter had training in engineering and thought in those terms. David Barrett was an aeronautical engineer and mathematician. By disposition, they are scientific and statistical thinkers. David Barrett's research deals with 2,600 pages of studies involving overall worldwide population characteristics, and the research done by these missiologists stands uncontested. They found that the most unevangelized areas of the world are also home to people living in the deepest poverty and experiencing the lowest quality of life. More details about this research can be found at www.world-christiandatabase.org, also in *World Christian Encyclopedia*, also in *Operation World*, and other publications. It is a public domain and a common knowledge concept in missiology.

Later, Luis Bush used the term "10/40 window" to popularize the concept at the Second Lausanne Conference in Manila in 1989, sponsored by Evangelist Billy Graham. From Lausanne, the 10/40 window concept became widely known and understood by evangelical leaders worldwide.

Their research concluded that 80 percent of the world's poor live in the 10/40 window. That area includes 84 percent of the world's people with the lowest quality of life. This area also experiences the least investment of Christian resources and the least sharing of the Christian message.

Two point seven billion Muslims, Hindus, Buddhists, Animists, and Jews live in the 10/40 window. The 10/40 window includes twenty-eight Muslim countries with a total population of over one billion, and two Hindu countries with nearly one billion people.

The Message

A royal princess who comes from out of the cellar—this message delivered to the king, his family and subjects was like no other news they had heard.

We have a message to give to the world that is like no other: *Jesus Christ is incomparable and supreme.*

Jesus Christ makes claims for Himself that no other religious leader dares to make. In all of our evangelism and discipleship efforts, we must be very clear about the uniqueness and supremacy of Christ Jesus. Christianity is the only religion in the world that rests its authority upon the sinless life, death, burial, and resurrection of its founder.

Jesus's claims about Himself exceed what any ordinary human being in his right mind would dare say:

- Jesus spoke with authority and laid claim to divine authority. He claimed that "all authority in heaven and on earth" had been given to Him (Matthew 28:18).

- Jesus took on titles given to God in the Old Testament, and He considered Himself worthy of honor due to God. (See Isaiah 60:20 and John 8:12; Psalm 23:1 and John 10:11; Isaiah 42:8 and John 17:1,5). More than thirty times in the Gospel of John alone, Jesus uses the term "I AM"—a direct reference to God (Exodus 3:14).

- Jesus claimed that those who believed in Him would receive forgiveness of sins and everlasting life (John 3:16).

- Jesus claimed a role as judge of humankind and said that people's eternal destiny depended on their relationship with Him. (See Mark 8:35–37 and Matthew 25:31–46).

- Jesus plainly stated, "I and the Father are one" (John 10:30). He said about a person who followed Him, "When he looks at me, he sees the one who sent me" (John 12:45 NIV).

- Jesus loved like no other person could love. Who else is willing to give his life for those who are his enemies?

C.S. Lewis, in his classic book *Mere Christianity*, noted that it was foolish to say, "I accept Jesus as a great moral teacher but I don't accept His claim to be God." Lewis wrote:

> "That is one thing we must not say. A man who was merely a man and said the sort of things Jesus said would not be a great moral teacher. He would either be a lunatic—on the level of the man who says he is a poached egg—or else he would be the devil of hell. You can shut him up for a fool, you can spit at him and kill him as a demon, or you can fall at his feet and call

him Lord and God. But let us not come with any patronizing nonsense about His being a great human teacher. He has not left that open to us. He did not intend to."

(Lewis, C. S., *Mere Christianity*, New York: Macmillan, 1952)

The writers of the New Testament were consistent in describing Jesus as fully human but sinless. (See Hebrews 4:15; 1 Peter 2:22, and 1 John 3:5 as examples). Those who witnessed His miracles glorified God and saw the miracles as evidence to support His claims of divinity (Mark 2:8–11, John 10:33). Miracles are not the only proof of Christ's claims, but they are one strong witness to His uniqueness and supremacy.

The foundation of the Christian gospel presented in the New Testament is Jesus, and central to the message of Jesus is His resurrection.

When the apostle Peter explained to the believers about the need for replacing Judas among the apostles, he said, "For one of these must become a witness with us of His resurrection" (Acts 1:22b, NIV). The resurrection was considered the final proof that Jesus was who He said He was.

The resurrection was and is:

- The cornerstone of the gospel message, from the time Peter preached in Jerusalem on the Day of Pentecost to now (Acts 2:24)

- Validation that God the Father accepted Jesus's death on the cross as the atonement for our justification (Romans 4:25)

- The foremost reason for our hope of heaven as Christians—the proof of Christ's victory over death.

The resurrection paved the way for first-century believers to receive the Holy Spirit. Those who saw and heard Jesus alive after His crucifixion were in the prime position to pray in unity until the Spirit came upon them.

Jesus is the One, according to John 16:7, who sends the Holy Spirit to those who believe in Jesus and receive Him as Savior. The Holy Spirit works in us to:

- Convict us of sin (John 16:8)

- Lead a believer in the path of righteousness (Romans 8:26 and 1 Corinthians 10:13)

- Produce the character of Christ in us (2 Corinthians 3:18; Galatians 5:22–23)

- Give us the power to resist temptations to sin (Romans 8:13)

- Confirm the preaching of the gospel with signs and wonders (Acts 4:30–31).

The apostle Paul said of his own ministry: "Christ has accomplished through me [the] leading [of] the Gentiles to obey God by what I have said and done—by the power of signs and miracles, through the power of the Spirit" (Romans 15:18a-19b).

In the end, Christ's supremacy and uniqueness rests on this point: Jesus did for us what we cannot do for ourselves and what no other person in history can do for us.

Jesus made it possible for a person to live in full reconciliation with God the Father in faith in that Jesus is the beloved and only begotten Son of God who died for our sins.

Religion says, "Strive to attain."

Jesus says, "Believe and obtain."

Religion says, "Attempt to live a good life."

Jesus says, "Receive the Holy Spirit I send to you and allow Him to produce goodness in you and lead you to love and serve others."

Religion says, "Try not to sin."

Jesus says, "Trust the Lord to help you at all times to resist evil and choose what is right before God."

Religion says, "Keep working at your spirituality."

Jesus says, "I accomplished all that needs to be done for you to be forgiven and cleansed of sin, and to receive the gift of eternal life."

Any time we stray from the centrality of Jesus to our lives, and to our ministry efforts, we err greatly. There must never be any substitute for Jesus. We must continually lift Him up as supreme and unique. Jesus said of Himself, "And I, if I am lifted up from the earth, will draw all peoples to Myself" (John 12:32).

We Must Never Lose Sight of the Message. The king's herald who joined the prince in his search for Cinderella had to keep the same focus upon the task given to him as the prince himself. He could not go fishing, take a nap, or do any other thing he preferred to do.

I believe the American church is in grave danger of losing sight of the message that Jesus is incomparable and supreme. Surveys conducted in 1999–2006 by Christian pollster George Barna and others have revealed startling statistics:

- In one nationwide survey among self-professed born-again adults, none of those interviewed said that the single, most important goal in life is to be a committed follower of Jesus Christ.

- Desiring to have a close personal relationship with God ranked sixth among twenty-one life goals tested in another survey, trailing behind such desires as "living a comfortable lifestyle."

- Although 67 percent of teenagers in one poll said they know the basic teachings of the Christian faith, 67 percent rejected the existence of Satan, 60 percent rejected the existence of the Holy Spirit, and 50 percent believed that Jesus sinned.

• Fewer than half of born-again adults (44 percent) said they were certain of the existence of absolute moral truth; only 9 percent of the teenagers in the survey felt certainty about the existence of absolute moral truth.

One of the clarion calls of this century must be this: regain a firm grasp of the truth revealed by Jesus Christ and passed down through the ages by Christian men and women!

The truth of our faith conveyed to us by our Christian ancestors cannot be passed to the world, or to the next generation, unless Christian adults today become more firmly entrenched in and convinced of the truth embodied by Jesus Christ.

The Nature of our Witness

The herald who joined the prince in looking for Cinderella could not simply join the prince but was expected to share the prince's enthusiasm for the task.

When my children were in elementary school, one of their favorite activities was "show-and-tell." Some brought their pets, dolls, and photographs. Even the quiet ones became quite articulate when they became emotionally involved in telling their personal stories.

In the same way, our Christian witness is not a mere matter of telling. Nor is it to be a matter only of showing. We are called both to speak and to live out the gospel. We are to be living letters of God's love, an open book for all to read.

Jesus taught plainly and repeatedly that His followers were to have "ears to hear" and that as they heard, they were to believe, tell, and embody His message. They were to have a 24/7 living faith that manifested itself in the smallest details of daily life. And so should we.

Words and Deeds Are One

In sharing the prince's enthusiasm for the search, the herald would also pass on his enthusiasm to friends and members of his own family. In the end, the whole kingdom would have a stake in the outcome of the prince's search.

From the beginning, Christian words and deeds have been inseparably linked. But how should our words and deeds fit together? That is a key question facing those who desire to win souls. It is a question we are wise to ask in America, and equally wise to ask as we reach out to the world as a whole. The fact that our words and deeds *should* be in harmony is not in question. Christ's message was always that faith must be expressed in words and lived out in deeds. A "silent" faith that does not express itself in words and actions will not win the lost or please the Lord. Jesus made this very clear:

> Therefore whoever confesses Me before men,
> him I will also confess before My Father who is
> in heaven. But whoever denies Me before men,
> him I will also deny before My Father who is in
> heaven.
>
> Matthew 10:32–33

Jesus fully expected His followers to live in such a way that others who heard them speak and watched how they lived would have no doubt that they were His followers—even to the point of persecution:

> Do not think that I came to bring peace on
> earth. I did not come to bring peace but a sword.
> For I have come to 'set a man against his father,
> a daughter against her mother, and a daughter-
> in-law against her mother-in-law'; and 'a man's
> enemies will be those of his own household.' He

who loves his father or mother more than Me
is not worthy of Me. And he who loves son or
daughter more than Me is not worthy of Me.
And he who does not take his cross and follow
after Me is not worthy of Me. He who finds his
life will lose it, and he who loses his life for My
sake will find it.

Matthew 10:34–39

Jesus certainly was not anti-family. His words above were a
Messianic claim related to the prophet Micah (see Micah 7:6).
Jesus was sending a clarion call to His followers that their devotion to Him meant whole-life, total-commitment, and perse-
vere-to-the-end devotion. Following Christ would involve a
change in all relationships, a reestablishing of all priorities, and
would bear upon every activity of life.

Integration of Belief and Behavior

The herald could not simply agree with the prince that looking
for the wearer of the glass slipper was a good idea. He had to
sacrifice every other pursuit until he and the prince had found
the object of their search.

The apostle Paul also taught the full integrity of belief,
speech, and action. Salvation, Paul declared, did not mean mere
intellectual assent.

One of the most famous verses of the New Testament tells
us, "With the heart one believes unto righteousness, and with
the mouth confession is made unto salvation" (Romans 10:10).
Throughout Paul's letters to the early church, we find references
to Christian conduct—especially putting off old behaviors and
putting on new, Christlike behaviors. And other New Testament
writers repeatedly admonish us to display the character of Christ
and to manifest godly behavior. The book of James states it clearly:

So throw all spoiled virtue and cancerous evil in the garbage. In simple humility, let our gardener, God, landscape you with the Word, making a salvation-garden of your life. Don't fool yourself into thinking that you are a listener when you are anything but, letting the Word go in one ear and out the other. Act on what you hear! Those who hear and don't act are like those who glance in the mirror, walk away, and two minutes later have no idea who they are, what they look like. But whoever catches a glimpse of the revealed counsel of God—the free life!—even out of the corner of his eye, and sticks with it, is no distracted scatterbrain but a man or woman of action. That person will find delight and affirmation in the action.

James 1:21–25 (The Message)

Through the millennia, the church has called its members to faithfulness in "thought, word, and deed"—to think pure, holy, and righteous thoughts, to hold loving and selfless attitudes, to boldly preach and teach the truth, and to live out lives of charity marked by the highest standards of morality, integrity, and justice.

Most Christians know the need to proclaim the message of the gospel in spoken and written words. However, few understand how to couple the Christian message with a Christ-honoring lifestyle in a culture different from their own.

The Challenge of Taking our Message to Other Cultures

Two issues are paramount in cross-cultural ministry. They may appear on the surface to be opposing issues, but in truth they are like two sides of the same coin.

Issue #1: The Culture of Christianity

Finding Cinderella was not simply the prince's pet project. It was a unique project for which his kingdom had no precedent.

It had a unique ending—finding the next princess and queen in the most unexpected place—the cellar.

First, we must recognize that the Christian message contains its own culture—and that this culture stands apart from all other cultures of the world.

Jesus wasn't an American. Neither was he English, German, Afghan, Russian, Chinese, Korean, or Indian. Jesus was Jewish, but he spoke of a culture that supersedes and judges all cultures, including the Jewish culture. *The message of Christ is supracultural. It affirms the good in every culture but also judges every culture.*

Our challenge as Christians is to live first and foremost in the culture of the kingdom of God, whether we walk the concrete pavement of an American city or help plow the rice paddies of rural India.

This does not mean that we necessarily reject the personal culture into which we were born or raised. When it comes to certain styles of expression, food, music, décor, language, and so forth there is much we can gain from every culture, and a great deal we can gain as diverse cultures blend together.

The aspects of personal culture that we must reject are those related to our race or nationalities that do not harmonize with the gospel.

We must reject anything that produces the "works of the flesh," which include inner attitudes contrary to God's love.

Paul listed some of these works of the flesh in Galatians 5:19–21:

> "Adultery, fornication, uncleanness, lewdness, idolatry, sorcery, hatred, contentions, jealousies, outbursts of wrath, selfish ambitions, dissensions, heresies, envy, murders, drunkenness, revelries, and the like." He made it clear that "those who practice such things will not inherit the kingdom of God."

Such conduct clearly does not belong in the kingdom.

On the flip side, Paul called upon the church to manifest "the fruit of the Spirit," which he characterized as " ... love, joy, peace, longsuffering, kindness, goodness, faithfulness, gentleness, self-control." He taught that "those who are Christ's have crucified the flesh with its passions and desires. If we live in the Spirit, let us also walk in the Spirit" (Galatians 5:22–25).

I remind you of what you no doubt already know deep within: we must monitor daily how we are living, and make certain that our words and behavior are one and the same.

Beyond our adherence to the culture of the kingdom of God, we must also become more sharply aware of human cultural differences. For many of us, the culture in which we grew up and the faith we adopted are inseparable. Many people have never fully reviewed what they do, why they do it, or how it is all related to what Jesus taught. They rarely stop to question why they dress the way they do, eat the foods they eat, study the books they study, hear the music they hear, or see the movies they see. To become effective witnesses for Christ wherever we go, we must grapple with this issue of our own culture; not only how our natural human culture may differ from the culture of the kingdom of God, but also how it differs from other human cultures.

Most of those on the front lines of evangelism today insist that Christians "rid the gospel of unscriptural western trappings." While we agree that we must shed unscriptural cultural baggage, not all of western culture is bad. A very large segment of the world desires the good aspects of western culture.

What repulses most of the world are blatant displays of immorality, heavy-handed power, and greed. Of course, all cultures display immorality, heavy-handed power, and greed—it is the blatant and excessive display of these traits that the world at large abhors.

The world wants to copy much of American life. The world wants to enjoy many of America's freedoms, but it wants to retain the right to choose those freedoms according to its own unique interpretation. The world wants America's prosperity, but not its crime rate. The world admires America's system of justice, free market, and educational system, but each nation wants to maintain its own cultural and national identity.

When humanity looks at the percentage of the world's natural resources that are consumed by Americans, it sees not only prosperity, but also greed. The Most Reverend Henry Luke Orombi, Anglican archbishop of Uganda, has said it well: "It is not enough ... to make poverty history. We must also make greed history."

I do not criticize the American way of life, nor do I believe that the vast majority of Americans are immoral, power-hungry, or greedy. Most Americans have fairly high moral standards, are generous toward those in need, and tolerate vastly diverse opinions and behaviors. However, what is projected overseas— through the export of our goods and circulation of our media images—is not a true reflection of the way most Americans live.

We must become aware of this before we go overseas to share the gospel, and closely examine not only how we live in light of God's Word, but how we are perceived to live by those whom we will encounter.

A good friend and colleague in ministry of mine is especially sensitive to this issue. Not long ago, on a mission trip to India, one of his team members was a man whose arms and torso were completely covered in tattoos. He had received all those tattoos while in rebellion against God, but he is now reconciled in Christ. Before they came to India, my friend instructed this man to always cover his arms and body with a long-sleeved and collared shirt. He completely understood and complied. He understood that his "liberty" in the US would have become a huge hindrance in proclaiming the gospel in India, where body art and piercings are associated with fetishes and signs of religious dedication within Hinduism. If the man had allowed these things to show, he would have sent a confusing and conflicting message to his hearers, not only to Hindus but also to Indian Christians newly converted from Hindu backgrounds.

Issue #2: Linking the Gospel to Practical Service. At the time they began their search, the prince and his herald did not know that the success of their search would help to right a terrible wrong, an injustice done to a young woman, Cinderella, deprived of her birthright by a wicked stepmother and her selfish daughters. Their relentless search would not just fulfill a romantic dream but have practical results, changing Cinderella's whole life in big ways they could not foresee.

The second great challenge we face in taking the gospel across cultural barriers relates to the role of practical service. We must come to grips with the importance—or lack of importance—of social service when it comes to spreading the gospel.

On the one hand, some believe that social action is the critical first step in telling others about Jesus. They hold that people don't care what you believe until they believe you care, and that it is virtually impossible for a hungry person to hear the gospel. This camp contends: heal the sick in body, and they will seek healing in spirit; feed the hungry, and they will desire the food of God's Word; lift up the poor materially, and they will desire to lift up Jesus.

This contention is only one side of the coin. If we don't heal and help, we cannot expect a response. But we don't heal and help thinking a positive response is automatic. We heal and help because this is what Jesus would do out of love.

Others, such as Susan Perlman of Jews for Jesus, urge evangelicals to "keep the proclamation of the gospel on the front burner." They believe that acceptance of the gospel message is the key to genuine social change. As Evangelist Luis Palau has noted, "Evangelism is social action." The approach is generally this: those who come to love Christ will have a new ability to love others around them, and a new desire to help others in practical ways—feeding, clothing, and assisting them in other practical, medical, and educational ways. Without a love of Christ at the center of social action, a "good deed" may or may not have eternal benefit to the recipient.

Most see the need to balance the two approaches. Let me offer these two premises for your consideration:

1. *All things done in Jesus's name have within them a seed of eternal benefit.*

Therefore, we must do everything we do with Jesus's name at the center of our activity (2 Corinthians 9:13).

We must never be reticent about declaring why we do what we do. We must serve others as if we serve Christ Himself, and to serve in this manner is to serve others "in His name." Jesus's love for us motivates us to reach out with His love in practical service to others.

The Urgent Call

1. Know what you believe and why you believe it. How would you explain, in your own words, the concepts below? Especially focus on how you might explain these concepts to a child or teenager:

   - The need for missions
   - The command of Jesus to spread the gospel message
   - The vital importance of proclaiming the uniqueness and supremacy of Jesus Christ
   - The culture of Christianity

2. What does the resurrection of Jesus mean to you?

3. Reflect on this critical question: to what extent does your life reflect full integrity of belief, speech, and action?

4. In what ways is the culture of the society in which you live different from the culture of Christianity? What challenge does this difference present to you?

5. How does "practical social service" go hand in hand with preaching the gospel?

6. Why is it important that we lift up the name of Jesus and raise up human potential simultaneously?

Since 1992, Indian Christian pastors, evangelists, and teachers have spent much effort in educating and uplifting the Dalits (often called "Untouchables") in the slums of a major city in north India. They provide education for children up to the fourth grade. Later, students take entrance exams to government schools that eventually lead to higher education. The children are taught the basics of reading, writing, and arithmetic. They are taught to read in three languages: Hindi (the national language), English, and the local state language. They are also taught the Bible and trained to memorize scriptures. They sing Christian songs, and are taught personal hygiene.

The result? These children consistently fare better than those children who spend their entire time in government schools. The families of the children who attend India Gospel Outreach schools have been transformed, and through those transformed homes their communities are transformed.

Two medical doctors organized our Bible college students to conduct surveys in one particular Ludhiana slum where we had extensive ministry and established a school. More than two hundred people in that slum believed in the saving power of Jesus and were baptized as believers in Christ Jesus. The research team surveyed more than four thousand families in all, and found that 1,300 of these families destroyed or removed their idols and were praying to and worshiping Jesus alone. The influence of the schools had been more far-reaching than we thought!

We also established a sewing center in this slum area. The women who trained at the center learned sewing and knitting and became skilled in knitting sweaters. We provided cycle-rickshaws to men who were demonized and alcoholics, and they became breadwinners for their families, enabling them to make a living and begin contributing to their communities. We provided medical clinics in various slum areas, and we helped the new believers establish churches.

We have openly done everything in these slums in the name of Jesus. On countless occasions radicals oppose us, asking, "Why do you want to meddle with what God intended?" They believe that God intends for some people to be downtrodden and poor because of a sin they committed in a previous life. They believe that those who are poor and disenfranchised from the larger culture should be left alone to suffer. They regard poverty as a means of purging bad karma. We have found that when the opposition rises up with this line of argument, the people who have been helped also rise up with a very different message. They say to the radical opposition, "You never came to help us and uplift us. You never came to teach our children. You never came to motivate us to do better. These Christians have come to help us, and to teach us about the love of Jesus Christ. We choose Jesus." (See Matthew 5:13–16).

This form of social action coupled with the gospel leads me to my second premise for your consideration:

2. *We must simultaneously seek to establish enterprises that lift up the name of Jesus and raise up human potential.*

What do we mean by "raise up human potential"? The premise here is that every human being experiences a higher quality of life and is better able to fulfill his potential if he is not shackled by poverty, illness, or ignorance.

Poverty, illness, and ignorance are the three giants that the church has faced from its beginning. Much of Christian missionary service comes as basic social services (food, clothing, and shelter), medical assistance, and education. Indeed, most short-term mission trips focus on one of these areas.

I once heard about a program designed to feed the homeless in a particular city. The director of the project, located in a Christian church, funded by Christian people, and staffed mostly by Christian volunteers, insisted that nobody mention the name of Jesus or pray in the name of Jesus. Why? "We don't want to offend those of Native American culture," she said. What a travesty! Christ-honoring services rendered by Christian people need to be rendered in the name of Jesus, freely and openly.

India is like the United States in that there are liberal groups in India who give help without calling attention to the name of Jesus. In fact, they adopt many non-Christian methods in their programs. But these groups and their efforts are not growing very much and are not as effective as those that lovingly declare they offer help in the love and name of Jesus.

From my perspective, after years of evangelistic work, nothing is gained by shying away from the name of Jesus. When the name of Jesus is lifted up, the Holy Spirit draws unbelievers to a saving knowledge of God's love and forgiveness.

Even Christians who work in oppressive and anti-Christian societies must ultimately tell at least a small circle of new friends that they come in the name of Jesus, or their work will never develop the eternal fruit of saved souls.

Every Christian Must Become Involved!

In the end, everyone in the prince's realm had a stake in the outcome of what happened to Cinderella. It would influence all their lives for generations and give credibility in their king to secure their welfare as well as Cinderella's. More than one person would have given their aid in the prince's venture to find his lady love.

You, as a Christian, must become involved. Make yourself available with whatever you have. God multiplies what we have. That is the lesson of the woman with the two coins and the little boy who offered his five loaves and two fishes to Jesus to feed five thousand people (Mark 12:41–44 and John 6:5–14).

It is not enough that a few leaders, or even a few laypeople, understand the need, command, message, and nature of witnessing related to missionary service. Every Christian from all walks of life must become involved! It will take all of us to carry out God's missionary command. The command is to every Christian. The message is one on which we all must agree. The nature of our witness pertains to the way Christians live out their lives, wherever on planet earth they may find themselves.

I often meet people who seem overwhelmed, even dazed, at the enormity of the challenge we face in winning a lost world to Christ Jesus. "I'm just one person," they lament. "What can I do?"

Let me encourage you: we each have a part to play. None of us can do everything, but each of us can do something. Each of us is called to a unique role, one defined by God. The fulfillment of our role is vital to the fulfillment of the *whole* of God's plan and purpose. It is our challenge to take up the task God has for us and to do His bidding with our whole heart, mind, and strength.

Neal Pirolo, in his book *Serving as Senders*, has pointed out, "In secular war, there is an acknowledged ratio of support personnel to frontline soldiers. In WW II, the military ratio to frontline soldiers was fifteen to one. In more recent conflicts, that ratio was expanded to fifty support workers per frontline soldier" (p. 165). Others are backing him up in what is called the "line of communication" (Neal Pirolo, *Serving as Senders*). In another illustration, to keep an F-17 fighter jet in the air, it not only takes a pilot but over two hundred people on the ground as well (Holmes Bryan, Vice President of Evangelical Development Ministries).

It will take *every* Christian to fulfill the Great Commission—each person contributing in his or her unique way.

What Might One Person Do?

Do you know your unique gifts and talents? If not, ask the Lord to reveal to you the special qualities He has built into your life from birth.

Then, ask the Lord how you might use these gifts and talents to present the gospel to those who have never heard it. Ask the Lord to give you His creative solutions to the needs He brings to your heart and mind.

Heavenly Father, forgive me for being an unfaithful herald of your kingdom. Forgive me of those times when I have placed one foot in the world and one foot in the church. I do not want to straddle the fence. Help me to live totally in the culture of Christ, fully aware of the power of His resurrection and fully embodying integrity of belief, words, and deeds. Help me to discover new ways in which practical service to others exemplifies the gospel "in action." Help me to help others—to encourage and raise them to the full potential that You placed within them. Help me to understand deep in my heart that whatever I have to offer You is always valuable in Your sight and that You will multiply it by your mighty power. I ask this in the name of Jesus, who always desires our eternal best. Amen.

Act on what you hear.

James 1:22 (The Message)

CONFRONTING 4 WICKEDNESS

In the story of Cinderella, the wicked stepmother consigns Cinderella to a life of drudgery.
She does this to promote the welfare of her own
daughters at Cinderella's expense.

By doing this, the stepmother is also perpetuating a lie. By keeping Cinderella out of sight
and assigning her servant work, the wicked stepmother gives the larger world the impression
that her daughters are the rightful heirs of the
estate and the manor house in which they live,
and that these stepsisters are equal to Cinderella
in lineage, goodness, and beauty. The stepmother's perpetuation of a lie and her mistreatment of
Cinderella make her "wicked."

The analogy to missions is fairly obvious. The foremost
enemy to missions work is someone far more sinister and
clever than a wicked stepmother, with far more resources at his
command. I speak of Satan, the adversary of Jesus Christ. He

would love nothing better than to consign the lost souls of this world to dungeons of oppression, and to divert the church's and all other people's attention to other matters. He rightly fears that the fulfillment of the Great Commission will mark the end of him and his dominion over the earth.

Satan's greatest power is his ability to deceive. He deceives us when we believe his lies instead of God's truth. So Satan pulls out all the stops, devising all kinds of deceptions that turn people from the truth. He is especially clever at appealing to human weaknesses and tendencies that produce evil, but which may give the illusion of promoting good.

Satan knows that humans like to feel comfortable—with themselves and with their environment. He knows that human beings have a tendency toward laziness. As much as possible, they like to live their lives like one long summer vacation spent in a hammock with a nice, warm breeze, a big pitcher of lemonade in hand (ice cold, please), and all the time in the world to do absolutely nothing.

Satan is very clever at suggesting arguments to help human beings justify their lazy tendencies so they can do as little as possible, all the while thinking they are doing something beneficial, and therefore feel good about themselves.

Satan works through a variety of methods, perhaps the foremost of which is apathy. He entices us to care about the "urgent" issues of life—some of which may seem demanding in the moment but eventually are transitory and temporary—and to ignore the truly important issues that have eternal consequences. He whispers to us, "Let others get concerned about missions." The excuse is all too often voiced, "I have enough concerns. I can't be concerned about everything." As a result, missions, like Cinderella, are pushed into the shadows of the church's vision and strategy.

Satan also uses clever and elaborate lies that we quickly swallow. In our day, the lies associated with universalism and relativism have blinded countless Christians, who feel that there is some degree of virtue in letting people believe whatever they want to believe. In this way we avoid responsibility for alerting people to the truth that what they believe may be a damnable lie. A failure to challenge universalism and relativism, and a failure to sound the good news, is a failure that has fatal consequences.

Overcoming Apathy toward Missions

In the story of Cinderella, her own father seems to have an incredible apathy about what happens to his own daughter. Somehow, the man allows his second wife and his wife's daughters to turn him into an ineffectual and powerless man. What kind of wiles could they have used upon him to allow them to persist in their cruel scheme of keeping Cinderella in the cellar performing the most menial of tasks when she had the birthright of nobility? He displays a terrible apathy.

Apathy is a lack of interest in pursuing a goal, or a lack of passion toward the accomplishment of a goal. Many people give lip service to the need for winning lost souls. Few actually overcome the distractions and detours of their daily lives to either give or go.

There are two main reasons for the apathy some people feel toward missions.

Reason #1: The Lack of Preaching and Praying about Missions.

Ask yourself, when was the last time you heard a pastor call upon the young people in his own congregation to commit themselves to extended overseas service for the cause of the gospel?

In addition to a lack of preaching, I have discovered in many churches across America a lack of prayer for missionaries and mission projects. When was the last time your church had a prayer meeting specifically for missions or missionaries? When was the last time the names of missionaries were included in the list of those for whom the church was interceding?

It is time that we re-emphasize and elevate the role of the missionary. We must address common misconceptions about missionaries:

- Missionaries are not those who go overseas to escape the rigors or stress of western life.

- Missionaries are not those who "opt out" of the cultural rat race in which everybody else finds themselves.

- Missionaries are not people who cannot "succeed" at home.

The truth is very different:

Missionaries are those called by God to fulfill what Jesus Christ says is the most important role a person can have: winning lost souls for the Kingdom.

- Missionaries must be multi-talented and good communicators, with a vision for how to accomplish God's plans and purposes.

- Missionaries must have tremendous courage and perseverance.

A good example is that of a young man who felt the call of God upon his life to work as a missionary in India. He faced rejection and ridicule from his own church elders. When he stood up to testify of his burden for the lost in India, he was told, "Sit down, young man, if the Lord wants to save the heathen in India, he can do it without your help."

While this young man understood the sovereignty of God, he also understood human responsibility. God has not assigned this task of announcing the good news to angels, but to weak, yet redeemed, human beings. This young man left his homeland of England never to return. He learned thirty-six languages during his lifetime, and translated the whole Bible, the New Testament, or gospel portions into those thirty-six languages. He produced the first English-Sanskrit and English-Bengali dictionaries. He established India's first daily newspaper, banking system, botanical society, and so much more. He did this all while grieving the death of his wife and son, and the loss of his home.

The man's name was William Carey—one of the most noteworthy people in modern history. Men and women such as Carey have tremendous courage and perseverance. It is time to honor missionary service, and to see missionary service as the greatest commitment a Christian can make. One can find numerous biographies on William Carey with more information (see Bibliography for recommended readings).

Today, you can go to any part of India and find schools, hospitals, orphanages, and leprosariums established by missionaries. Very often missionaries do not limit their work to the establishment of churches. They often motivate their converts to do tremendous work that gives an opportunity for the Christian message to penetrate the greater society.

Reason #2: We Have Denied the Prospect That All People Face Eternity When They Die. Cinderella's father must have been in terrible denial of what was happening in his own house with his own flesh and blood. This brings us to another reason for his profound ineffectiveness.

The second reason for our apathy related to missions is less obvious but far more insidious and more difficult to correct: we have stopped believing that people are in danger of dying and going to hell. This is why many no longer support missions or seek to send missionaries abroad.

The lie is at the core of a philosophy called universalism. At its core is its close-cousin philosophy, relativism.

Standing Against the Rising Surge of Universalism

The Philosophy of Universalism. Universalism is the teaching that all people will be saved and go to a paradise after death. Rather than stand staunchly against universalism, many Christians have invited universalistic teachings into the church. Some churches openly welcome people of other religions to come to the communion table as an expression of "community building." Vacation Bible school programs in some Christian churches invite children to explore the rituals and traditions of false religions—not merely for information purposes, but so the students might practice the rituals and experience their spiritual impact. For decades now, the seminaries of a number of denominations have taught universalism or have presented Bible classes from a universalistic viewpoint. In turn, countless pastors are preaching universalism—albeit under the cloak of Christian compassion.

Univeralism plagues the churches in India as much as it does in America. The truth is that universalism is an anglicized name for Hinduism! Hinduism openly embraces many gods and many approaches to them. Hinduism offers methods intended to purify the spirit of man, but offers no guarantee that such purification is either possible or effective all the time. Religions that advocate reincarnation believe that past sins are atoned in the future, whereas universalism contends that there are no sins that require atonement! Both reincarnation and universalism teach an "inevitable good end."

The bottom line of both Hinduism and universalism is the same: no need for a Savior and no need, therefore, to spread the gospel.

Very specifically, the brand of universalism we routinely encounter in North America and Europe is a philosophy that grew out of post–World War II writings among theologians and philosophers. In many cases, these writings came about because of growing opposition to European colonialism. The prevailing thought was this: all people have the right to their own destiny, the validity of their own cultural expressions, and the use of their own national resources. European nations must cease to impose their culture and political systems upon the nations of Africa, Asia, and South America. At the same time, European nations must cease the pillage of national resources from these nations, and enter instead into a more equitable trade relationship that benefits the indigenous people. Education and opportunity must be equalized around the world.

Certainly there was good reason to stop many of the practices related to colonialism, especially those practices that brought economic hardship and a lack of justice to the colonial areas. For example, in India, wool, silk, cotton, and many other products were taken to Great Britain, where they were processed and then sold at higher prices back in India. In Indochina (modern-day Vietnam, Laos, and Cambodia), rubber was taken to France for processing, only to be sold at a higher price in the colonies.

Not all activities of colonialism, however, were negative. Those efforts aimed at modernizing society, improving health care and educational systems, and extending the gospel were very positive. India's colonial government helped to establish schools, hospitals, and the democratic forms of government that continue to benefit India today.

Theologians bent on reversing colonialism, however, did not draw a distinction between the baby and the bathwater. As an extension of this anti-colonial approach, European theologians concluded that not only are all people and cultures created with innate validity (true), but because religion is an expression of culture, all religions are created with innate validity as well (false).

Universalism pictures a huge global pool of love, joy, and peace lying just under the surface of humanity. Various religions tap into that pool in various ways, just as oil rigs tap into oil reserves under the surface of the earth. Supposedly, all religions help people experience love, joy, and peace, and seek after God. All religions, therefore, have a universal common purpose. The conclusion: all religions are good and all are equal paths to deeper spirituality and the ultimate knowledge of God. This simply is not scriptural, nor is it what the church has taught historically from the beginning.

These attitudes are based upon sentimentality, not reality, and certainly not the holy love of God that sacrifices Himself for another person. This sentimental picture of reality overlooks the radical differences in religions and is based more upon emotionalism rather than reality.

What *is* universal? The human desires for love, joy, and peace beat in the heart of every human being as "universal" desires. People around the world have a universal hunger for truth and freedom from feelings of guilt and shame. The conclusion that "all religions result in eternal life" is not truth, and therefore, in the purest of definitions, it cannot be universal.

Universalism has produced such statements as:

- "It doesn't matter what you believe as long as you believe consistently and fervently."

- "There are many paths to God—you have your way, I have my way."

- "God honors all religions equally as long as the heart is sincere."

- "All roads lead to heaven."

At the root of universalism is a firm belief that a loving God would never "send" a person to hell, which becomes something of a circular argument. Universalism advocates that individuals have great autonomy in making their own choices regarding religion and in making decisions that determine their own destiny; however, individuals seemingly can't choose to reject God and separate themselves from Him.

A Close Tie to Relativism. Cinderella's father treated his step daughters as equal or superior to his own flesh and blood because he seemed to recognize no difference between having the birthright and not having the birthright of nobility. As a practical matter, he was a relativist in his thinking. Perhaps he thought he was being fair, loving, open-minded, and tolerant toward his second wife and her daughters, but in the end he wound up being as cruel as the crafty stepmother herself in the practical results of his inaction.

Universalism is closely allied to relativism, the idea that all religions are equal. The relativist rejects absolute truth; therefore, relativists reject the idea of sin, and they resist the idea that something may be judged as "good" or "evil." To them, such judgments reek of "intolerance" and even "hatred." They resist the possibilities of moral and personal accountability. They regularly speak of "love" but rarely of "righteousness," and they especially accuse Christians of being "bigoted," "self-righteous," and "judgmental" for saying that Jesus is the only way, and the Bible is God-inspired. It results in statements such as: "You have your truth, I have my truth;" "You're okay, I'm okay, and together, we're all okay;" "Who am I to discount your experience or to invalidate your religion?"

Can you see how such beliefs and statements come into direct conflict with the concept of "winning the lost" and "making disciples of all nations?"

To the universalist and relativist, there is no lost person! To the universalist, it is the height of presumption to seek to make a disciple of your faith, rather than simply seek to help that person live a better life and more fully embrace the cultural religion of his ancestors.

Universalism offers "good works" as the proper outcome of all religious belief. Holistic concerns for health, education, and justice are not only regarded as admirable, but are openly advocated. Universalists insist, however, that good works must never be done in the name of Jesus! They do not believe that Jesus is the name above all other names. For them, the name of Jesus is not unique and incomparable, but only one name among many.

Universalism Is Enemy Number One. Universalism is widespread. It is the number-one enemy of missions.

J.I. Packer, senior editor of *Christianity Today*, wrote this in a foreword to Ajith Fernando's book, *Crucial Questions about Hell*: "Emphasis on the lostness of the lost has come to be almost taboo. The shift is startling."

Universalism Has Infected the Church and Missionary Outreach
Even more insidious than the general garden-variety type of universalism prominent in Western culture is the adoption of universalism by certain Christian spokesmen and denominations. The core belief is that Jesus died on the cross for all sin—past, present, and future—and that every person born after His death and resurrection is automatically the recipient of God's full pardon and forgiveness.

There are two main camps in Christian universalism:

One camp states that the unrepentant will be punished only in proportion to the degree of sin they have committed. The punishment is regarded as temporary, and the suffering associated with the punishment is what enables a person to move beyond his sin and be in full and right relationship with God.

Another camp contends that there is no punishment after death for sin, only a "loss of reward."

At this writing, a media frenzy regarding universalism has arisen over controversial writings of Rob Bell, founder/pastor of a large church in Michigan (featured in *Time Magazine*, April 25, 2011, p. 38). If nothing else, response to his writings have dramatically revealed the deep cultural divides of our day and widely differing approaches toward missions even among some evangelical churches.

Certainly you do not need to become an expert in universalism in order to refute it. Rather, you need to become an expert in God's

Word! Jesus spoke about heaven and hell very clearly. He taught that heaven was a place prepared for redeemed people. Hell was a place intended for Satan and his angels. But He also taught that those who intentionally rebel against God and reject the salvation offered through Jesus Christ will share the punishment of Satan and his angels. (He will judge us according to the knowledge we have received and what we do with it. Hell is reserved not for those who lack knowledge, but those who rebel against God. God is the best judge of those who fall into this category.)

Universalism and the Denial of Evil. In letting the wicked stepmother get away with her schemes, Cinderella's father denied the presence of evil in his household and conspired with her in perpetrating the worst of injustices. In so doing, Cinderella's father demonstrates what takes place in this world time and again, and to which even the church itself can become an unwitting tool if it does not stay true to the King's Word.

Universalism is a false belief because it fails to take serious account of the presence of evil in the world and its consequences for those who perpetuate it. If God is simply love and not righteousness and justice, and all people are saved in the end, does that mean that St. Francis of Assisi and Adolf Hitler will both enjoy the eternal bliss of heaven? Something in the heart of all thinking people resists this conclusion.

In the end, for all peoples regardless of lifestyle to have the same destiny means that evil and good are equal in the eyes of God. It is no coincidence that true universalists have less motivation to recognize evil in the world or contribute to missionary or charitable causes. They believe there is nothing from which to be saved. Goodness is that which is defined by his own fickle emotions.

There are few evils in the world worse than India's caste system. This heinous system of social structuring has existed in India for at least three thousand years, probably created by conquering Aryans to structure and dominate society.

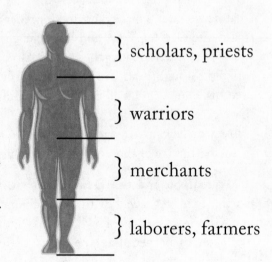

The Hindu View of Creation

Brahma, the creator god, created people out of his own body.

} scholars, priests

} warriors

} merchants

} laborers, farmers

Dalits (outcastes)

The Indian caste system operates under the theory that the creator god, Brahma, created people out of his own body. At the top are the scholars and priests, followed by warriors, merchants, laborers, and farmers. The lowest group includes the so-called "outcastes" who were not created out of any part of Brahma's body and are thereby considered less than animals and "unborn." These outcaste people number almost 25 percent of the Indian population, or three hundred million, equal to the entire population of the United States. (Note: "Dalit" is a self-designated word used by India's outcaste or "untouchable" population. Theoretically, the concept of "outcaste" and "untouchable" was outlawed by the Indian Constitution. Therefore, you will not find the word "Dalit" in India's government documents or census figures because according to the government documents, such people no longer exist. Reality is another matter. The number of Dalits equals the sum of people in all the hundreds of what are referred to as scheduled castes, backward castes, and tribal groups. This amounts to about 25 percent of the entire Indian population, or over 300 million people.)

Caste determines one's occupation, spouse, status, and place of residence. In India, a Hindu cannot advance from one caste to another. His way of life and the lives of his descendants are fixed in perpetuity.

After the caste system became institutionalized, it became justified in Hindu scripture in a similar way that slavery became justified in the American South by pro-slavery ministers and theologians. Those in the dominant castes justified their exploitation of lower castes and kept them in line by saying that karma from previous lives determined their low estate, but if they humbly accepted their present state and gained merit to overcome bad karma, they could advance to a higher caste in the next life. This teaching is nothing more than a means to manipulate the slaves into subservience.

This caste mentality permeates all of Indian society. In the West, where the individual is considered important and upward mobility is the "American dream," it is impossible to fully understand the mindset that would regard any human being as worthless and sub-human.

For good reason, the outcastes of Indian society do not call themselves "outcastes" but "Dalits," meaning "oppressed ones." They are daily humiliated and de-humanized in ways that we would consider intolerable.

- Dalits are not permitted to cross into high caste sections of town without risk to their lives.

- Dalits must drink from clay cups instead of glass cups to keep from mixing cups and contaminating "better" people.

- Dalits are forbidden to use village wells or enter village shops and non-Dalit homes on pain of death.

- Dalit girls are routinely raped, even those thirteen and under.

- Most Dalits make less than one dollar a day.

- Dalit children must sit separately in government schools and receive little or no help from teachers. They cannot use the facilities used by others.

- Dalits have no recourse to the law—no rights in the courts, ignored by the police at best or attacked by them at worst.

- Dalit women who resist injustices of the non-Dalit world are stripped naked, paraded in public, gang-raped, and murdered to punish them or family members, or as a prerogative of an upper-caste male.

- Dalits are denied basic health care.

- Dalits are denied normal sources for food, so malnourishment is high among Dalit children, who experience high incidence of polio and leprosy.

- Dalit girls who are missing, probable victims of sex trafficking, number nearly one million.

- Dalit women have a literacy rate of only 2 percent.

- Dalit communities are regularly burned.

- Dalits are subject to summary executions without trial, often by burning alive.

- Dalits are regarded as Hindus whether they like it or not, but they are denied access to Hindu scriptures, temples, and pilgrimage sites.

Numerous websites give much information about the Dalits. Among them are www.christiancouncil.in and www.dalitnetwork.org.

These general facts are only a hint of the suffering Dalits endure. The millions of individual stories make up the real tragedy. For example, take the story of the Dalit laborer accused of stealing a wristwatch. No one actually saw him steal the watch, nor did they find him in possession of a watch, but that did not prevent a group of doctors from spending an entire afternoon beating him, cutting off his hair, and forcing him to drink urine. (For this and similar stories, see the following websites: www.christiancouncil.in and www.dalitnetwork.org. Both websites give numerous illustrations similar to these.)

In the state of Rajasthan, Dalits were prevented by high caste villagers from using the village well because they would "contaminate" it. They were forced to get water from a source with toxic levels of fluoride.

In one village, a Dalit family tried to resist unfair treatment from high caste farmers. In retaliation, four family members were violently dragged from their homes and beaten. The women were stripped naked, paraded through the village square, gang-raped for hours, and then publicly beaten to death. Surviving relatives were unable to achieve justice.

In 2003, in the state of Haryana, five Dalit young men who registered as leather tanners were lynched by police with the approval of local Hindu radicals. At the time of their death, their truck was loaded with animal skins, headed toward a leather factory. The police accused the young men of killing and skinning a cow along the side of the road, a crime according to Hindu statutes. The police did nothing to help the investigation. The vice president of the World Hindu Council justified the lynching on the grounds that the life of a cow is more important than the life of a Dalit. This illustration about five Dalit men took place in 2003 while I was ministering in the city of Ambala, in Haryana, not far from the incident which was reported on local TV news.

How many Dalits are kept in the cellar all of their lives, like Cinderella, because of an unjust social system that violates God's intentions for them? How many Christians live their lives without a thought to this terrible injustice?

A Dalit child may be a prodigy. He may have outstanding abilities to become a great artist, statesman, scientist, business leader, doctor, or computer programmer. But it doesn't matter. Once a Dalit, always a Dalit. Beginning at age five, he will scavenge, clean sewers, and sweep streets, while others of higher caste but lesser abilities spit in his face, kick out his teeth, and rape his mother. Chances are, a Dalit child with outstanding gifts will never know he has them. He will never dream about the possibility of his giftedness, because the caste system has squashed all such dreams from his soul. When asked what he wanted to be when he grew up, a seven-year-old Dalit boy responded, "I can't be anything."

It is safe to say that in degrading and discriminating against Dalits, the caste system deprives India of at least 25 percent of its highest potential. And what about the possibilities for leadership that lie in the lower castes that comprise another 50 percent, or 600 million, of India's population? The caste system awards positions not on merit but on birth, a major reason why there is so much gross incompetence in India's national, state, and local leadership. This incompetence causes all of India to suffer at many levels of life.

> The most banal of human faults—the failure to imagine the life of another.
>
> —Richard North Patterson, "Exile"

Of course, the caste system of India dehumanizes not only those at the bottom, but also those at the top. It obligates people to serve at tasks for which they may be totally unsuited or unmotivated. It isolates them from rich relationships with most of their countrymen. It leaves them with a constant fear that lower castes will one day rise up against them in unspeakable violence. Every advance of a Dalit, no matter how tiny, is cause for deep paranoia.

There is no other way to say it—the caste system of India is evil. It is not just a cultural alternative, but a wicked system concocted in the depths of hell to destroy and degrade the men, women, and children made in God's image.

Though they do not always have theological foundations for self-worth, the Dalits themselves know that something is wrong. God has placed within their hearts the knowledge that they are worth more than what their masters tell them they are. In recent decades, the Dalits have made increasing efforts to break free of the system that has enslaved them for three thousand years. Growing movements of Dalits seek the freedom they instinctively know is their right. By experience, they know that the caste system is evil.

Just as Cinderella knew there was something terribly wrong in an arrangement that left her, as the rightful daughter of noble birth, in a cellar with menial tasks, so the Dalits know that they have become victims of a system that was not divinely ordained. In recent years, that realization has become stronger as the gospel of Jesus Christ has come to them, and as the gospel has even influenced men and women who have not yet come to Christ. One of them was Mahatma Gandhi.

Mahatma Gandhi, father of modern India, recognized the evil of caste systems. He gave Dalits a name—"Harijan"—meaning "children of God," and he strongly advocated an end to the caste system. To make his point, he enlisted the services of Dr. B.R. Ambedkar to become the chief architect of the Indian Constitution. Dr. Ambedkar, a Dalit, was one of the first to get an education. He excelled in his studies, attended the University of Bombay and Elphinstone College (in Bombay), and obtained degrees in political science and economics from Columbia University in the United States. Ambedkar's hopes for the Dalit community were ignited by what Gandhi did for him and his people. Tragically, Gandhi was assassinated by a radical Hindu who opposed his ideals. Unfortunately, Gandhi's successors did not keep Gandhi's promises, and the caste system continued as it had for centuries. Out of sheer frustration and anger, Dr. Ambedkar publicly denounced Hinduism for all its evils and embraced Buddhism just two months before his death in 1956. Since that day, the number of public denunciations of Hinduism by Dalits has increased, with mass conversions to other religions.

Few people in this world are more open to the gospel than the Dalits of India. The Dalits are on the verge of a major turning to Christ, provided that they hear the gospel. The gospel is beautiful music to the ears of a Dalit. It is unbelievably good news to a Dalit to know that God made him and all people in His image; that in God's eyes there is no high caste, low caste, or "outcaste;" that the same salvation is offered to all regardless of background; and that Jesus's grace is strong enough to break the power of his bad karma.

India Gospel Outreach has a strong ministry to Dalits. Our evangelists experience a high response among them. We give a clear presentation of the gospel, and we provide practical ways for Dalits to escape the cycle of poverty and exploitation. For example, in the city of Ludhiana, Punjab, our evangelists offer literacy schools to Dalit children up to the fourth grade, giving them opportunity to enter government schools. Dalit women have opportunity to learn skills in tailoring and sewing to greatly enhance their families' ability to earn a living. They are also taught how to establish a budget. They are amazed that they receive help from Christians. In the process of learning academic and vocational skills, most of the children and members of their families discover Jesus Christ. The gospel frees them from the lies that have bound them and their families for thousands of years.

None of this miraculous transformation among the Dalits through our evangelists' gospel witness would take place if we were universalists. To the true universalist, oppressor and oppressed have the same destiny and same reward. They are morally equivalent. Why rock the boat in trying to change the status quo when all religions are equal, and everyone gets the same reward in the end?

What Must We Do to Confront Universalism? As we have already pointed out, Cinderella's father made the grave mistake of treating his second wife and her daughters better than his own daughter. Perhaps he thought he was being fair and open-minded, but in reality, he was creating an unthinkable injustice. Without realizing it, those who hold to universalist thinking are encouraging and perpetuating the same kind of injustices, causing untold suffering around the world and affecting the eternal destinies of millions.

What are the essentials for confronting universalism and winning the battle against its insidious effects?

First, we must know what we believe and why we believe it. Only one thing will put an end to the encroachment of universalism into every area of life: a strong proclamation of the gospel of Jesus Christ. We must know the Word as individual believers. We must put ourselves into a position to hear the truth of God's Word preached with boldness and the anointing of the Holy Spirit. We must read the Word faithfully, study the Word diligently, and be quick to speak the Word whenever the opportunity arises. We must pray for discernment about what to say, when, and how, so that we can use the Word with maximum effectiveness in presenting Christ.

Hebrews 4:12 tells us, "The word of God is living and powerful, and sharper than any two-edged sword, piercing even to the division of soul and spirit, and of joints and marrow, and is a discerner of the thoughts and intents of the heart." It is the Word that uncovers and exposes impure motives, false teachings, and sinful behavior.

We each must have a ready argument, a solid line of defense when we encounter the deceptions of universalism. We must know what we believe and why. We must be skilled in our use of Scripture to counteract lies.

Second, we must be certain that those who pastor us have a sure understanding of Jesus Christ as the way, truth, and life, and a personal testimony of salvation.

Hundreds, if not thousands, of churches across the United States have senior pastoral leadership that is steeped in universalism. A recent George Barna poll revealed that only 51 percent of all senior Protestant pastors have a truly "biblical worldview," defined as a worldview based on these criteria:

- Believing that God is all-knowing and all-powerful
- Believing that Jesus Christ never sinned
- Believing that Satan is real
- Believing that salvation only comes through faith in Christ and not by good deeds
- Believing that the Bible is accurate
- Believing that absolute moral truth exists and is described in the Bible
- Believing that Christians should share their faith with nonbelievers (Duin, "Public Christian Symbols Backed")

Universalistic church leaders and pastors do not believe that Jesus Christ is the only way to the Father. They do not believe that the Bible is the authoritative Word of God. Therefore, they do not believe the words of Jesus as recorded in the Gospels can be trusted as truth. They are people who are led by their own intuition and self-justifying arguments; they cannot be truly led by the Holy Spirit because they do not proclaim Jesus as their personal Savior. (See John 14:15–18.)

If you are part of a denominational structure that appoints pastoral leadership on a congregation-by-congregation basis, make sure you ask the tough questions of your pastoral candidates. Make sure your pastor knows Jesus as his Savior and has a heart for following Jesus as Lord. Insist that your denomination send out as pastors only those who truly love the Lord Jesus Christ, have a love for God's Word, have a passion for reaching lost souls, and who know that they are born again. Look for fruit of evangelism and discipleship in their lives.

Unless those who are in pastoral leadership in your church have a heart for winning the lost—and are truly convinced that the world is filled with lost people who need to be won to Christ Jesus—you will not have a leader who values or promotes missionary work beyond your church doors.

Third, we individually and personally must be able and willing to give a personal word of witness about Jesus Christ.

In addition to a solid understanding of what Jesus taught as evidenced by the Gospels, and what the New Testament as a whole teaches us about Jesus and what it means to be a Christ-follower, we must be quick to share our personal testimonies of salvation and conversion whenever we have an opportunity. If you call yourself "Christian," you should be able to tell others how you became a Christian and what Christ has done for you *personally*. You must be able to share succinctly, directly, and clearly what it means for you to have a Savior and to follow Jesus Christ as your Lord. You must know how to lead another person to a saving relationship with God through belief in Jesus Christ.

There is tremendous power in a simple and forthright personal testimony, especially in the developing world. Countless people have told me how they came to know Jesus as their personal Savior after hearing a personal testimony and how grateful they are for the sacrifice Jesus made on the cross on their behalf.

The Power of Personal Witness. Cinderella's father was unbelievably hesitant, shy, and awkward in facing up to his wife and bringing justice to his daughter. Did he fail to speak the truth in love, in fear of offending her? Did he mistakenly believe that by keeping quiet he would maintain peace? If so, he was a deluded, cowardly, and unjust man. Passivity is always the companion of evil.

During my thirty-eight years of ministry in the United States, I have become increasingly aware that many who call themselves Christians are hesitant, shy, awkward, ashamed, or otherwise reticent in telling me how they came to know Jesus as Savior.

I do not know why this is so. Is it because they are unsure about their personal salvation? Is it because they are so concerned that they might offend another person that they hesitate in proclaiming what they know to be personally true? Is it because they believe such conversation does not belong in polite company? These same people would be very quick to tell me all about their favorite sports teams or their reason for purchasing the cars they drive. A friend of mine in the Midwest will talk to you all day about his business and recruiting other people for the company, but when it comes time for him to offer a prayer or share a brief testimony within the confines of the church, he freezes. Why the reluctance to talk about the most important event in their lives, especially if talking about their salvation might assure another person of a heavenly home for all eternity?

In our movement in India, we place a strong emphasis on a person publicly telling his or her own conversion story. Every time people tell their conversion stories, they build up their own

The Urgent Call

1. How would you summarize the enemy philosophy of universalism to someone who believes that "all religions are equal paths to God"?

2. Examine your own beliefs. Has universalism crept into your own belief system?

3. How does the gospel of Jesus Christ stand in opposition to universalism?

4. Ask someone today about his or her personal conversion story. Ask, "How did you come to believe in Jesus as your personal Savior?" Be quick to share your story in reply.

5. If the person you ask does not have a conversion story, do you know how to lead that person to accept Jesus as his or her Savior?

faith and they increase their ability to articulate their faith with boldness. We encourage a time of sharing testimonies every Sunday. Those who give testimony to Christ's life-changing power find that they are much more aware of Christ's working in their lives. They are looking with great joy and expectancy for the Lord to do tremendous things for them, in them, and through them to others. Their boldness and confidence grows. Their witness is enlarged.

Our evangelists usually hold open-air meetings, where they not only share their personal conversion stories, but also invite others to share their stories. In addition, we encourage the sharing of personal stories that portray the power of Jesus Christ in the life of the believer. The result is a continual stream of stories of how the Lord delivered them from fear, demonic possession, illness, and other kinds of transformation experiences. Some of them have told stories of how their enemies tried to poison them because of their faith in Christ, and how God miraculously saved them. These stories are voiced to the unsaved as well as to the church. This stream of miracle stories is a tremendous blessing to the believers who hear the stories, and a compelling witness to those who have not yet accepted Jesus as Savior.

Every person in every Christian church in the United States should have an opportunity to publicly tell his or her conversion story—to declare publicly what God is doing in his life—at least once a year. In telling our personal salvation stories and our ongoing "following Christ" stories we encourage other believers, reinforce the tremendous importance of what Jesus did for us, and make the possibility of a life-changing, destiny-altering decision known to unbelievers. For the sake of brevity and clarity, a person who goes on a short-term mission trip should be able to say in one hundred words or less, "This is why and how I accepted Jesus as my personal Savior, and this is what my salvation means to me."

Having words to say, and even rehearsing those words to yourself, is insufficient. You as a believer in, and disciple of, Jesus

Christ must have the courage to speak. Eloquence is not always necessary, but a willingness to give voice to what you know is necessary. After all, Moses stuttered and felt like a coward. In the end, he recognized that God was with him to voice what he knew was necessary. Jesus gave these words of encouragement to His followers, "Now when they bring you to the synagogues and magistrates and authorities, do not worry about how or what you should answer, or what you should say. For the Holy Spirit will teach you in that very hour what you ought to say" (Luke 12:11–12). Jesus was not saying that His followers should be unlearned in the Scriptures or unprepared in their messages, but rather that they could count on the Holy Spirit to inspire their speech and direct their thoughts. We must boldly open our mouths to speak. We must rely upon the Holy Spirit to give us the best words to say.

When you develop your testimony and place it in the Lord's hands, you can be sure that God will use it to bring people to Him.

What Might One Person Do?

Read and study your Bible consistently and diligently.

Ask the Holy Spirit to quicken to your heart and mind as to which verses and passages of God's Word that you are to commit to memory, so that you will have a ready arsenal of scripture at your disposal should you find yourself in a situation that warrants your giving witness to Jesus as the Christ.

Find a friend with whom you can role-play potential scenarios for sharing the gospel. In other words, set up potential "How I would respond to someone who said…" scenarios. You might want to do this in a small-group setting. Talk to your small-group leader or pastor about setting aside a portion of your small-group time for such role-playing.

Write down your personal testimony. Gain a clear understanding in your own mind about how to succinctly and clearly present the essential points you would want to share with a person you were attempting to lead to Christ.

Talk to your pastor about various ways the people of your church might be given an opportunity to share their personal testimonies of salvation in the presence of at least two or three other people who are also believers.

Heavenly Father, forgive me for my complicity in perpetuating injustice in the world by allowing the philosophies of men to dilute and deny the uniqueness of Christ. Forgive me for being passive and apathetic to evil in pursuit of a false peace. Help me to know that Jesus is utterly holy, unchallengeable, and unchangeable. Purge me of any teaching that is not one hundred percent in line with Your Word. Help me to become more focused about what I believe and why.

Give me greater courage and boldness to speak Your words and to give my personal testimony to others. I want to be Your witness—help me, Lord! Give me a steadfast spirit in face of difficulties. Free me from all fear of the enemy and give me the ability to discern quickly when I am being ensnared by the enemy's lies. I ask this in the name of Jesus, who alone is the truth, the life, and the way. Amen.

Jesus said to His disciples... "Do you not say, 'There are still four months and then comes the harvest?' Behold, I say to you, lift up your eyes and look at the fields, for they are already white for harvest! And he who reaps receives wages, and gathers fruit for eternal life, that both he who sows and he who reaps may rejoice together. For in this the saying is true: 'One sows and another reaps.' I sent you to reap that for which you have not labored; others have labored, and you have entered into their labors."

John 4:35–38

BETWEEN THE CELLAR AND "HAPPILY EVER AFTER"

Cinderella's story is popular worldwide because it has a happy ending. But a lot of things must take place before Cinderella is permanently transformed from an object of scorn and pity into a royal princess and queen.

She needs the intervention of the fairy godmother.

She needs the assistance of an array of unlikely characters to get her to the ball.

She must overcome the wiles of the wicked stepmother and her equally wicked daughters, as well as her passive father.

She must win the heart of the prince.

She must depend upon unplanned but fortuitous occurrences, such as the losing of her glass slipper, which will give the prince an important clue as to his beloved's identity.

She must depend upon the determination of the prince to leave no stone unturned in find-

ing her, not even the diversionary tactics of the
wicked stepmother.

She must depend upon the prince to communicate his intentions so effectively to all young
women of noble birth that even Cinderella in
her obscurity will know about it.

She must depend upon the prince's continued
love and patience toward her as she comes to live
in the palace and become used to a completely
different way of life.

In short, she must depend upon grace—and a
whole lot of other people.

Kind of sounds like the Christian life, especially in places and among people where there
seems to be no way "out of the cellar."

———◦◦◦———

Persistently, Satan does a number of shameless things to keep
people in the cellar. He does this by trying to keep Jesus's
emissaries from succeeding on the mission field in reaching the
rightful people whom God has intended to hear His good news.
Satan intends to keep those who are lost from ever emerging
into the fullness of Christ's purpose for their lives—to keep the
lost in drudgery and bondage, without hope, without miracles,
and without the joy of salvation. In this, he has been very effective, just as the wicked stepmother was effective in keeping
Cinderella in the cellar for a long time. One of Satan's foremost
tactics to keep missionaries off the mission field is to define the
concept of "missionary" in such narrow and confining terms that
people not only see missionaries as dull and boring but cease to
seek out creative ways of proclaiming the good news.

Before the 1970s, missionaries usually were trained to work
in a designated nation or region of the world, raise support
from their respective denominations, and go to the mission field

with their families to work and live among those they hoped to evangelize and disciple. Generally speaking, a person, couple, or family expected to spend the remainder of their lives overseas sharing the gospel and planting Christian churches. Frequently, they also established a school or medical clinic adjacent to or sponsored by the church. In the mid-twentieth century, with advances in transportation systems, it became customary for missionaries to return home every few years to report on their progress, renew their support, rest, and renew their relationships with extended family members and friends. Nevertheless, the commitment was perceived to be a lifelong commitment.

In the last forty years, technology and widespread air travel have greatly changed the definition of missionary service, opening up the possibilities for new types of creative evangelism. Let me share with you three examples of missionaries with whom we have had the privilege of working with in India.

Joel and Kathy (names changed) came to India in 2008 to teach at India Bible College and Seminary and Punjab Bible College. Their area of expertise is campus ministry, a ministry that is greatly underdeveloped in India. Only about five hundred out of twenty thousand campuses in India have any Christian ministry representation. My figures on Christian outreach in Indian universities are based upon my own extensive ministry contacts and personal involvement. I have frequent contacts with evangelical campus staff of Campus Crusade, Evangelicals Union, Evangelical Union Students of India, Intercollegiate Prayer Fellowship, Blessing Youth Ministry, and YWAM. Most seminaries and Bible schools in India do not offer any courses dealing with campus ministry.

Joel and Kathy were with us for ten weeks. The training they offered was greatly needed and well received. They enjoyed good cooperation with both faculty and students, and they proved to be very adaptable to Indian culture and customs. They respected the work accomplished by our evangelists, and they learned from us even as we learned from them. Plus, their two-year-old daughter turned out to be a real hit with students and faculty.

In another situation, a medical team of four medical doctors from a supporting church in southern California provided medical aid following the disastrous tsunami of December, 2004. This natural catastrophe killed more than fifteen thousand Indians and left hundreds of thousands of Indian people homeless. The team provided medical aid, working harmoniously with a team that included more than twenty Indian doctors and nurses, as well as graduates and students of India Bible College and Seminary. The team offered both medical assistance and spiritual guidance. In all, more than seven thousand people received individual help in several places and in a variety of ways. In many cases, team members prayed with the people as they provided medical help.

Many of the people they helped came from Hindu backgrounds. They were deeply impressed by the team. In the aftermath of this tragedy, countless people sought out Christian solutions to their problems. More than 1,200 people asked for Christian Scriptures and are still receiving ministry from our evangelists.

This medical team came to us with a true attitude of servanthood. The seeds of faith planted in a very short period of time are still growing into a harvest.

In a third example, Gary Doyle (name changed), an American pastor and a supporter of our ministry, has come to India Bible College and Seminary several times over recent years. He, and two American professors of psychology and counseling, teach on the nature of Christian counseling, another area lacking in most seminaries and Bible schools in India. They have a good relationship with members of our faculty and see themselves as team members, cooperating in a common purpose of meeting needs in the name of Jesus. Their servant attitude, coupled with their counseling skills, has greatly impacted our training program.

Each of these three missionary endeavors was for a different length of time, and for a different purpose. The success of each endeavor was rooted in the coupling of a genuine servant heart with practical information and skills.

I believe that each of these people represents a major new type of missionary work that has emerged in just the last four decades. Each of them knew their role was that of a specialist who comes in for a limited time and leaves after students are trained and ready to go throughout India.

Different Roles for Different Goals

The prince made sure that all young women of noble birth effectively heard the decree so that they would have their fair chance to try on the glass slipper. Though Cinderella worked in the cellar, away from all others, even she knew of the royal ball and later, about the decree that would eventually set her free. *We have to credit the prince for a communication job well done.*

In the same way, we need to make sure that the good news is communicated effectively to all who need to hear it. Because human beings live in many kinds of situations, that means we cannot be satisfied with just one method or language to accomplish the task. We may have to invent dozens, hundreds, and thousands of ways to make sure that everyone hears the gospel. What works well in one situation or for one generation may not necessarily be right for another time and place. There must always be room for improvement in means and methods.

Missions work today tends to fall into one of two categories: long-term, full-time missionary work by ordained clergy, or short-term, part-time mission work by laity.

In many ways, mission work has become like much of church-related ministries: full-time trained professionals and part-time laity who are partially trained or untrained. The part-time laity has been mostly involved in either evangelism programs or practical service projects that employ specific skills, such as medical work, educational programs, and construction or agricultural

at the emotional level: birth and death, marriage and divorce, wealth and poverty, health and illness, strength and weakness, love and hate, and care and abuse. It happens most often that when bad things overtake us, we undergo the greatest anguish and are most likely to question our assumptions. Many of us can testify that our periods of greatest growth have come in times of adversity when pure reason fails.

In nearly all cases, the language barrier is a major issue for many of those who participate in short-term missions. Those who give their witness often require translators. Given the time constraints and limitations that may exist on the part of both those speaking and those translating, the messages presented are often personal testimony or very rudimentary presentations of the gospel message. This is fine for basic evangelism, but does not truly allow for discipleship of those won to Christ.

The Technology Factor. The particular missionary mentioned previously also conveyed a problem that many medical experts have when they go overseas. American medicine is rooted in science and relies heavily upon laboratory tests and advanced equipment, nearly all of which require a steady source of electricity. Overseas medicine, especially in the neediest areas of the world, rarely has the lab support, electricity, or equipment to support the work of Western-trained physicians and surgeons. Most of the "medical" work involves vaccinations, dental care, and instruction related to basic hygiene and nursing techniques. This presents good news and bad news. The good news is that many laypeople can be trained fairly quickly to provide these practical health-care services. The bad news is that physicians, who often can afford to go on short-term missions—both financially and in their work schedules—are overqualified for the tasks they are able to perform owing to technological limitations.

The Cultural Factors. Another major issue to consider in short-term missions is the lack of understanding on the part of many short-term mission participants when it comes to geographical and cultural boundaries. If the church is truly going to reach the two billion people on the planet who have not yet heard the gospel, short-term missions is not the most effective approach.

Few seem to recognize that the people who have not yet heard the gospel are those who tend to be the most insulated against other cultures, and are often the most wary of other cultures. They have a closed mindset that precludes the notion that anything of value can come from the outside world. This is true not only of remote areas of Africa, South America, and Asia, but also of nations in the grip of fundamentalist Islam or cut off by their geographic remoteness, such as areas of Mongolia and western China. For that matter, some neighborhoods in inner-city America also have an insulated world view not easily bridged or addressed by short-term visitors.

To evangelize these out-of-reach peoples, a missionary must live among the people long enough to learn their language and culture, and to win their confidence and trust.

Research has repeatedly shown that the credibility and trust factor with missionaries begins only after the seventh year (Covey 2006). The whole book discusses the importance of trust and the global crisis of trust in the world today. Trust takes time, the author says, and is the issue of the decade. The author gives a full discussion of the issue in this book. Low trust is the greatest cost in life and in organizations, including families. Low trust slows everything—every decision, every communication and every relationship. On the other hand, trust produces speed. Jim Burke, former CEO of Johnson & Johnson, says, "You can't have success without trust."

A 2005 Harris Poll in the U.S. revealed that only 22 percent tend to trust the media, only 8 percent trust political parties, 27 percent trust the government, and only 12 percent trust the companies.

Relationships of all kinds are built on and sustained by trust. Low trust is the very condition of a bad relationship. The percentage of students who acknowledged that they cheated to get into graduate school include: liberal arts students, 43 percent; education students, 52 percent; medical students, 63 percent; law students, 63 percent; and business students, 75 percent.

In all these areas, establishing trust is based upon relationship, integrity, personal capabilities, expertise, and track record. The other person must know you have a trustworthy record and do not have a hidden agenda. All of this takes time to discover. In his book, Stephen Covey discusses this topic thoroughly. Our own experience with missionaries verifies everything that Mr. Covey discusses. (See also page 84 regarding the experience of William Carey.)

When people perceive you as a "hit-and-run" worker, you do not earn their trust. Also, full language proficiency takes ten to twelve years to develop. That means church planting must be seen as a long-term or a lifetime commitment. Our own experience with the thousands of evangelists that we have trained and sent as well as working closely with those involved in Bible translation in India has enabled us to arrive at this figure.

What about Church-to-Church Missions?
A corollary to short-term mission is the concept of "partnering"—meaning an established church in America or elsewhere partners with an indigenous church overseas to reach out to the lost. These partnerships involve indigenous pioneer missionaries, who tend to live close to the unreached people, and sometimes live among them. This is wonderful in theory. But in truth, such partnering rarely occurs. Indeed, it is rarely possible. One of the foremost reasons is that indigenous missionaries—the career or professional clergy in other nations—tend to be leaders of fairly young churches. These churches are still being raised up and the people in them are still being discipled. Evangelism in the immediate area of the church is still underway. There simply are

no time, resources, and available trained and mature Christian personnel to extend outward to a nearby people group, tribe, or unreached area.

Suppose that a new church work in a major US city was established in a largely Asian immigrant neighborhood that was "across the freeway" from a similar, largely Hispanic immigrant neighborhood. The Asian church is likely to have an Asian pastor, perhaps someone trained in a larger Asian church elsewhere or in a Caucasian church. The new Asian-neighborhood church may have started only a few months earlier. Evangelistic outreach continues in the Asian neighborhood in a small rented building as a church meeting place, with various fledgling Bible study and ministry programs. To ask that Asian church to "partner" with a group of Caucasian upscale short-term missions participants for outreach into the unreached Hispanic neighborhoods would leave the Asian Christians baffled and overextended.

"But," you may say, "you are dealing with two different cultures and races of people in your example." True. But that is exactly the point when dealing with unreached people groups in overseas locations. Although the people might occupy land along the same river or live "just over the mountain," and appear to be of similar ethnicity, the unreached people group may have a different culture, different language or dialect, different history, a different awareness level of the outside world, and a very different degree of openness to outside influences.

Geographic proximity does not mean cultural proximity.

The truth is, most short-term mission participants minister not to the unreached but to the already reached. Their work largely supports fellow Christians. It is rarely truly evangelistic, and is often limited when it comes to discipleship.

Let me share with you a fairly startling fact: *even if all ministry were to be done by Christians who belong to the same ethnic people groups as their non-Christian neighbors, some 6,872 people groups without any Christian witness would still remain unreached.*

In other words, there are still 6,872 people groups without anyone to communicate the gospel to them, even from members of their own ethnic group. They are people of distinct tribal status with their own unique cultures, languages, and histories—who have never heard the gospel. These unreached peoples will not hear or understand the gospel unless someone communicates to them in their heart language. This can happen only by actually living among them on a long-term basis and getting to know them closely. See further statistics for this at www.joshuaproject.net/great-commission-statistics.php. Note: Joshua Project is one of the most reliable research agencies that statistically measure the Great Commission task that remains before us. According to their website statement of purpose, "Joshua Project is a research initiative seeking to highlight the ethnic people groups of the world with the least followers of Christ. Accurate, regularly updated ethnic people group information is critical for understanding and completing the Great Commission."

In one of His parables, Jesus said that the kingdom of God would expand in similar fashion as leaven, which a woman "works into" a loaf of bread (Matthew 13:33). Such leaven is spread evenly in a lump of dough from within. Just as sprinkling a little yeast on top of a lump of dough does not cause the bread to rise, so short-term missions will not bring about effective church planting and discipleship.

The Benefits of Short-Term Missions

My analysis of short-term missions should not be taken as a denunciation of all short-term missions work. Far from it! Many wonderful things can occur through short-term mission outreaches. The key is for the team to have a genuine servant's heart, desire to work alongside indigenous pastors and evangelists in a mutual exchange of ideas and skills, and to have an appreciation for the culture and expertise of those being served. We find it particularly helpful for short-term mission groups to have highly focused areas of expertise or information in areas where the church is weak, such as medicine or teaching.

When these short-term mission groups return to their churches, they bring important information and an expanded vision for missions to their own congregations and parishes. The level of awareness of the lost, awareness of other cultures, and the awareness of missionary needs is raised. All of these are positive benefits for the church as a whole.

Where short-term missions fall short is in their ability to establish new works: new churches, new schools, and new ministries. Both time and long-term commitment are required to plant a new venture and nurture it to maturity.

Prayer-Based Short-Term Missions

Some people may not have special skills, but they have a burden and willingness to pray. Many such people have gone to different parts of the world and engaged in surveying the cities, walking through the streets and praying for the city. In several places, we have seen breakthroughs for the gospel and miraculous doors opened for the ministry. I call this ministry "pre-evangelism." Prayer should always precede evangelism. This includes prayer before a person leaves for a mission field, as well as prayer on site before beginning to proclaim the good news publicly. In our own ministry, we have commenced a 2020 Prayer Vision for India to ask the Lord to break down all spiritual barriers to enable the gospel to saturate all of India.

An Overview Appraisal of Long-Term Missions

The prince was committed in the long term in reaching the rightful wearer of the glass slipper, in this case, Cinderella. If this was noble and noteworthy for the attaining of an earthly crown, how much more noble is it in joining long-term with God in His work of reaching all of His loved ones so that they will attain the crowns to which He has eternally ordained for them!

Long-term missions involves a life commitment. It is generally the arena of "professionals" who are trained for mission work in a particular area, either through formal education or more practical internships or apprenticeships. Professional missionaries are trained in language, culture, customs, and various aspects of church building and church growth, in addition to Bible-training.

Career missionaries from North America are needed now and for the foreseeable future, and they are indispensable. Both Western-based missionaries and missionaries from the developing world must work together to complete the tasks of evangelism and discipleship.

The long-term, full-time missionary is called to two roles: evangelism and discipleship. Evangelism involves presenting the gospel so that people might accept Jesus as Savior. Discipleship involves training the new convert to follow Jesus as Lord.

> God does nothing but in answer to believing prayer.
> —John Wesley

The Most Effective Means for Overcoming a Parochial Mindset

The wicked stepmother and her daughters tried to limit the possibilities for the prince and his herald in giving Cinderella her right to try on the glass slipper. First, they tried to deny that there was any other daughter in the house. When that failed, they tried to deny that Cinderella had a foot small enough to fit the glass slipper.

In similar fashion, Satan tries to deny a fair hearing for the gospel for those whom God has intended it by limiting the possibilities. One of his favorite methods is to create parochial mindsets that become barriers to hearing the truth.

A parochial mindset is highly suspicious of influences and peoples outside of the tribe, and it tends to be closed to all things new and foreign. This may be the result of a narrow-minded attitude, longstanding prejudices, or bad treatment in the past from outsiders. In places such as Orissa, India, tribal people are often exploited and mistreated by outsiders, so there is a natural tendency to protect themselves, especially if the mistreatment has taken place over a long time.

To win the confidence of a group of highly ethnocentric people, one needs to live among them long enough to discover the cause of the parochial mindset: their fears, prejudices, past experiences, and anxieties. The evangelist must earn their trust and win their respect. He must say and do things that make sense to them and incrementally take them from what they know to what they do not know. The missionary or evangelist needs to stay with the people long enough to help them not only accept a new idea, but come to accept it as their own idea and not something foreign. This is a slow process that passes through stages of "resistance" and "tolerance" before reaching "acceptance."

Among Orissa's tribe people, there is great suspicion of outsiders. At the same time, they need outsiders to teach them essential things that their worldview makes it difficult for them to learn. For example, tribal people drink water from the same source used by cattle for drinking and defecation. This greatly increases human susceptibility to disease and death. When they learn this vital connection, and that foreigners have just helped to save their lives and the lives of their children, they are more likely to listen to other ideas, including the lifesaving good news. When they gradually see that outsiders are trying to help them, not overpower and control them, they are more likely to become open to other foreign ideas.

Long-Term Missions for Discipleship

The stepmother's power to deceive extended only as far as her ability to keep Cinderella in the cellar and her attempt to deny Cinderella her right to try on the glass slipper. Once Cinderella left home and took up residence in the palace, the wicked stepmother was powerless to do anything more, though Cinderella still had to make huge adjustments to a new way of life.

But after we become believers in Christ, we don't immediately take up our residence in God's heavenly palace. Usually, we remain on earth, where Satan's attempts to deceive continue. Because of Satan's crafty ways, each new believer needs effective training into our new roles as members of God's royal family.

Let us consider the matter of discipleship more closely. The Great Commission of Jesus includes a command to disciple the nations. Jesus said…

> Go therefore and make disciples of all the nations, baptizing them in the Name of the Father and of the Son and of the Holy Spirit, teaching them to observe all things that I have commanded you; and lo, I am with you always, even to the end of the age.
>
> Matthew 28:19–20

I invite you to note four important things about that brief statement of Jesus:

1. *Discipleship Lies Beyond Evangelism.* Jesus told His own disciples to go and make disciples. The challenge was not to tell the gospel, but to teach and preach the gospel so that others might not only accept Jesus as Savior, but follow Jesus as Lord. The challenge we face in missions is not merely to get others to come forward in a rally and pray the sinner's prayer, but also to go back into their neighborhoods and live Christ-honoring lives. It is not enough that others convert to Christ and are saved. We must teach others how to live a Christian life.

In dealing with missions overseas, a person must be aware that evangelism is not the beginning and end of a missionary's work. The *making of a disciple* is a missionary's work.

Discipleship places an emphasis on the uniqueness of Christ and His ability to change the inward heart, not merely change outward forms and rituals. In India, the work of discipleship focuses upon the teachings of Christ Jesus, such as those in the Sermon on the Mount. We have also found it effective to have a teaching focus on the Ten Commandments because such teaching addresses the overall health and spiritual wellbeing of the individual, family, society, and nation. We do our utmost to expose new converts to the whole counsel of God, seeing that God desires a change of heart that results in change of behavior. Simply changing outward forms does not produce inner change.

2. *Baptism Involves Acceptance of a Completely New Identity.* Jesus called His followers to baptize disciples in the name of the Father and Son and Holy Spirit. To be baptized in a name—in this case, the full name of the Trinity—is to be baptized into the *full identity* of the one named.

In India, baptism is a process that involves a fairly extensive period of instruction prior to the baptismal service. Baptismal services are conducted in public places, such as a river or lake, where people congregate to wash their clothes. Those being baptized recite the Apostles' Creed and each person being baptized declares full allegiance to Jesus Christ. For the new believer, baptism reflects a complete change of spiritual identity.

Read the second and third chapters of the book of Acts, and you will readily conclude that Peter and the other apostles of Jesus were obedient to the Great Commission that Jesus Christ gave to "make disciples of all the nations, baptizing them in the name of the Father and of the Son and of the Holy Spirit" (Matthew 28:19). Baptism was far more than a mere cleansing ritual or rite of passage. In his day of Pentecost sermon, Peter called men and women to, "Repent, and let every one of you be baptized in the name of Jesus Christ for the remission of sins; and you shall receive the gift of the Holy Spirit" (Acts 2:38–39).

This meant that the earliest believers, the vast majority of whom were Jewish, went into the waters identified as a son or daughter of the Law, and came out of those waters identified as a son or daughter of Christ Jesus! They were cleansed of not only their sins but also their sin nature by God the Father, according to the atoning sacrificially shed blood of Jesus Christ. They were sealed into their new life of forgiveness and called to new life of gospel-based, loving service by the power of the Holy Spirit. Baptism for the new believer in Christ Jesus was a matter of *total identity change*! The purpose involved forgiveness, but also a call to a radically new way of believing and living, and to a new type of godly service to others.

Those engaged in cross-cultural mission work must recognize that a new convert's commitment to Christ Jesus involves a total identity change—a cleansing from sin, but also a call to a new life that includes service to others, as the Holy Spirit both empowers and leads that person. Baptism acknowledges that Jesus is *Savior*, and it prepares a person to be led by the Holy Spirit in following Jesus as *Lord*.

Those who grow up in the United States often do not fully understand this matter of total identity change. Although the American culture is shifting, much of the American culture is still decidedly Judeo-Christian when it comes to matters of law, and it is certainly culturally Christian when it comes to many customs and traditions that, for the most part, are taken for granted. In the United States, even the nation's money states, "In God We Trust," and the nation sets aside certain Christian holidays (such as Christmas) as federal holidays.

A person in another nation without such a Christian cultural foundation faces a tremendous challenge: how to live a Christian life and live as a person of his own race and culture, especially when his race and culture have for a millennia opposed Christ Jesus either openly and adamantly, or through lack of information. Culture has tremendous impact on every human being. The change required is equally tremendous. To become a Christian means to become immersed into the full identity of Jesus.

A person in another nation or culture comes to know this in a powerful way. Let me tell you the story of Dr. Kishore Jeevan (name changed). He came to Christ a few years ago from a Hindu and high caste Brahmin background. Kishore is the only son of his parents who were highly accomplished professionals in their fields. Most of his family members are medical doctors. Dr. Kishore Jeevan himself is a medical doctor. He accepted Jesus as his Savior after a friend shared his testimony and explained the gospel message to him.

After coming to the Lord, Kishore obeyed the Lord in water baptism and was faithful in Bible study. Sometime later, his mother died. As the only son of the family, he was asked to perform several Hindu funeral rituals. To do this would have meant bowing to idols and performing acts that would violate biblical commands and his personal testimony.

I spent a lot of time with Kishore, sharing the scriptures with him and praying, and also introducing him to others of similar backgrounds. This encouraged his faith. He took a strong stand and he shared his testimony with his family, friends, and Hindu priests in a loving way, and gave reasons why he could not perform the expected rituals. Nobody in his family understood him fully. Some became very angry. Others would not speak to him. The few who were close to him barely tolerated him.

Rather than become bitter or angry at their reaction, Kishore responded in love, but remained true to his new experience in Christ Jesus. The result is that he now openly proclaims an even greater identification with the death, burial, and resurrection of Jesus Christ. He knows what it means to die fully to one's past and rise to a new way of living. Baptism was and is for him a vivid and meaningful, outward and visible act representing a very real and inward reality.

3. *Discipleship.* Jesus said that discipleship was a "teaching process" (Matthew 28:20). More specifically, it was a teaching process of what Jesus commanded.

Evangelism is a matter of sharing with others the good news of what Jesus did; what He accomplished by His sacrificial and atoning death on the cross; what He secured in His resurrection from the dead; and what He promises to every person who will turn to Him: forgiveness from sin and life everlasting. Evangelism is a matter of *believing*.

In contrast, discipleship is a matter of *learning*. It is a matter of knowing what God's Word says, and knowing as well how to apply God's Word to the believer's daily life. In terms of our Cinderella analogy, discipleship is training to help us keep from returning to "cellar thinking" and going back to what we should have left behind. It is amazing that Satan's lies are so effective that we so easily go back to what we should reject!

Jesus said that disciples were to teach others to observe all that Jesus commanded. That word *observe* means "to do, keep, and/or live by." Those who observed the Law in Jesus's day were strict keepers and doers of the Law. To "observe the commands of Jesus" means that a person not only knows them, but he lives by them. He is a doer of the Word and not a hearer only. He is a living example of Christ Jesus walking among his peers.

The commands of Jesus are active. Jesus was not merely concerned that people have a right attitude and right set of beliefs, but right speech, right deeds, and right ways of treating one another.

A disciple is one who is an active doer of an active life of "loving God" and "loving others as he loves himself." To love is to give. It is to serve in an unselfish, generous fashion.

Any effort at evangelism that does not include teaching discipleship is only a partial fulfillment of the Great Commission, and therefore, it can be only partially successful.

The most successful form of teaching and learning in discipleship is a method educators call "modeling." The successful rabbi in Jesus's time was a person whom others followed daily, walking and talking along life's highways and byways in times both festive and mundane. The true disciple learned not only from what the rabbi believed and taught, but also from how the rabbi lived. The true disciple adopted the lifestyle of Jesus. The disciples of Jesus were trained through daily actions over months and years to live as Jesus lived, to speak as Jesus spoke, and to act as Jesus acted.

Modeling is how full-time professional missionaries teach best. They "walk the talk" before others. Their lives become the living textbook for the new Christian to read daily. Whatever the missionary preaches and teaches is seen within the total life of the missionary.

Our evangelists in India preach that Jesus Christ expels fear from a person's life. They "live out" their lack of fear in a real and observable way. In north India, especially, our evangelists who are new to a community seek to rent a house that no one has occupied for years. The lack of occupancy is usually the result of a strong belief that the house is filled with demons or has been cursed. The community as a whole expects that any person who lives in such a house will become ill, die, or face some form of terrible tragedy. In the face of these beliefs, the Christian evangelist openly prays for God's protection and moves in! The people watch closely, expecting something terrible to happen. When nothing bad happens, the people are much more quickly convinced of the power and authenticity of the gospel!

4. *Discipleship Embodies a New Worldview.* Since we are told that Cinderella lived with her prince "happily ever after," we know that her relationship with the prince continued to blossom. Instead of growing old and stale, their relationship became more joyful and giving and exciting as they came to know each other better and shared the joy of raising children and being of service to others. Her new and expanded way of life gave her a new perspective that kept her from wanting to return to her former life as a scullery maid. She became devoted to her prince because he prepared her for palace living instead of cellar living. This brings us to an important point of Jesus' concept of discipleship.

Jesus certainly did not take this matter of discipleship lightly. It was His supreme challenge to His apostles, both during His lifetime and as He entrusted His life and ministry to them.

The Gospel of Luke gives a succinct and very powerful set of statements that Jesus made about discipleship. Jesus said:

> If anyone comes to Me and does not hate his father and mother, wife and children, brothers and sisters, yes, and his own life also, he cannot be My disciple. And whoever does not bear his cross and come after Me cannot be My disciple. For which of you, intending to build a tower, does not sit down first and count the cost, whether he has enough to finish it—lest, after he has laid the foundation, and is not able to finish, all who see it begin to mock him, saying, 'This man began to build and was not able to finish.' Or what king, going to make war against another king, does not sit down first and consider whether he is able with ten thousand to meet him who comes against him with twenty thousand? Or else, while the other is still a great way off, he sends a delegation and asks conditions of peace. So likewise, whoever of you does not forsake all that he has cannot be My disciple.
>
> Salt is good; but if the salt has lost its flavor, how shall it be seasoned? It is neither fit for the land nor for the dunghill, but men throw it out, He who has ears to hear, let him hear!
>
> Luke 14:25–34

Let me summarize this passage for you in missionary terms.

1. *Total Devotion and Love.* Jesus certainly wasn't anti-family; however, He understood that a person's loyalties and priorities

move either toward God and our eternal royal family in heaven or toward human beings and our temporary human families on earth. Every person moves toward what that person loves. Those who love God make God's commands their priorities. Just as Cinderella adopted the prince's royal family as her own, we adopt God and His royal family as our own. We forever seek ways to move closer to God and fulfill God's claims and call on our lives. To live as a disciple is to value what God says more than what other people say, even if they are members of our earthly families.

This is a critically important concept in missions. People newly converted to Christ often face intense criticism from other people—especially from the people they love the most: their parents, spouses, and other family members. Jesus's call of discipleship is to love God fully and to pursue what God commands regardless of what others say.

The new convert in India faces many social and family pressures. For instance, the new Christian must remove Hindu amulets that he or she may have worn for years. Amulets are created by a particular caste in India, and the piece of jewelry is engraved with names or symbols of Hindu gods. This is the way they write the name of their god and address him. Wearing an amulet is thought to bring good luck and to be a sign of devotion to a god. An amulet very often becomes a fetish, which is an object that is worshipped in itself and is thought to have magical powers.

For the new convert to Christ, the removal of an amulet or fetish is a sign of removing former spiritual influences. For many, it is also an open sign of separation from a longstanding family devotion to a false god. Many new Christians are ostracized by their families and neighbors in their village when they openly remove their amulets.

New believers need new families of loving and supporting Christians who offer shelter and encouragement in those times of distress and abandonment, when their own flesh and blood have disowned them. When I grew up in the twin cities of Hyderabad-Secunderabad, all my neighbors were Hindus. One son became a Christian, and he was literally kicked out of his family. His parents disowned him, never again admitting that they had given birth to him. I knew a woman who became a Christian and her husband not only beat her but required her to hold fiery coals in her hands.

The new convert faces persecution not only from his or her immediate family, but also from local witch doctors, priests, and shamans. The Bible gives us an example of Paul being persecuted after he delivered a young woman from a fortune-telling demon. What happened to Paul happens today in India. Indian society includes much palm-reading and fortune-telling. When a person becomes a Christian he realizes that his future does not lie in the position of the stars or arrangement of tea leaves, but rather in the hands of the one who made the stars and tea. The new convert no longer needs to consult a fortune-teller or witch doctor.

Hinduism is a religion based upon fear. Hindus seem constantly engaged in behavior that they hope will appease the anger of some particular god. A family may worship a particular god, for example, but then conclude that other gods are causing harm to come to them. Since their chosen or favored god is unable to protect them against these alien gods, the person takes it upon himself to appease the god. The result? They must constantly appease competing deities to avoid catastrophe.

But when a person opens his heart to Christ, He dispels this fear. Of course, this represents a huge threat to the person's former witch doctor. Often, the witch doctor or local fortune-teller will do their utmost to re-instill fear and superstition. One of the most powerful forms of witness a new convert can display is a refusal to cave in to this pressure from those who practice the occult. If a Christian believer stands strong in the face of threats from a witch doctor or fortune-teller, his witness can have tremendous impact.

2. *Total Submission to Christ's Demands.* Once Cinderella became a princess, she became totally devoted to the prince and the royal family. Even her blood father had no more power over her. Power takes many forms. Very few nations, tribes, or cultures around the world are democratic. Individuals in most nations do not have personal rights to free speech, free worship, or even free assembly. To submit oneself totally to Christ Jesus is to put Him above the current power structure. That didn't sit well with Rome during the first century, and it still doesn't sit well in many parts of the world today. Persecution of Christians is often intense and fully sanctioned by those who are in power. To "bear one's cross" in following Christ is to be subject to what Christ commands—not just some of the time or at convenient times, but all of the time.

While this conflict with prevailing powers can become an experience for those who live in an increasingly secularized United States, it is a far greater issue to those in other nations who seek to follow Christ. The new Christian is constantly swimming upstream against the current of his prevailing culture, and often against the forces associated with the false religion to which he once gave allegiance.

Christ commands the new believer to submit to those in designated leadership positions and at the same time to stand for a higher law than that which human governments enact or enforce. Achieving a balance in this area is sometimes difficult. Civil disobedience is sometimes necessary. The goal, however, was made clear by the apostle Paul: we are to live in peace as much as possible, so that we might do our work of evangelizing others in peace.

The Christian missionary teaches from the Word of God, which is revolutionary in and of itself. In many cases, the missionary's witness and work among those in leadership creates an environment in which the gospel flourishes.

When a person sees a missionary turn the other cheek, not strike back in anger or vengeance—sometimes accepting personal loss of property without pressing charges—that's radically different, revolutionary behavior!

When a person sees a missionary go the second mile rather than demand service—such as bandaging the wounds of an Islamic terrorist—that's radically different, revolutionary behavior!

When a person sees a missionary engaged in sacrificial giving rather than seeking a gift—such as sharing what little food the missionary may have with an even poorer person—that's radically different, revolutionary behavior!

Such behavior is subversive and turns the norms upside down—or perhaps better stated, right side up.

3. *Perseverance in Commitment and Ministry.* Once Cinderella married the prince, we can assume there was nothing half-hearted about her commitment to her new role. Neither is there anything half-hearted about truly living the Christian life. Jesus made consistency between belief and behavior a matter of integrity and reputation. He told them to "leave what you know and follow Me." To one who asked what he had to do to become a disciple, Jesus said, "Go and sell all and follow Me."

People do not judge what another person begins. Rather, they judge what another person finishes. And in truth, all discipleship ventures of any kind are never fully finished. There is always something more to learn, some additional teaching to apply, or some new application to improve. Nevertheless, the more we mature in Christ, the more God's work of refinement and maturity is accomplished or finished in us. Thus, the more we grow in Christ, the more we are subject to judgment by those who do not follow Jesus. We should not be surprised when we are judged or when this judgment turns into persecution! When persecution occurs, we must persevere.

How do we learn to persevere? By observing those who persevere. Perseverance happens over time. A reputation for integrity and perseverance does not happen instantly. It comes as a person's life is observed in a variety of situations, many difficult and involving suffering. Perseverance is the price of success for the missionary. William Carey, the great missionary to India whom I mentioned earlier, had to wait more than seven years before he saw his first convert. It took seven years for him to build trust with that person and those who followed after him (see page 73). He persevered until that day!

4. *Total Obedience and Allegiance.* We can be sure that when Cinderella married the prince and lived happily ever after, that she was expected to obey her husband and prince, but her obedience and allegiance toward her prince and king was based upon love. The world at large functions according to channels of authority. So do we as Christians. We are called to obey God fully and to count the cost of our allegiance. We who obey live at peace with God, our superior in all things. We do not rebel against what God commands, either outwardly or inwardly. We do not make war with God: we do not seek to tempt God or to dance along the edge of sin's abyss. We do not argue against God's Word or seek to justify behavior that we know in our hearts is contrary to God's commands. We do not obey God out of fear but out of love.

For most of us, a true change of heart and allegiance does not happen overnight. With each new command of Christ—each new insight of the Word—comes a need for further confession, repentance, and renewal, knowing that God accepts us in love.

Cinderella had to learn a lot of things about living in a palace. It did not come overnight. Rising instantly from scullery maid to princess and then queen is a real culture shock. Could any of us do it without some errors in protocol along the way? But the prince must have been very patient and loving with his new bride and encouraged her along the way to insure that her new life truly would be happy forever-after. In so doing, the prince plays the role of Jesus and the role of the Holy Spirit in mentoring us and in helping us to mentor others who are growing in faith.

At salvation, we receive a new nature with which to make wise decisions. That new nature is received in an instant. A baby birthed from the womb suddenly has a new nature that requires the infant to use its lungs to breathe, be subject to the laws of gravity, and to eat. In similar fashion, the new believer is set free from the bondage of sin and its attendant guilt and shame, and is empowered to choose what is right. But the newly saved person is not perfected in a moment. The born-anew spiritual infant is not made instantly mature. Paul writes extensively about the process of growth into the "full stature" of Christ. Renewal is an ongoing process of living in total obedience and allegiance every hour or every day of every week of every month of every year for the rest of a person's life.

People may adhere to a philosophy or ideal—even to a religion. But people by nature are loyal to people. This remains true in the world of missions. Those who come to Christ

> Humanity does not progress beyond Jesus Christ.
> —Samuel Taylor Coleridge, English poet and philosopher

follow those who led them to Christ. The role of a full-time missionary is not easy, nor is it always safe. New Christians may feel alone and powerless in the face of these former authorities and the larger community that once nourished them. They need to know at the bottom of their hearts that they are not alone but are empowered by the Holy Spirit within them to bear the love of Christ to these new believers. How important are words of Jesus: "Lo, I am with you always" (Matthew 28:20)?

A Christian teacher, T.P. Suresh, comes from a high-caste Brahmin family. Once, he was an assistant priest in the temple, and his father remains a priest in the largest temple in an Indian city. Following his conversion, he encountered a very dramatic series of events that led him to trust Christ above an earthly father. This new convert eventually wound up on the streets and faced many kinds of problems. But he discovered that the presence of Jesus Christ became even stronger and more real in his life because of his continued faith in the face of persecutions. He felt the strength of the Holy Spirit enabling him to overcome the tremendous family and social pressures coming against him. When T.P. Suresh speaks about Christ's sustaining power and the reality of the Holy Spirit enabling a person to withstand persecution, he speaks from personal experience. When he speaks about the rewards that come from total obedience and allegiance, others listen.

5. *Purity and Righteousness.* Jesus used salt as a metaphor for the disciple's life. Salt can lose its flavor in only two ways. It can lose its saltiness by becoming contaminated by dirt or other chemicals. Likewise, a person can become contaminated by sin to the degree that he or she no longer has effectiveness in ministry, nor even a reputation as a believer. Salt can also lose its saltiness by becoming so diluted with water that there's no hint of flavor left. Likewise, a person can become so enmeshed in the world's systems and the world's mindset that he or she no longer has a distinctive witness for Christ Jesus.

The disciple of Christ Jesus, therefore, is called to a life marked by total devotion and love. He totally yields himself to God's directives. He totally commits himself to persevere in whatever God commands until God's purposes are fulfilled. He lives in total obedience and allegiance to God, and in total purity.

Purity is a standard unknown by most of the world. The world does not have the ethical or moral values that match a truly Christ-centered life.

The Holy Spirit living in a person makes impurity uncomfortable and unacceptable. The Holy Spirit cleanses the thoughts and hearts of the new believer. But when it comes to a practical application of morality and ethics, the new believer is often adrift. He has a sense of what is wrong, because the Spirit has convicted him thus. But he does not have a clear vision of what is right. Again, the teachings of the apostle Paul give witness to this truth even among first-century believers. It is the role of the missionary, in many cases, to model what is pure in God's eyes.

In India, we have seen powerful examples of the gospel resulting in a "purifying" of human behavior. My grandfather once led a major revival in Kumbanad, a city in Kerala, south India. Hundreds of people accepted Jesus as their personal Savior, and their lives were dramatically transformed. Advertisements and sales of liquor and tobacco in the area ceased. Entertainment standards changed dramatically. People got out of debt and stopped applying for loans, choosing instead to live simpler lives and pay cash for their purchases. Even today, there is less borrowing of money in this area than in any other area of Kerala.

We have also seen tremendous transformation in the lives of those who have come to know Jesus as Savior in Nagaland and Manipur. Thieves and headhunters have turned into honest and trustworthy neighbors. Many people in these regions feel such a strong sense of trust for their neighbors that they no longer feel a need to lock their homes. They share readily. Manipur now has an established legal code of moral and ethical standards for those who run for political office.

Purity attracts many people while repelling others, especially those whose material lifestyles profit from impurity—those who will lose wealth and power if their society becomes more Christian. This is a major reason why Christian witness is both gaining new believers and drawing persecution in places like India today.

The Modeling Challenge

Cinderella's prince must have been a remarkable and wise young man to help her adjust happily to life at the palace. It could not have been only the material wealth and power of royalty that made her happy, but their relationship of love that made all the difference. Maybe they faced trials, but the prince would have been a model of love to his bride to which she happily submitted. He would never tire of her, nor she of him, so they continued to grow in love. It is this growth in love that is key to living "happily ever after."

It is the challenge of the full-time missionary not only to speak about a life of discipleship to Christ Jesus, but to live this life as well. Such modeling doesn't happen on a two-week trip. It takes years to convey—by example.

In many ways, Indian culture lends itself to learning through modeling. The Indian model of *guru* and *shishya*—master and disciple—is a method, not a religion. At India Bible College and Seminary, every faculty member is responsible for a certain number of students. Students go to their faculty mentor to observe how to minister in different contexts. They move from observation to helping and assisting in various ways. Then the students are given opportunities to share and minister with the assistance of their mentors. Finally, the student moves to taking a central role in a particular ministry. The next step is to launch out and establish a new ministry based upon the successful model of the mentor.

Long-term Missions are a Demanding and Difficult Challenge.
The story of Cinderella doesn't fully bring out this truth, but "living happily ever after" did not mean that serving the King and living in the palace was not without sometimes severe challenges. It was love that made all the difference, enabling them to persevere and experience enriched lives.

Why don't more people accept the challenge of full-time missionary service, even if it means serving a loving King? Because it is often extremely difficult. Becoming a full-time missionary means, first and foremost, living as a genuine disciple. It means giving up much of what is known, comfortable and conventionally successful. It means taking on a dangerous challenge. It can mean years of work with little observable fruit and virtually no fame, either overseas or back at home. Most people are simply not willing to give up known comforts for unknown blessings that may come only in an indefinite amount of time.

The potential rewards, however, are tremendous, beyond earthly riches and fame. Great revival movements are born out of full-time mission work, and nations are changed as great revival movements turn into great discipleship movements. Where the gospel takes root and grows, social changes follow in due course: schools are built, hospitals and clinics are established, the poor are helped, widows and orphans are cared for, and economies begin to flourish. This is not pie-in-the-sky wishful thinking. It is observable fact in any honest reading of history in virtually any nation on earth. True Christianity changes cultures in positive ways when it is established on the basis of genuine discipleship. The process of discipleship produces amazing transformation:

- Single-hearted love and devotion to God spills over into love for others, and love is marked by generous giving aimed at meeting needs. George Muller offered his love and life to care for thousands of orphans. William Booth rescued thousands of the poor and needy on the streets. These two missionaries embodied the generosity of Christ's love in meeting practical human need.

- Submission to Christ results in a mutuality of submission within the Body of Christ, which creates an atmosphere of mutual respect that enhances the giving and receiving of spiritual gifts. A church body made strong by the free exchange of spiritual gifts is better equipped to reach out with respect to others. As people in the broader community receive respect, they tend to show respect. As a community increases its value for one another, amazing things happen.

    Let me add this information about what I said previously regarding Nagaland. Proportionately, Nagaland has more Christians than any other place on earth. In just one generation, the entire society was transformed from a land of headhunters to a civilized community. Today, four to five generations after the awakening began, there is a tremendous sharing and support for one another among the people.

Wherever there is a true Christian awakening, crime rates drop, litter is picked up, graffiti disappears from buildings, and people are generally quicker to engage in random acts of kindness—even without a prevailing political initiative or campaign to spur on such outcomes.

• Perseverance in ministry produces lasting change, not only in the church but outside the church walls. Good works take root and "stick" long enough to grow and produce good fruit. The school that is established as part of the new church produces literate people who, in turn, provide a higher level of goods and services. At the same time, they provide a reason and resources for building more schools and new schools that provide more advanced instruction. Children from the broader community are brought into these schools, and eventually schools are established in the area and staffed by Christian teachers.

The same trend happens in health care. Clinics conducted by mission stations turn into hospitals over time, which in turn create more clinics and more hospitals.

The greater the health care and educational level of the prevailing community, the greater the quality and productivity of the business enterprises. The overall quality of life rises so that people might move beyond their community boundaries to reach their neighbors up river or in the next valley.

• Obedience and allegiance lead to establishing lines of authority within the church, which provide a model for the peaceful ordering of a greater society. At the foundation are the commands of God's Word, which are not only known but lived out. The application of God's law to individual lives leads to greater morality, which results over time in the establishment of laws and justice that are in keeping with God's law.

As a very practical example, when people begin to live out the law "thou shalt not covet," crimes associated with theft and robbery decline. Neighborhoods become safer. When people begin to live out the Christian principles of fidelity in marriage, sexually-transmitted disease rates drop, fewer children become AIDS orphans, and children raised in happy, functional families establish new norms of excellence in a society.

- Purity in one's personal life becomes purity in the life of a family, a church, and eventually the larger community. Wherever Christianity has taken root, there have been tremendous changes in society, such as the abolition of slavery and a vast improvement in women's rights and equality.

Can you see how Christianity—bearing the marks of Christ-following discipleship—truly can change a tribe, a society, and a nation?

Certainly the heavenly rewards associated with souls saved and lives changed are beyond calculation. Time and again, those who have given their lives to full-time missions work state very boldly that their lives have a sense of deep meaning, purpose, and fulfillment they can't imagine experiencing any other way. This is the story of missionaries such as William Carey, Amy Carmichael, and many others. Full-time missions work not only spreads the gospel and enriches the lives of others, but it also changes, enriches, and deepens the life of the full-time missionary.

An Overview Appraisal of Mass-Media Approaches

The prince succeeded in winning Cinderella's hand because he communicated his intentions well. He communicated his message effectively to all who needed to hear it. Anyone who heard Cinderella's story knew that the prince's motives were for genuine love, and what marriageable young woman doesn't want her possible husband to show this?

Similarly, mass media efforts in evangelism and discipleship are part of mission methodology. Modern technology offers much to those who desire to spread the gospel.

People who lived a century ago would be stunned to see how a relatively few people can daily reach millions of people around the world with the message of Jesus Christ. Satellite communications, cell phones, the Internet, instant translation systems, and small solar-powered devices capable of receiving and displaying messages in visual or audio formats are changing the way we communicate from culture to culture and nation to nation. The potential impact on communicating the love of God and developing His kingdom is immense.

Strengths and Opportunities in Mass Media

Today's technology offers three tremendous advantages in spreading the gospel and teaching God's Word.

First, the preaching of the gospel and the teaching of Christ's commandments can now happen in private settings. A person does not need to attend a large public rally or go to a public meeting place in order to hear the gospel message. This is a critically important factor in nations that have a national law or policy against Christian ministry or proselytizing (the attempt to "forcibly" convert somebody to a religious faith or doctrine). In many nations today it is illegal or even dangerous for believers to gather together openly. Most of the world does not have freedom of speech, freedom of worship, or freedom of assembly laws and rights such as those guaranteed to Americans by the First Amendment and the U.S. Constitution.

The ability to broadcast, podcast, or internet-stream the gospel directly into private homes and to personal hand-held devices means that a person can hear the gospel and grow in his or her understanding of Christ's commands even in the most oppressive political or religious climate.

Second, these media systems allow for the best preaching and teaching to be made available on a widespread basis. Those whom God has gifted to preach and teach His message are no longer limited geographically or by the size of an auditorium.

Third, these media systems make available a wide variety of expression and a tremendous quantity of data. The gospel can be presented in dramatic pageantry, complete with soul-stirring underscores and elaborate costuming and set design. The gospel can be presented in song—stirring concerts involving dozens of musical groups or hundreds of musicians or intimate expressions of a single voice and guitar. The gospel can be presented with accompanying visual text of Bible passages to further underscore the dynamic preaching of a speaker. Our evangelists in India frequently do these things.

Literally tens of thousands of sermons and Bible-based lessons and lectures can be stored on databases and accessed according to the recipient's level of understanding, specific problems currently being encountered, or topics of interest. Chat rooms, blogs, text messaging, and other interactive methods can provide Christian encouragement and might be used for Christian counseling and tutorials.

The challenge we face as Christians is not *whether* to use mass media in evangelism and discipleship efforts, but *how best* to use mass media. To know how to use the media to full advantage, we must recognize its limitations as well as its strengths.

The Gaps Remaining to Be Filled

There are at least four great weaknesses to current mass media outreach.

Weakness #1: Lack of Reception. To successfully communicate the gospel does not mean having only good technology but *appropriate* technology. Just because something is broadcast doesn't mean that it can be received. Gospel messages are presently circling the globe in great number. But the truth is, the vast majority of the world cannot tap into those messages. Most media devices, at present, require electricity. A significant percentage of the unreached people around the world do not have electrical power, nor do they have media-related devices for receiving the messages invisibly available all around them. We need to make certain that the evangelistic messages conveyed by the mass media can be received!

Weakness #2: Few Languages Being Broadcast. The messages being broadcast or sent by Far East Broadcasting Company, Trans World Radio, and other organizations are, for the most part, in relatively few languages. As is the case in face-to-face missionary efforts, language translation is critically important. The more languages the better!

Weakness #3: American Metaphors. Many of the messages being broadcast are often loaded with references or metaphors related to American culture and products. This includes messages from American culture such as offensive women's clothing and styles of music. For maximum effectiveness, media messages need to be adapted to cultural contexts, or at least be made culturally neutral.

Weakness #4: No Follow-Up. A media message cannot replace live preaching and teaching or, more important, live interaction among believers. The flow of spiritual gifts from believer to believer is vital to balanced, healthy, vibrant Christianity. We were intended to function as communities of believers; more specifically, as the body of Christ. When the surrounding culture is anti-Christian, it is very difficult to live healthy Christian lives without personal, direct, physical contact with Christians of like mind and heart.

Live communication within the body of Christ is essential for maximum spiritual growth and balance, but live modeling of the gospel—real-time, real-world role models who show how the gospel might be "lived out" in a particular culture and environment—is still the most effective method for establishing a platform for evangelism and providing instruction in discipleship. Mass media can give exposure to the gospel message and insights into Bible-teaching, but it is not an effective means of discipleship, modeling, or personal mentoring. Discipleship is a one-on-one process. We err greatly if we ever assume that it is sufficient to simply tell a person how to become a Christian or develop a godly lifestyle. We must show others how to embody Christ, and to do so by deeds as well as words.

Christianity is relationship-based and involves all the senses and all of one's being: spirit, mind, and body, both in the individual believer's relationship with the Triune God and in relationships with others in the church. God created us to fellowship with one another, to pray together, to eat, laugh, cry, and sing together, to praise God together, to work together, and to minister to one another as the Spirit leads us. We do not worship according to what we see and hear alone, but also by fully activating all the physical senses and spiritual discernment beyond the physical senses. We are to relate to one another not only mentally, but also emotionally and spiritually. Knowing Christ is not an objective experience, but a subjective one, and for the most part, the media offer only an objective experience.

Maximizing Effectiveness: Ask When, Where, and What

The challenge ultimately lies in our developing an understanding of which missionary methods work best in the culture where we are attempting to communicate the gospel. Let me offer these suggestions as to prompt your own thoughts and prayers:

Find the Method That's Right for Each Person and Situation
Remember this important truth: principles are few; methods are many. Principles never change; methods often do.

First, each method has a good and proper use. Do not focus upon only one method. As much as possible, match yourself with the methods that best suit your spiritual gifts and talents, and with your call from God to work in a particular nation, profession, or area of need. Think outside the box of your own church or denomination. Think outside the box of what you have always done to explore what God has truly gifted you to do!

I recently heard about a nurse who always feared the unknown. One evening she felt convicted that this fear of the unknown was keeping her from fulfilling what God purposed for her life. She explored the possibility of going on a short-term mission trip to eastern Africa. While on that trip she used her skills and experience as a nurse and nursing instructor, and felt a real call to full-time mission work. She left her career in the United States, sold what she had, and today supports herself as a nurse in a mission station that by even Africa's standards is remote and primitive. She reads by a kerosene lantern after nightfall and lives in a small and primitive hut that she cannot secure against either animal or human predators. She has had malaria, and has experienced dysentery more times than she can count. Even so, she wouldn't trade her life for anything else. She frequently writes to friends about her joy working among the people there and passing on her nursing skills to a few young women in a three-village community of believers. Today, her greatest fear is that she might not receive a periodic shipment of paperback books on Bible-related topics. This nurse no longer fears the unknown because she found herself in the place that God prepared for her. He caused her to prosper and experience peace under the very conditions she feared most. Each of us has our own fears. Trust God, and He will provide in amazing ways to overcome our fears. His ways vary according our various abilities and experiences.

Establish Longer Terms of Short-Term Service

We need to challenge people to accept longer terms of missionary service. Certainly, we need to renew the challenge to today's youth to give a lifetime of Christian service in unreached areas of the world. At the same time, we must not live in fantasyland; few young people will accept this challenge. The cultures with the most to give are also increasingly among the most hedonistic and self-absorbed. Often, young people with the most talent to give to the gospel are the first to resist the challenge.

We can still challenge people to give "mid-range" missionary service; either multiple years of service or multiple trips to the same area and role. This challenge applies to both young and old.

For example, we wisely encourage missionary service as a second career for those who have retired from their secular careers. Literally hundreds of thousands of people who retire after twenty or thirty years of career work find themselves in their fifties or sixties with good energy, good health, and relatively little reason for living. What a wealth of experience and wisdom these people represent; especially if they have lived, worked, or traveled overseas, and if they are biblically mature believers! These are prime believers to target with the challenge of full-time missionary service.

The Urgent Call

Choose a nation. Begin to read about the people of that nation. If the nation has more than one tribal, language, or cultural group, focus on one group of people within the nation. Become an expert on that culture. Even as you read about the culture, seek a way to get in touch with someone in that nation. Pray for an opportunity to make an international friend, and especially pray that God will open the door for you to present your personal testimony about your relationship with Jesus Christ with that person.

Might just one person, with God's help, leap an international and intercultural barrier with the gospel? Absolutely!

I recently heard about one couple that retired from corporate executive positions after thirty-five years. They left their financial portfolio intact to grow for another ten years, sold their home and invested half of what they earned in what they perceived to be safe investments, and used the remaining half of their home sale to fund ten years of full-time missionary service! In those ten years they helped establish five schools and an orphanage associated with a growing church. The orphanage and school were linked so that tuition from a growing middle class in that area funded schooling for the orphans as well as maintenance of the orphanage. The couple kept active in the church; the husband helped supervise several building projects as well as a water purification system available to all church members. The wife taught a women's Bible study that grew to three hundred women in regular attendance.

God is ready to work creatively and miraculously in the lives of all those who commit their lives and fortunes into His hands. Not only will they discover the meaning of true abundance, but they will provide meaning and abundance to countless others—blessings that far surpass the narcissistic values of today's society.

Another couple leased their home, cashed in part of their savings, and took on the challenge of starting a Bible-training center in an overseas location. They expected to be there for at least five and possibly seven years. They envisioned developing a two-year program to involve up to one hundred students a year. They challenged each of these students to give the first five years of their post-study time to missions before settling in to a career and family life.

Yet another couple sold everything they had acquired, cashed in all of their financial portfolio holdings, put a down-payment on a condo in a retirement area (which they promptly subleased to another couple, hoping that fifteen years of subleasing would pay off the fifteen-year mortgage), and headed for what they hoped would be fifteen years of active missionary service—from age sixty to seventy-five. If they ever return to their condo, they said, it will be so they can evangelize the "old folks" who live there. This particular couple started a small handicraft center in a village. The handicraft center supports a number of AIDS widows and their children. They work closely with full-time missionaries in a variety of church roles, including mainte-nance of the church van. (The husband has auto mechanic skills, even though he worked as an electrician.) One of their projects involves developing a small electrical plant linked to a nearby rushing stream of water.

Each of these three couples is highly educated, highly skilled, and highly committed. They availed themselves of specific train-ing in key areas during the years immediately before their depar-ture as missionaries. All three couples have now served on their respective mission fields for at least two years, and all six indi-viduals tell of having greater purpose, better health, and a deeper spiritual life than they experienced in all their previous years.

Another model of missionary work for those able to take time off from professional commitments: give four to six weeks of service a year to the same locale year after year. I know of one surgeon who embodied this model for twenty years. He gave six weeks a year—his "tithe and offering of time"—to take clinic appointments and perform surgery on a remote south Pacific island where health care was minimal. Because he went to this location year after year, he developed ongoing relationships with professional staff and fellow Christians on that island. He spent part of his time each year teaching others what he knew of the Scriptures as well as the latest medical techniques. His profes-sional colleagues in the United States were motivated by his example, some also giving of their time. Others gave of their financial resources to help build a more advanced clinic and hos-pital to serve the people.

I also know of a dentist who goes for three-week terms twice each year, and has done this for eight years. Again, because he comes at the same time each year and has been consistent in his commitment, he has developed outstanding relationships with both dental-care and medical professionals, as well as church leaders in the area where he serves. He stays in touch with both his professional associates and his church friends by e-mailing messages on an almost daily basis. As he hears about specific needs, he mobilizes stateside resources to provide answers and solutions.

Professors and teachers often find it possible to give six, eight, or twelve weeks of their time to teaching in overseas mission schools. Some of them teach the children of full-time missionaries. Others teach Bible or language classes. Still others give their skills to alleviate the pressure on those who work full-time in church-related schools or training centers. Some of these professors and teachers offer short courses to indigenous teachers to further their teaching skills and information base.

The Strength of Each Method

We must identify the strengths of each method and exploit those strengths while minimizing any negative aspects of the method.

As stated earlier, the short-term mission is not the best method for evangelizing unreached people or providing ongoing discipleship training. This form of mission, however, can have tremendous impact in strengthening the existing body of Christ. Indigenous leaders and believers are greatly encouraged by practical gifts of service, as well as by smiles and tender expressions of godly love. A short-term mission group that blesses a local church or group of churches sends a message to the greater community that Christians love one another. Such love is very attractive to unbelievers.

Short-term mission projects can effectively build and equip facilities for ongoing indigenous church groups to use. These missions projects can also provide information and motivation for church people back home to make financial gifts in support of specific programs or projects. For example, several churches from across the United States currently work together to build and outfit a vocational training center for a consortium of churches in an overseas nation. The American churches send teams of people in rotation to build and equip this facility. When complete, the churches will send teams of people to teach various specific skills—again in rotation as part of an ongoing curriculum. The vocational center will provide practical training in computer maintenance, health care, and mechanical engineering by day. The center will be used at night to conduct Bible-training classes. Both the material and spiritual needs of church members are being addressed. In the end, a model is being established that truly will build up the church in that location so it might impact the entire nation.

Short-term missions are also excellent for medical relief efforts, for offering short courses in highly specialized areas of instruction, and for sharing musical skills and songs. Music teams on short-term mission trips often have great impact upon young people by drawing attention to the gospel message.

We need to use media to its full advantage but place it within a social structure whenever and wherever possible. We need to download programs for groups of believers to watch together, so they might interact and encourage one another in direct relationship to the material they have heard or seen. We need to produce programs that lend themselves to a presentation of the gospel within a house church or small-group setting so that indigenous believers might invite their family and friends to learn more in a safe environment, and without requiring the host of the event to be an expert in either the Bible or the church.

Finally, we must use the Internet to establish Christian friendships across cultural boundaries. As the availability of computers and digital communications expands, millions of people will find themselves able to talk to people they have never met, who live thousands of miles away and come from cultures vastly different from their own. Individual believers will increasingly interact with nonbelievers without any regard for geographical boundaries or need to travel. We in the church must explore this opportunity for one-to-one evangelism and discipleship training, especially the broader ramifications of entering into genuine intercultural and international friendships in order to win others to Christ.

- What do Christians in the United States need to know about people from other nations?

- What cultural factors do we need to address?

- How might we present the gospel to those who have advanced technology but no knowledge of Christ Jesus?

- How might an individual believer reach out to an unsaved person in a high-tech society?

    In our own ministry, we minister to the high-tech people of Hyderabad and Indian high-tech people in southern California. In the United States, we are mobilizing Indian believers in high-tech industries to reach their fellow workers.

    It is not only the "primitive pagan" who needs to hear the gospel. Many in technologically advanced societies do not know why Jesus died on a cross and rose from the dead. We face the challenge of telling them—one at a time, from one computer to another, one friend talking to another friend.

What Might One Person Do?

1. Stop to consider: who discipled you in the teachings of Jesus? Who were your spiritual mentors? How important

was one-on-one mentoring to your growth as a believer in Christ Jesus?

2. Whom are you discipling? What methods are you using to help a person become a follower of Jesus as Lord?

3. What meaning did your baptism in water have for you?

4. What do you believe your allegiance to Christ Jesus will cost you? Have you truly counted the cost?

5. What does the word "purity" mean to you? What do you possess in terms of wealth, health, talents, and/or spiritual gifts that, when place in God's hands, can help to bring purity to another family, community, or nation? What have you done about it?

6. How do you personally determine which methods to use in reaching another person with the gospel?

7. In what ways are you feeling challenged to get involved in a missions outreach—short-term, mid-range, or long-term?

Heavenly Father, purify me. Remove from my life any behavior, any attitudes, and any beliefs or values contrary to Your Word and Your desire for me. I want my life to count. Make me a soul winner, Lord. Give me a heart for the lost. Lead me into the paths of righteousness for Your name's sake and for Your glory. I ask this in the name of Jesus my Savior and Lord. Amen.

I have not hesitated to proclaim to you the whole will of God.

*Acts 20:27 (*NIV*)*

THREE GREAT 6 NEEDS, THREE EXCITING OPPORTUNITIES!

We have already spoken of what had to happen to Cinderella between the cellar and the conclusion of the story that states simply, "And they lived happily ever after." We know from the story that Cinderella and the prince married and that Cinderella moved to the palace. We know nothing, however, of the transition that was necessary for a char-girl cinder sweeper to happily become a part of the royal family. She no doubt received a new wardrobe, learned new customs and protocol, and experienced things that she may have only dreamed about.

Part of her smooth and happy transition must have involved the prince's ability, and that of his royal family, to speak and understand Cinderella's points of reference, her experiences and perceptions of life. Understanding these things would enable them to better help her at those points of adjustment that might otherwise prove difficult for her. Also, every person in the palace, whether royal or commoner, in large ways and small, was involved in Cinderella's smooth transition, helping along the way with friendly encouragement and constructive advice.

Every new convert to Christ Jesus also undergoes a transformation process that includes significant learning, growing, and changing. The new Christian becomes increasingly aware of the importance of knowing God's Word and applying it to daily life, of experiencing the power and presence of the Holy Spirit, and of discovering when, where, and how to share the gospel with others.

Mission work is not limited to evangelism or pastoring. Other vital aspects of the work present tremendous challenges and excitement for those called to enter these areas of ministry.

In the last chapter, I suggested how our great adversary, Satan, tries to curb the effectiveness of missions by narrowing the options by which the gospel is taken to every people as Jesus Christ commanded. Our great adversary, Satan, tries to curb this effective transition by narrowing every option by which the gospel is taken to every people group. As far as Satan is concerned, the fewer people involved in missions, the better.

One way Satan seeks to thwart the Great Commission is by fostering the impression that only designated missionaries—often clergy-based or part of church teams—can participate in the proclamation of the gospel. People who buy into that lie see little need to get involved, have little interest in getting involved, and therefore do not get involved! In the last chapter, we explored a number of ways in which laity might proclaim the gospel.

The truth is that every person has a critical role to play in the fulfillment of the Great Commission. An important way to discover your role is to learn the continuing needs that must be met to fulfill the Great Commission. As you pray about these needs, I believe the Lord will reveal to you where He wants you to serve.

The Concept of "Go" or "Send"

If any member of the prince's royal family or retinue had responded to Cinderella with the attitude, "it's none of my business what happens to this new princess," Cinderella's experience as a new member of the royal family would have been less than living "happily ever after."

A friend told me recently that when she was growing up in an evangelical church, she heard a principle stated so often that it became deeply engrained: if you can't go or aren't called to go, you must help send someone in your place.

Oh, that every church in America would continue to proclaim this message loudly, frequently, and insistently!

God does not call every person to full-time missionary service. Not every person can go on a short-term mission. But every person can help provide for those who are called, in very practical and yet profound ways.

Every missionary I know faces three areas of need on a daily basis:

- The need to have the Word of God available in the language of the people being served;
- The need for an adequate understanding of the prevailing "belief obstacles" that must be confronted and overcome;
- The need for adequate funding.

Let me address each of these.

Need #1: The Whole Bible in Every Language

Most likely, Cinderella succeeded in her transition because the prince knew how to speak the language of love to his beloved. How well do the diverse people of the world understand the language of love intended for them by Jesus Christ unless they hear it in a way they can understand?

There are at least six thousand and nine hundred distinct languages spoken in the world today. Some of them are what we call "dialects," a regional variety of a language with distinct differences in vocabulary, grammar, and pronunciation.

The New Testament—or portions of it, such as the Gospel of John—has been translated into more than a thousand languages during the last four hundred years. Nearly half of the world's language groups have access to the words of Jesus. But that's only half.

There's still much work to do. As of 2010, only 457 of the world's six thousand and nine hundred languages have a full translation of Scripture.

Of these six thousand and nine hundred languages, almost two thousand and one hundred do not have a single verse translated into their language as of 2010. These languages are spoken by three hundred and forty million people (Wycliffe Bible Translators).

A Renewed Emphasis on the Whole of the Bible

Cinderella probably lived happily ever after because the prince and his family held back nothing that would help Cinderella make her transition smooth and pleasant. Even the things that at first glance seemed unimportant had their place in the culture of the palace, and these things were also taught to Cinderella.

Leviticus is probably not the first book of the Bible that comes to your mind when you think about evangelism. The book of Leviticus, however, was the key to a significant evangelism success story in West Africa in April 2005.

The first ten chapters of Leviticus were read aloud to an audience of the Lobi, a people of subsistence farmers, animistic mask-makers, and poison-arrow warriors. The reading took place in Burkina Faso, and the Scriptures were read in the Lobi language.

Many in the listening crowd marveled at the similarities between the sacrifices mentioned in Leviticus and those of the Lobi religion. The public reading infuriated the son of a Lobi priest, who forbade the reading to continue. His reason? It is taboo to speak of Lobi religious practices in public. Another listener countered, "Yes, but this story means that we, too, are descendants of this High Priest, aren't we?"

That one question opened the door to a full sharing of the gospel by the translators who were reading to the Lobi. Jesus was understandable to them first as their High Priest, a concept that often eludes even the most ardent evangelical believer in America who has no experience with an active priesthood.

Bible translators are increasingly discovering that many of the world's unreached people have great similarities with the Old Testament Israelites when it comes to sacrificial and legal systems. I certainly can confirm that this is true in India. A patriarchal society similar to that of ancient Israel is found in almost every village of India. Genealogy is very important. Indeed, the entire caste system in India is based upon genealogy. This system divides society into priestly, warrior, merchant, and laborer segments, with very little individual mobility allowed from one category to the next. In many cases, an entire village consists of just one caste.

The story of Old Testament sacrifices connects with tribal groups in Andhra Pradesh, Orissa, and Bihar because sacrifices still occur there, sadly including child sacrifice. In Andhra Pradesh, the concept of sacrifice is common in rural areas, especially the sacrifice of live chickens to a goddess. The blood of chickens and goats is often applied to new cars as a means of seeking protection from the gods. During large construction projects, one or two deaths are nearly always reported. Often, however, these deaths are human sacrifices intended to ensure that the project is successful. As late as 2007, the Indian media have reported human sacrifices in Andhra Pradesh and Orissa. The concept is strongly ingrained in Indian thinking in these regions.

Such disturbing news could cause us to make false assumptions on how to present the gospel to these peoples. How do we share Christ with people who continue to live like ancient Canaanites? Here again, the story of Cinderella may offer us an unexpected analogy.

Great Gospel Value in the Old Testament

To happily become a part of the royal family, Cinderella would have had to become aware of the royal family history and tradition and feel that she was a part of it. But at heart, she was still a subject. That is the way she had lived her whole life. She could not make the change overnight. The prince and the royal family would have to help her make the bridge smoothly from subject to royalty. Apparently, she succeeded well in blending her background as a subject with royal tradition until one day, she could say from her heart as well as her mind, "I really am part of the royal family." She did not feel she was sacrificing her self-identity to become part of royalty. She could not have lived happily ever after in any other way.

This is a fairy tale lesson we must take to heart in the real life of presenting the gospel. Often, we take an either-or approach to things that are not helpful. In presenting the gospel to unreached peoples, we have been so eager to make unreached peoples aware of the good news and their potential membership in God's royal family; we have not taken into account where they are actually coming from.

"The assumption was that the New Testament alone was adequate, because it held the gospel message and would be sufficient for evangelization," said Ralph Hill, international translation coordinator for Wycliffe Bible Translators. This assumption, coupled with shortages of personnel and resources to take on the Old Testament's intimidating size, created the "translation gap."

All that is changing slowly, but nevertheless changing.

Don Pederson, director of field ministry for New Tribes Mission (NTM), believes that "effective evangelism among unreached people groups needs to start with Genesis. It is through the story of God's interactions with humankind that His character is fully understood, that people understand their dilemma, and that they need a Savior." NTM focuses on planting churches among the unreached, and as part of that effort it currently has one hundred and twenty translation projects that start with Genesis and then proceed through translations of key Old Testament passages en route to the gospels. These "chronological" translations provide a framework of salvation history.

We have found that groups coming out of animism (belief ascribing conscious life or a soul to all natural objects or nature in general) or polytheism have a much better understanding of God and sin when they encounter the gospel with an Old Testament background. The ancient Israelites' ritual sacrifices, patriarchy, and agrarian practices come from a lifestyle these people groups understand. As they hear or read about the Israelites, the stage of their hearts is set for a greater understanding of the sacrifice of Jesus, the fatherhood of God, the agricultural-based parables and teachings of Jesus that describe the kingdom of God. This is especially true among people in Southeast Asia, Central Africa, and Central Asia.

The Old Testament also connects powerfully with Muslims. We see this routinely in India. Muslims are attracted to Old Testament characters partly because they coincide with characters in the Koran; Abraham is considered the father of Islam as well as the father of Judaism. Muslims have a strong sense of "clean" and "unclean" and also engage in sacrifice. The Koran includes stories of Adam and Eve and their fall into sin, Noah and the flood, David and Goliath, Solomon, Jonah, and Jesus, but the stories have a different twist from what is found in the Hebrew Scriptures and they are not in the same historical order. As a very young man traveling with a relative to the area now known as Israel, Mohammed heard stories from the Hebrew Scriptures, but only in part. His conveyance of those stories was garbled because no one in Mohammed's circle of family and friends had information about these stories. The stories remained as he dictated them, without verification or any check of accuracy.

Natalia Gorbunova, of the Moscow-based Institute for Bible Translation, has commented, "Muslims are already familiar with the characters of the Old Testament.... the Old Testament becomes a bridge into the New Testament." The Institute seeks to take the Bible to one hundred and thirty non-Slavic language groups living in Russia and Central Asia. It presently has twenty-two Old Testament projects aimed primarily at Muslim audiences. A recent translation in Crimean Tatar, called "Prophets," contains selections from Genesis, Exodus, and other Old Testament books, and tells stories of biblical characters known in both Islam and Christianity, accompanied by relevant New Testament excerpts.

I agree with Gorbunova. One of the main ways to reach Muslims in India and elsewhere around the world is through the Old Testament stories found in the Koran. They can become a bridge to sharing the gospel. Christians need to know that Jesus is actually called "Messiah" in the Koran (Sura 3:45). Most Muslim religious leaders don't know this fact of the Koran, and many who do know it refuse to acknowledge it.

The Entire Bible Is Necessary for True Discipleship
Making Cinderella's transition smooth would have involved not just knowing a part of royal tradition and family but the whole

of it. Even her knowledge of royal genealogy would help her to understand her prince and what brought him to this deep love for her. This would enable her to feel like a true member of the family, not like an outsider torn between living in the palace and living outside it, hating palace living but imprisoned by it.

Those who see a great need for more Old Testament translation recognize it as a means of ensuring long-term health and growth for newly established churches. Phil Towner, director of translation services for United Bible Societies, has said, "Since churches must go beyond evangelism, they need the whole picture and the whole Bible. It's not just a matter of evangelism. It's a matter of being in this Christian adventure for the long haul."

As I have stated in previous chapters, it is not enough to bring only salvation knowledge. Maturation is a process that will continue through this life and throughout all eternity. It is not enough to be satisfied with salvation knowledge alone any more than it is to simply give birth to a baby. We must also train and nurture the baby to healthy maturity. Long-term discipleship is what brings a new believer to a level of maturity beyond spiritual babyhood. (See 1 Peter 2:2, Hebrews 5:12–14.)

Others see Old Testament translation as a means of moving beyond "syncretism" in Africa and other parts of the world. Syncretism is the practice of adopting and implementing one set of beliefs—in this case, Christianity—while retaining old beliefs and practices. A number of African and Asian groups claim Jesus as Savior, but still hold to ancestor worship, blood sacrifices, and other pagan rituals. These groups have laid Christianity on top of their old religions. But they cannot and must not do this. They must renounce their old beliefs before they can accept the gospel and the unique work of Christ. (See Galatians 5, Hebrews 10.)

We battle syncretism daily in India. Many forms of syncretistic Christianity are entrenched. A few years ago, we started a work in the pilgrim city of Varanasi. The rebuilt Roman Catholic Church there has prayers inscribed into the marble façade. These prayers are addressed to Jesus, to Mary the mother of Jesus, *and to a Hindu god*! In some so-called Christian churches in that city, coconuts are broken and cut into pieces and passed out as a part of the communion sacrament. This sharing of a coconut is a Hindu ritual.

The Old Testament narratives help lay a conceptual foundation that helps the new converts replace old pagan practices with a genuinely Christian lifestyle.

Old Testament translation also helps people understand Jesus better. In many cultures, it is very important for a person to know someone's ancestry before he can accept fully what that person says and does. In India and throughout Asia, it is common to ask people "What is your family name?" Family origins and descendants are much more important in third-world cultures than in the West.

The Challenge We Face
The prince must have offered patient mentoring of Cinderella into the ways of the royal family. This would enable Cinderella to become effectively involved in royal leadership herself. No teaching was regarded as too unimportant, something to skip over.

What does this growing importance of the Old Testament have upon us as we seek to be more involved in world evangelism?

First, we each should become challenged anew to know the Old Testament for ourselves. This means not only knowing the "stories" of the Old Testament, but understanding the key ways in which those stories are linked to Jesus and the message of the New Testament writers. Such knowledge not only deepens our own faith. It also gives us a greater depth and breadth of knowledge from which to draw as we encounter unbelievers in our own culture, and specifically as we share the gospel with Muslims who are from other nations as well as young Americans who have converted to Islam. We need to know the whole of God's Word so we might speak to others about Jesus as God's Word.

Second, we each face the challenge of assisting this effort of Bible translation—and specifically of Old Testament translation—overseas. Missions need experts in various Old Testament books, the cultures and customs of Old Testament times, and the Hebrew language to assist on a short-term or long-term basis in translation institutes. There is an equal need to fund translation students who are doing the translation work, often far from their homelands.

You may not be an Old Testament scholar, but rest assured, there are many facets to the challenge! Overseas language institutes and translation facilities have a tremendous need for people to help with the practical requirements of the students, everything from meal preparation to assistance with child-care. There are countless office-related needs. If you have typing, accounting, or advertising skills there's a role for you.

Only stories are really readable.
—Rudolf Flesch,
Readability Expert

Increasingly, Old Testament translation projects use national translators. In fact, nationals now comprise 90 percent of the world's translation force. These translators produce higher quality translations at a faster pace, because they know their own language and culture well. Many translation agencies use Western missionaries primarily as "quality checkers" and advisers, especially for comparing translations against the original Hebrew and Greek.

The ideal model appears to be national translators who know Hebrew and Greek and can translate straight from the original biblical text into their own languages. This requires Hebrew and Greek scholars, since only about 10 percent of national translators currently have biblical-language skills.

Halvor Ronning, founder of the Jerusalem-based Home for Bible Translators, has caught the vision for training people from other nations in Hebrew so they might better translate the Old Testament into their own languages. He has found that the speed of learning and retention of biblical Hebrew is better when translators from other nations learn and speak modern Hebrew. His program has offered advanced biblical language training to seventy-four translators from twenty-six nations, who speak forty-four different languages. His students have led translation efforts in Kenya, Togo, Nigeria, and other nations.

Translation schools are sponsored by a number of organizations in various nations. Wycliffe sponsors schools in the Philippines, Thailand, Kenya, and Cote d'Ivoire. Word for the World offers a mobile two-year program, which, in 2005 alone, trained 175 translators from seventy-three language groups in Ethiopia, Tanzania, and other African countries.

We are blessed in our work in India to have more than 10 percent of our translators with master's degrees and a good working knowledge of both Hebrew and Greek. We find that it takes an average of fifteen years for a person to become a truly excellent translator. Many translators in India also know three or more modern languages. They compare the translation of the Bible in all of those languages. Even so, there is a need for more translators and more teaching of Hebrew and Greek.

Having the entire Bible available to missionaries—and available to new converts—in every language of the world is a mission goal that can and must be reached in our lifetimes.

Need #2: Understanding the Beliefs of the Foreign Culture

For the prince to effectively help Cinderella get used to royal living, he had to have full understanding of her prior experience even if he did not have that prior experience himself. He had to know how to speak in analogies that would help her to understand better what was happening to her in her new situation. He had to know how to address the possible obstacles she might face. This was imperative for her to living "happily ever after."

This is not unlike the situation faced by today's missionaries. In addition to learning a new language and becoming familiar with the intricacies of a new culture, missionaries face the chal-

THREE GREAT NEEDS, THREE EXCITING OPPORTUNITIES!

lenge of confronting the strong beliefs of false religions, which have often prevailed for thousands of years. These "belief obstacles" are perhaps the foremost challenge a missionary faces.

In India, our work of evangelism involves mostly work among the Hindu people. Certain religious barriers—which have great cultural ramifications—must be overcome as the gospel is presented. I share these only as an example of the types of "belief obstacles" a missionary must hurdle as he or she presents the gospel and disciples the new believers. Foremost among the Hindu beliefs are these four that stand in sharp contrast to Christianity:

- *Polytheism.* Hinduism has thousands of gods, and each of them is considered worthy to be revered. Christians face a challenge in presenting the supremacy of the one Jesus, God the Son.

- *God is unknowable.* None of the gods of Hinduism are human representations who have experienced human life with its struggles, suffering, or its joys. The unknowable nature of God leads the Hindu to search for knowable gods that he can see and touch, such as idols which are prominent in Hindu ceremonies and rituals. Christianity stands in sharp contrast. God is knowable through Christ Jesus. Christianity presents God Incarnate, who is thoroughly familiar with our human experience.

- *Reincarnation.* Hinduism advocates reincarnation; death occurs, but there is no finality to life on this earth. Life forms are "recycled" and never fully end. The Christian pastor or missionary faces the challenge of presenting the truth that life on this earth does end, and future, everlasting life is possible only if one believes in Jesus as the Savior.

- *Progressive perfection.* Part of the process of reincarnation in Hinduism is a process of potential improvement as one passes from one life form to the next. People are rewarded for their good deeds and diligence in revering the gods by living in a higher caste in their next lives. The Christian pastor or missionary faces the challenge of presenting a total cleansing of sin made possible by the atoning, sacrificial death of Jesus on the cross, and that this cleansing of sin is not based upon the good deeds of the human being, but rather upon the overflowing mercy of a loving God.

As these four main beliefs are confronted, a number of other beliefs are called into question. These include the validity of a caste system. Another is the power of evil. Many Hindu gods are thought to have great power to inflict pain and suffering if they are not revered properly. Still another belief called into question by Hindus is the nature of the Trinity. These religions question whether Christians serve one God or three gods. Others question the sense of urgency about accepting Christ, since there is no urgency in Hinduism.

The good news is that these belief obstacles and others like them are the points of belief that make Christianity ultimately appealing and exciting to the Hindu convert. There is tremendous joy in knowing that God made Himself knowable in Jesus, forgives sins completely and immediately, and paves the way to heaven through Jesus Christ.

Missionaries who work among other religious groups face different dominant belief obstacles. Those who work among Muslims, for example, face tremendous belief obstacles regarding the divinity of Jesus and the nature of the triune God. The incarnation of Christ is of tremendous importance in presenting the gospel to Muslims, as is the definitive salvation offered by Christ Jesus. Islam offers no assurance for remission of sins or of life in heaven. The best a Muslim can hope to obtain is a "maximum opportunity for favor" after death. Forgiveness is not a tenet of Islam, only the refinement of character through good works and the keeping of various religious disciplines.

Furthermore, Islam does not recognize the Holy Spirit. Jesus is perceived to be a prophet, and Allah (Islam's name for God the Father) is perceived to be the Creator, but there is no ongoing presence of God made available to individual people as comforter, counselor, or helper to live a redeemed and renewed life. These obstacles hold within them the seeds of those things most appealing to the Muslim convert: the assurance of forgiveness and relationship with God, assurance of heaven after death, and assurance of experiencing God on a daily basis through the indwelling of the Holy Spirit.

Missionaries in Africa, as well as China and other Confucian societies, often face tremendous belief obstacles related to ancestor worship. It is not uncommon for new converts in these areas to seek a means of continuing their ancestor worship alongside their worship of Jesus. The missionary faces a tremendous challenge in teaching new believers to place all their faith and trust in Christ.

Knowing the belief systems of another religious group does not require detailed immersion in the subject. To know the basic belief systems, however, is very valuable in "targeting the truth." There is tremendous value in focusing on those things that are most problematic—and, in turn, most beneficial!

Concerns for Every Christian

We can assume that Cinderella's healthy adjustment to living in the palace was a legitimate concern to every citizen of the realm, and every commoner in the royal household, not just to the prince and his royal family. In the end, what happened to her in becoming an influential person would have an effect on them, too, and generations who followed. Therefore, every effort was taken to remove every obstacle to her healthy adjustment.

Why be concerned about belief obstacles if you are not a full-time missionary?

First, knowing more about what a missionary faces empowers you to pray with greater focus and intensity for that missionary, especially for his or her wisdom in discerning how best to present the gospel. There is tremendous power in intercessory prayer aimed directly at releasing the stranglehold of other religions.

Second, if you are considering a role on a short-term mission team, or are anticipating a mid-range length of missionary service, you must know the prevailing belief system of the people to whom you are going. Take materials about the gospel with you to address the belief obstacles predominant among those you seek to evangelize.

Third, having at least a cursory understanding of various religions will better prepare you to share the gospel with people you encounter in the United States who either come from nations where these religions are dominant or who practice these religions in America. You can communicate the gospel without referring to other "false" religions. Modern mission literature should convey truth without using attack language, especially if it is to be widely read and reviewed. In this day and age, with travel so easy and economies becoming increasingly global, the mission field may be at the cubicle next to yours in your corporate high-rise office! People of other religions and belief systems likely live in your neighborhood. Vast numbers of people of all ages in the United States unknowingly adopt non-Christian beliefs. You must be wise to both know and communicate the differences.

In the end, the belief obstacles of other people should be in the interest of all of us. It is easy to overlook these things, but such areas of neglect have ways of biting us in the end. Little ways of trying to understand now can prevent huge misunderstandings and even tragedies later on.

Need #3: The Need for Adequate Funding

It is safe to say that the prince had every financial resource he needed to accomplish his mission of finding Cinderella. For the prince, no cost was too great, no expense too lavish, to find the woman of his dreams.

Unfortunately this is not true when it comes to finding the world's most lost and unreached peoples. As a whole, missionary work is under-funded around the world. Of every one hundred dollars contributed to the American church, ninety-four dollars is used for the upkeep of church buildings and programs, while only six dollars is used for overseas outreach. *Of this six dollars, only a few cents is used to reach the majority of the world's unreached people* (Barrett 2001).

I personally do not know of a qualified missionary or a worthy missions project that presently has all the money necessary to meet all of the basic needs in order to do a fully adequate job. I'm not referring to the funding of luxuries or "wouldn't-it-be-nice-if" projects. I'm referring to sufficiency in the basics for life—individually and collectively.

Reasons that Missionary Work Is Underfunded.
First, missions fall into the category of "offering" for many individuals and churches—it is not considered part of a person's tithe. In that light, an overall drop in mission giving may be linked to the fact that many people in the church believe mission giving is optional. Certainly, this is not a biblical conclusion. Jesus was critical of the way in which the religious leaders of His day gave their tithes and offerings. He renounced their public show of giving, but He did not negate tithing and the giving of special offerings. Jesus taught on numerous occasions about giving generously and about doing the will of the Father. Jesus certainly never intended the Great Commission to go unfunded!

The Lord often may ask of us more in offerings than in tithes. I know of a couple who recently gave 46 percent of their income in response to the Lord's leading. This amounted to 10 percent of their income in tithes and 36 percent in offerings. This shows the couple's sensitivity to the nudge of the Holy Spirit.

Second, the common method of funding missionaries in the last one hundred years was through a denomination "missions board." These denominational bodies screened candidates for missionary work, authorized missionaries and specific overseas projects, and often served as a clearinghouse for finances and material goods. Missionaries traveled from church to church within a denomination, casting their vision for a particular people group or project. If their presentation was approved by the local church, a percentage of that church's annual missions giving was designated for the missionary and his family.

Much of this has gone by the wayside. Denominations still have mission boards and missionaries, but overall they are not increasing in numbers of churches as rapidly as "nonaffiliated" churches who do not have mission boards.

Third, the decrease in giving is related to how Americans perceive developing nations and unreached people within their own borders. With the rise of communications technology, many Americans assume that the gospel can be communicated in this decade to all nations through mass media. So they give their mission dollars to large mass media ministries that have global broadcasting abilities.

They reason that many people in the United States have plenty of opportunity to hear the gospel. There are churches everywhere, Christian television and radio broadcasts available 24/7, bookstores aplenty with religious sections. Most people have no excuse not to see and hear the gospel if they are hungry for truth, they reason. Doesn't this apply to media ministries abroad as well?

But these massive media outreaches don't reach everybody, not even in the United States. Most American Christians are not aware of the millions of unreached and less reached peoples within our own borders. The 2010 edition of *Operation World* (p. 868–9) speaks of large immigrant groups, international students, Jews, Muslims, South Asians, cult members, and the US prison population—all of whom have sub-cultures and/or language barriers preventing them from having little, if any, contact with these vast media efforts to spread the good news here at home.

Conservatively, their numbers may add up to fifty million or more in a nation of three hundred million—one out of every six people.

If our vast media outreach in America has failed to reach one-sixth of our own population in the United States, what about the hundreds of millions of people who live in the 10/40 window who have absolutely no opportunity to hear the truth of the gospel unless someone comes to them from the outside? In words that Oswald J. Smith often said and which have been oft-quoted since, "Why should anyone hear the gospel twice before everyone has heard it once?"

There are other American perceptions of developing nations and unreached peoples here at home that affect our giving and involvement with them. Other Americans resent what they perceive to be the ungrateful hearts of many in overseas countries who denounce America's presence in their nations, even as their leaders greedily accept American dollars to further their own causes and personal desires. Still other Americans believe strongly that indigenous people should evangelize themselves, that nations with a growing middle class should win their own people to the Lord.

All of these reasons are understandable and perhaps even justifiable on some levels. But we are left with the prevailing conclusions drawn earlier in this book:

- Hundreds of millions of people around the world are still unreached. They will never have an opportunity to hear the gospel unless someone personally goes to them.

- Mass-media broadcasting of the salvation message is not a substitute for human interaction and ongoing discipleship of the entire body of Christ.

- Many nations, even those with a growing middle class, cannot fully fund ongoing evangelistic efforts at present. In some cases, the middle class that is growing in a particular nation is a non-Christian middle class. In such cases, of course, the middle class people who might be able to financially sustain an evangelistic effort are not inclined to do so.

• We have not yet fulfilled Jesus's command to go and make disciples of all nations!

For more information read *The Hole in Our Gospel* by Richard Stearns, and *Attacking Poverty in the Developing World* by Judith M. Dean; Julie Schaffner; Stephen L.S. Smith, editors.

We must remember that fulfilling the Great Commission takes place in numerous ways. We make disciples by verbally preaching the gospel. As Saint Francis of Assisi put it, "Preach the gospel always; when necessary, use words." In other words, our preaching becomes effective only after we demonstrate it with appropriate actions.

It is no accident that there are almost two thousand verses in Scripture that are concerned about poverty and justice. The entire Bible is a single message, and all these two thousand verses are directly related to the Great Commission.

George Bernard Shaw, Irish playwright and political activist, hinted at this relationship when he said, "The worst sin towards our fellow creatures is not to hate them, but to be indifferent to them; that's the essence of inhumanity."

Most evangelical Christians do not regard themselves as indifferent or inhumane. But do people of developing nations regard western Christians as inhumane? Many of us become defensive at such a question. Maybe that is because we do not understand life from their point of view. Though it is difficult to put ourselves in their shoes, a few facts and figures from Richard Stearns' *The Hole in Our Gospel* may help us to better understand. Consider:

- The poorest 40 percent of the world's population possesses only 5 percent of the world's income. The richest 20 percent accounts for 75 percent of the world's income.

- Almost one in seven people on earth—854 million—are in constant danger of malnutrition and starvation. Every day, 25,000 people die from hunger and related causes. These people are found in the developing nations.

- 1.2 billion people drink water filled with parasites and waterborne diseases, killing five million every year. Again, these people live mainly in developing nations.

- HIV/AIDS infects 33 million people worldwide, 70 percent of them in Africa. It has taken more than twenty-five million lives since 1981, with no cure in sight.

- The ongoing war in one developing nation, the Democratic Republic of Congo (a war mostly ignored by the media), has taken more than five million lives, with more than forty-five thousand people dying each month.

- The United States spends $1,780 per person on primary and secondary education; Uganda spends five dollars per person.

As Richard Stearns has put it, "If you don't believe Satan is real, come with me to Africa, or Asia, or for that matter, anywhere the poor are marginalized and exploited. Then you will see the face of evil alive and active in our world."

The trouble is that we are so surrounded by affluence that most of us live in a bubble of ignorance about these people. For the most part, we are oblivious to the way the world really lives. Given the few statistics I have listed here, is there any good reason that the people of developing nations should love us? Most of these people see us as Christians, but most of them are not followers of Jesus Christ. Why should we expect them to have ears for the gospel if we do not hear and feel the pain of their hunger and suffering?

The late Ralph Winter, missionary, scholar, professor, and founder of the U.S. Center for World Missions, once said, "Obedience to the Great Commission has more consistently been poisoned by affluence than by anything else."

Let's face it: affluent people tend to judge the amount of their wealth in comparison to their *neighbors*, not in comparison to the *world at large*. Such comparisons give us a false picture of reality.

Let's say you make only $25,000 per year. That is not wealthy by western standards; it's the poverty level for a family of five in the continental United States. But you still make more money than 90 percent of the entire world. And if you make $50,000 per year—still not wealthy by western standards—you make more money than 99 percent of the world's population. Next time you don't feel rich, consider the standard of living where 74 percent of the world's people live: Asia and Africa (Stearns 2009).

Does all of this mean that we should feel guilty about our great wealth? By no means! God has shed His grace upon us. In many ways, our wealth is the direct result of the influence and application, however imperfect, of traditional Christian values in our government and society. We have reaped the benefit of wise and godly men and women who have gone before us.

But God does not expect us to enjoy our blessings alone. He expects us to share our blessings with others. He does not expect us to make an idol of our wealth and what it can buy us. He has entrusted it to us to invest in His purposes. He wants us to join Him in His work of shedding His grace upon others who are still in darkness and suffering. That way of grace comes through fulfillment of the Great Commission and doing the works that Jesus did, including feeding the hungry and healing the sick. All of this takes a clear vision of the *real world*, great expectations from God, and the willingness to entrust our wealth back into His hands.

How well are we doing this? Not well, I am afraid. The wealthiest churchgoers in the world are American Christians. According to George Barna, they have a total income of $5.2 trillion. With wise administration, it would take slightly more than 1 percent of that vast income to lift the poorest one billion out of extreme poverty. Since American Christians control about half of the world's Christian wealth, lack of money is not our real problem.

The truth is, only about 9 percent of Christians who call themselves "born again" tithe their income, and only 24 percent of evangelical Christians do. That leaves 76 percent of evangelical Christians who do not tithe. In terms of actual giving, the average American church member in 2005 gave only 2.58 percent of his income to the Lord and His purposes. This is down from 3.3 percent in 1933, at the height of the Great Depression when most people were struggling to make ends meet. Of the money that Christians do give, only 2 percent of that 2.58 percent goes for Great Commission purposes—just six cents a day (Stearns 2009).

The average person in the developing world does not know all these facts, but they feel them deeply. Is it any wonder that many of them have grave doubts about the God we say we love and serve, and even wonder if the good news is not so good?

What Can and Must Be Done?

We need to openly address the concerns associated with funding and working together, across denominational ties, in developing a comprehensive strategy for evaluating and prioritizing various projects and addressing specific needs. Together, we need to distinguish which groups are most different, difficult, and distant. Within those groups we need to determine which groups are receptive and which are resistant. Each of these different groups needs a different plan. For the purpose of the Great Commission funding, one size does not fit all.

We must place a renewed emphasis on missions as part of each church budget. We must elevate the awareness of missions and the Great Commission commands of Christ in every congregation. Each congregation must become involved in the Great Commission. We must get involved in reaching people overseas with the gospel even as we are reaching nominal or non-Christians at home. It is not "either/or" but "both/and."

We must especially send an "include missions" message to every church.

William F. High, writing in the *Christian Research Journal*, states, "The current economic climate and a resulting drop in giving have caused Christians to pull back and reexamine their views on the financial support of ministry."

High, President/General Counsel of the Servant Christian Community Foundation (www.servantchristian.com), states that demographic trends "have significant impact for churches and charities." He points to four generations of American Christians whose support for Christian ministry varies widely:

- *The War Generations* (GI Generation, born 1905–1924, and Silent Generation, born 1925–1944) "understood giving their lives and money to a cause. They worked hard, saved diligently, and gave to causes consistent with their values. These generations have been the backbone of some of the country's oldest ministries." But, he points out, these generations are passing from the scene, and with them their financial support.

- *The Boomer Generation* (born 1945–1964) "might be known as the rebellious generation. Think Woodstock, war protests, sit-ins, love-ins, and the events of the 1960s. While the legacy of the Boomers is still being written, it does not appear that it will maintain the generosity of the War Generations."

- *Generation X* (born 1965–1984) "saw the excesses of the 1980s and became disillusioned. Whereas the Boomers rebelled, Generation X detached itself, and 40 percent left the church as they reached adulthood."

- *The Millennial Generation* (born 1985–2004) "represents upcoming opportunity. [They] appear to have the promise of being the most cause-oriented ... [W]ith education and training they may be one of the greatest missions-minded generations in history. On the other hand, if they do not reach their promise then we should ponder the consequences."

Those consequences may include a dramatic decline in support for the church's Great Commission task. "The facts tell us," says High, "that the largest givers in our history are heading toward death and retirement and will be replaced by a generation of non-givers."

He suggests several ways the churches must respond:

1. Return to a proper theology of money: everything belongs to God; the tithe is just the beginning of giving.

2. Reach the coming generations with a clear biblical stewardship message. Because everything belongs to God, we are responsible to Him for all our income, not just the tithe.

3. Think about money, giving, and givers in new ways. The War Generations will pass in the next few years, and church leaders must challenge them to leave a significant portion of their wealth to Great Commission ministries.

4. Establish endowments to provide a sound economic base for ministry. The secular world is aggressively pursuing this endowment strategy; it's a matter of wisdom for Christian ministries to do the same.

5. Consider new forms of gifting: real estate and other property, financial investments, and estate transfers.

6. Enterprise funding: income from fees for service—businesses that channel profits to ministry support so long as they are a separate entity (otherwise there is risk of losing non-profit status).

In all of this, we must recognize, like George Barna, that more and more Christians who should give to missions are acting and thinking no differently from the rest of the culture in which they live. Increasingly, there is little discernible difference between believers and nonbelievers. This includes their attitudes about money.

Again and again, the Bible reminds us that Christ must become Lord of our lives in the use of our money. If our priorities are not the same as His, we have no right to call Him our Lord. Our use of what He has given us reveals our true spiritual state.

In the Bible, seventeen of thirty-eight parables deal with money and possessions. More Scripture verses deal with possessions than any other topic: three times more than love, seven times more than prayer, eight times more than religious belief. At least 15 percent of God's Word (2,172 verses) deals with our use of money and possessions (Alcorn 1989).

The church needs a revolution in generosity. In fact, *Revolution in Generosity* is the title of a recent book edited by Wesley K. Willmer, vice president of university advancement and professor at Biola University. The subtitle describes the theme of the book: "Transforming Stewards to be Rich toward God."

Willmer says that, as believers in Christ, our lives should become a journey in which our actions reflect a progressive deepening of our understanding of God's love and generosity. God reveals His generosity through Christ's incarnation, death, and resurrection (Philippians 2:5–11). As God has given Himself to us, we learn to give ourselves to others. In 1 Peter 4:10 we read, "As each has received a gift, use it to serve one another, as good stewards of God's varied grace ..." The gifts we have in time, talent, and money are entrusted to us by God to use as He directs.

As Neal Pirolo states, "The world's believers spend 0.09% of their income to non Christians in reached people groups, where a church movement has already been planted. But the world's Christians spend only 0.01% on reaching the remaining people groups" (*Serving as Senders*, pg. 173)

Richard Halverson, former Senate Chaplain, reminds us, "All through Scripture there is an intimate correlation between the development of a [person's] character and money."

Jesus reminds us of the nature of this responsive generosity in His observation of the poor widow: "I tell you the truth, this poor widow has put more into the treasury than all the others. They all gave out of their wealth; but she, out of her poverty, put in

> If a person gets his attitude toward money straight, it will straighten out almost every other area of his life.
> —Billy Graham

everything—all she had to live on" (Luke 21:3–4). She had every earthly good reason to give nothing, but she freely gave everything to God because God was more real to her than the riches of this world.

Why is it that Christians are not more generous with their money? Howard L. Dayton, Christian financial adviser and author, believes it is because as believers, we have underestimated and marginalized God according to the ways of the world.

We have marginalized God's power by underestimating it. We say that God creates all things and owns all things, but we act as if our possessions were ours and ours alone. When we truly grasp God's ownership, we no longer ask, "Lord, what do You want me to do with my money?" Rather, we ask, "Lord, what do You want me to do with Your money?"

We have marginalized God by thinking He is not interested in our welfare. We fear that God will hold out on us if we put everything into His hands. We fear His will for us will benefit us less than what we wish for ourselves. Many believers seem to be unaware of passages such as Psalm 112:5 and Proverbs 22:9 that promise God's blessing on those who are generous. Unknown to most are passages such as Philippians 4:17, in which Paul writes to those who gave to him: "Not that I seek the gift, but *I seek the fruit that increases to Your credit.*"

We have marginalized God by limiting His character. We have assumed that His perfect attributes do not apply in the fallen world in which we live, but to a far-away heaven. But Christ's incarnation and life and the presence of the Holy Spirit in each of His children should convince us that God's eternal character has everything to do with here and now. God's eternal character should help us develop a long-term perspective on our material goods rather than our usual short-term perspective.

We marginalize God by limiting His righteousness. The portrayal of life in the media often seems more real to us. For the moment, events in the world seem to favor the unrighteous, but God promises that in the end He has always been in control and that His righteousness will prevail. If we truly trust God, that promise will govern the way we see His cause in the world and our giving to it. If our generosity is lacking for God's cause, we are really saying that He is not sufficiently righteous to fulfill His word and bless those who put their trust in Him.

We marginalize God when we think He has not given us practical, effective instructions in His Word for managing what He has entrusted to us. He has given us our work as a blessing. He has given us our aptitudes, interests, and abilities. He helps to promote us. He instructs us as employers and employees. Too often, we think that God is looking for something that comes from us when His first desire is His best for us. We cannot receive His best when our hearts are enslaved by money and possessions.

Many people do not give generously to missions and to the poor because their giving seems so small while the task seems so large. They unrealistically expect their money to "fix everything." They are dismayed when, after they have given, things seem to appear pretty much the same as they did before they gave. They do not see any return for their investment.

If Jesus had had this attitude, He never would have come into the world as a human being. For the better part of His earthly life, He was known to few outside of Nazareth. Even after His triumphant resurrection, He left an unimpressive band of one hundred and twenty disciples and friends who seemed totally inadequate for the task of taking the gospel to every part of the world. The pagan Roman Empire continued for another three hundred years. Pilate remained as the pagan governor of Judea. The Sanhedrin continued to hold sway over the religious life of the people. As far as the world was concerned, Jesus's mission as Messiah must have looked like a dismal flop.

But Jesus did not see himself as a failure. He knew this was only the beginning. Two thousand years later, we see the growing fruit of His mission, and it will not end until He has returned in power and glory.

It is important to remember that Jesus's mission originated in love and generosity toward sinful humanity in need of a Savior. He gave everything on our behalf even when it seemed to accomplish nothing. He did it with joy in His heart because He anticipated the victorious outcome in spite of the short-term appearance of ineffectiveness and failure.

In the story of Cinderella, the prince anticipated the final outcome, discovery of the beautiful woman who would become his bride. That anticipation caused him to spare no expense. How many homes did he or his servants enter before they finally found the young lady who could wear the glass slipper? But faith in the final and glorious outcome caused him to make the necessary sacrifices.

Do we really believe that the rest of the world needs Jesus Christ? Do we believe that God was doing something in the world that would make a difference to millions imprisoned in sin and degradation? Are we convinced that Jesus Christ has the last word, even with people who presently refuse to believe in Him? Are we truly impressed with the generosity of God toward us? Down through the centuries, God has truly been rich for us and desires every good thing for us. Do we really believe that Jesus Christ will come again in triumph?

We do not give generously because our giving will fix everything. We give because our giving is in keeping with the generous character of God. In the end, He will triumph, and so will we.

This generous attitude is not merely a theory. Not long ago, I read the story of Craig Kielburger, a seventh-grader from Canada, who learned of a twelve-year-old Pakistani boy trapped in a job to pay off family debts. Forced to work twelve hours a day for several years at low wages, the boy had never received a basic education. Craig discovered that millions of children around the world lived like this.

Motivated by the need, Craig started a homegrown movement called "Free the Children" that gathered support from one hundred thousand students in thirty-five countries. He traveled to many countries to see the situation first-hand. He even had a one-on-one meeting with Canada's Prime Minister, Jean Chrétien, to make him more aware of the situation and challenge him to do more about it. In the end, Craig's efforts helped him to start three hundred and fifty schools that rescued more than twenty thousand children.

Did Craig Kielburger's impressive efforts "fix everything?" No. Terrible child labor conditions continue in many countries throughout the world. What counts is Craig's spirit of generosity and his desire to make a difference, one life at a time. Craig Kielburger's experience became an example for many others in his desire to drop everything to help those in need. This is the spirit of Jesus.

Those who request generous and sacrificial support for their God-given mission must likewise live with a spirit of generosity like that of Jesus Christ. They must live as examples to others in the way they live within their means, give of their best to God, and open their lives and homes to neighbors and friends. Like Jesus, they must demonstrate that they believe in His mission and that God will faithfully work through them to accomplish it.

I know of a recently established, nondenominational, growing church that made a commitment to tithe to missions the amount that the people contribute to the church. Tithe refers to 10 percent. The board of this church prayed diligently and chose to contribute to four distinct outreaches: in Africa, South America, rural America, and Asia. To give away 10 percent

The Urgent Call

1. Reflect upon what it would mean to your spiritual growth if you had little or no scripture available to you.

2. How vital is knowing the Word of God to your knowing God in a personal way through Jesus Christ?

3. Focus on a missionary or a mission organization and:

   • Do research into the "belief obstacles" that missionary groups face;

   • Commit to praying for that person or organization every day for the next thirty days.

4. How might you reach out to a person in your community who doesn't know Christ?

5. Reevaluate your personal giving to missions. Is your giving generous? What more might you do?

of its income was a sacrifice for this church, but as the board implemented the policy, they made an amazing discovery. Giving among the people increased! Membership also increased as word got out that the church was a "giving" church. Eventually, the board chose to increase the level of mission giving to 15 percent. The church still has enough money to meet its needs, and membership is still increasing. There's no telling what the ceiling might be as this church continues to give and grow.

I also heard about another small nondenominational church that recently hosted a missions-minded retired pastor to speak on a Sunday morning. It was the first missionary speaker this church had hosted in its five years of existence. This man so ignited a passion for missions among the one hundred members of that congregation that the church voted to make missions a part of its annual budget. Just a few months ago, this church sent out five of its members on a short-term mission project to help build a training center that will offer both job-skill and Bible training—and also serve as a meeting hall for Sunday services.

Check the budget of your own church. Is missions work included? If not, seek the Lord's guidance to what your church can do to make up for this lack.

What Might One Person Do?

Reevaluate your own financial giving to mission projects or to specific missionaries. Ask the Holy Spirit to speak to you about your level of giving. Be open to what He prompts you to do, and obey His leading.

Consider getting involved in the funding of translation projects, or of sharing with your church the possibility of a short-term mission trip to assist with a language-translation project. A good resource to help you learn about translation projects is The Bible Society of India: www.bsind.org.

Pray diligently against the forces of evil associated with other religions. Learn enough about other religions to be able to address key issues with a practitioner. Ask the Lord to lead you and to use you as a witness to non-Christians.

Heavenly Father, how grateful we are for Your Word and how readily accessible the Bible is to us. Help us to do more to get Your Word into the hands of every person around the world, especially to those for whom it is not available at all. Give us insight into how we might better communicate the gospel of Jesus Christ to those who do not know You. Give us boldness when it comes to our giving to missions that we might be willing to give generously and even sacrificially to reach those who do not know or love You as You desire to be known and loved. I ask this in the name of Jesus. Amen.

Jesus went about all the cities and villages, teaching in their synagogues, preaching the gospel of the Kingdom, and healing every sickness and every disease among the people. But when He saw the multitudes, He was moved with compassion for them, because they were weary and scattered, like sheep having no shepherd. Then He said to His disciples, "The harvest truly is plentiful, but the laborers are few. Therefore pray the Lord of the harvest to send out laborers into His harvest."

Matthew 9:35-38

More Powerful than the Fairy Godmother!

Cinderella could never have escaped her life of poverty and slavery without the workings of her fairy godmother. The fairy godmother possessed the unusual powers necessary for equipping Cinderella to attend the ball. She created for her a wonderful ball gown. She turned a pumpkin into a royal coach. She transformed field mice into coachmen.

Because of the powers of the fairy godmother, Cinderella was transported to a world beyond her imagination. And in return, an entire kingdom gained a princess.

———◆◆◆◆———

There is a power greater and more real than the powers of the fairy godmother. That is the power of the Holy Spirit, accessed through prayer.

Many people, including Christians, often have misguided notions of prayer and vainly use it for selfish or ungodly purposes. But when properly understood and used, prayer can and will change the world in ways that make any fairy godmother's power pale in comparison.

In this chapter, we will discuss seven kinds of prayer that God delights in answering. As you learn to pray these prayers, prepare to be amazed and excited about what God might do in and through your life to help others.

Experiencing Miraculous Answers Routinely

If Cinderella didn't believe in miracles before her experience, she certainly did afterwards. Miracles are not just a matter of intellectual assent, but of experience.

Once while I was studying at Fuller Theological Seminary I needed four dollars for stamps, but we had no money, not even four dollars, so I was unable to mail my letters. I prayed. In past years, a family had sent a card to me every week, and they had included a one-dollar bill in each card. I hadn't heard from this family for three years, but a letter from them arrived exactly on the day I needed to mail my letters. Enclosed with their letter were four one-dollar bills!

On another occasion, we needed money to pay our rent of $145, but we had no money. We prayed. The next day we received a check for $152 from a friend who had never given anything to me before that time. The person told me that God had told him to send me the money. We paid our rent and had a little left over for the week's groceries.

These may seem like small and isolated examples to you, but I have recorded several hundred times in my life, and in the lives of my family members and our ministry, when we prayed and the Lord intervened in practical ways, often in extremely precise timing.

For example, when we were involved in purchasing land for a Bible college in Punjab, we needed all of the money necessary for the deal on a certain day. Two days before the deadline, less than half the money had come in. On the last two days, the entire remaining amount arrived in our office. Within hours of the deadline, we received the largest gift India Gospel Outreach had received up to that time. We had a similar experience when we purchased land for campus expansion of India Bible College and Seminary.

On yet another occasion, we needed a bus for our evangelistic team to use. I prayed that all of the money necessary would come in before I left the United States to minister in India. The bus cost $42,000, but when I left for the airport to fly from California to India, we had received only $7,000. A moment before the door closed on my flight out of Atlanta, I received a call from a board member that a church had notified our office that it would give $35,000 toward the purchase of the bus.

I have absolutely no doubt that God releases His power and provision when we pray. The more we pray, the more power He releases. When we fail to pray, we experience no power.

God Delights in Answering Prayer

Clearly, in the story of Cinderella, the fairy godmother delighted in helping Cinderella escape her unjust role as a cinder maid. If this was true of the fairy godmother, how more true is it of our heavenly Father who is filled not only with infinite power but infinite love for us?

In the 1800s an English clergyman and theologian, Richard Trend, wrote, "Prayer is not overcoming God's reluctance; it is laying hold of His highest willingness."

I am continually reassured and encouraged by this truth that I see throughout God's Word, in my own life, and the lives of other faithful believers. God delights in giving to us what He knows is for our eternal benefit and for the eternal benefit of others. There is nothing as powerful as uniting our will with God's will, and then expecting His will to prevail.

Surely a person can pray with tremendous faith, knowing that he is praying fully in the will of heaven for transformed lives, for new churches, for people to learn the commandments of Jesus Christ, and for the proclamation of the gospel far and wide— frequently, skillfully, passionately, and effectively. The book of James should encourage each of us:

> The effective, fervent prayer of a righteous man avails much. Elijah was a man with a nature like ours, and he prayed earnestly that it would not rain; and it did not rain on the land for three years and six months. And he prayed again, the heaven gave rain, and the earth produced its fruit.
>
> James 5:16b-18

- Prayer prepares hearts for service and for reception of the gospel. How this happens is one of the mysteries of God, but we know that it happens. Just as the air force clears out what it can before a ground-troop assault, water prepares the soil and helps seeds to sprout, so intercessors in prayer have a role in creating a path of light in the darkness so the gospel might be proclaimed with greater power.

- Prayer reveals to us the father heart of God, enabling us to approach Him with courage and boldness with our personal requests. As God meets our needs, He enlarges our hearts to include others.

- Prayer imparts to us a vision for what God might do, and gives us a heart to understand what God desires to do. Many a ministry has been "birthed" in prayer!

- Prayer emboldens those who preach and teach the good news of Christ Jesus. Prayer strengthens the hands of the weary. Just as Aaron and Hur helped Moses in the

Israelites' battle against the Amalekites by holding up his arms with the miraculous rod, so we must hold up the arms of those who proclaim the gospel. (See Exodus 17:8–13.)

- Prayer focuses our attention on needs, and on Christ's power and authority to meet those needs. When we pray for a specific need, we must always pray with faith and with praise that God not only can meet the need in His strength and power, but will meet the need because of His great love. Prayer assures us that we will be victors in any battle against the enemy of our souls. Prayer gives us confidence to take on a problem and know with assurance that we can do all things in the strength that Christ will impart to us. (See Philippians 4:13.)

- Prayer compels us to take action. A person is much more likely to take steps to confront an evil situation after prayer than without prayer. Prayer compels us to speak up. Prayer is never a substitute for action. Rather, it is the precursor to action.

- Prayer creates an atmosphere for receptivity of the gospel. Prayer welcomes the Holy Spirit of God into any situation so that He may do His work.

I have been to more large meetings in my life than I can count. A few of them were secular in nature, a few associated with the mission of the church but secular in atmosphere, and many vibrantly alive with the unseen presence of Almighty God. What makes the difference in the atmosphere of these meetings? Prayer! When any event or rally is soaked in prayer, both before and during the actual meeting time, that event or rally takes on a climate that reflects the presence of the Holy Spirit.

Prayer is not a substitute for evangelism. Rather, prayer is the first and vital step in evangelism. People are won to Christ because they hear the preached Word of God; however, when prayer is the atmosphere for that proclamation of the gospel, hearts are more receptive to receiving Christ.

Seven Specific Areas that Warrant the Fervent and Effectual Prayers of Righteous Men and Women Everywhere:
The scriptures tell us of ways in which we can and must pray if we are to accomplish His purposes:

1. *Pray for the Lord to send laborers into the harvest.* Jesus Himself told us to pray this prayer. He said to His disciples: "The harvest truly is plentiful, but the laborers are few. Therefore pray to the Lord of the harvest to send out laborers into His harvest" (Matthew 9:37–38.)

This prayer goes far beyond asking the Lord in a general way to send out more missionaries from your local church or denomination. It calls upon a person to see the potential harvest from God's perspective. The harvest is not what we determine in our own logic will be a successful place to evangelize. We must pray first and foremost to see the world as the Lord sees the world.

There were no doubt hundreds of very ill people in Jerusalem on the day that Jesus went to the pool of Bethesda and encountered a man who had been waiting by the pool's edge for a very long time. This man had been hoping against all hope for a miracle cure. He was lying there among others who were also hoping for the angels to come and stir the waters and for someone to help them be the first into the waters to experience a supernatural healing. Jesus went to this one place on that one Sabbath to encounter that one man. His focus was very specific. (See John 5:2–9.) What a wonderful example of God's sovereign love, mercy, and grace toward the individual!

Thousands upon thousands of people in Samaria were among the "unreached" of Jesus's day. Jesus stopped by a well outside the Samaritan town of Sychar and there spoke to one woman. (See John 4:1–26). He revealed to her that He was the Messiah. She, in turn, made two simple statements to the leading men of her town, "Come, see a Man who told me all things that I ever did. Could this be the Christ?" (John 4:29). The men acted on the woman's words and, the Gospel of John tells us, "When the Samaritans had come to Him, they urged Him to stay with them; and He stayed there two days. And many more believed because of His own word." They concluded, "We know that this is indeed the Christ, the Savior of the world" (John 4:42b).

The harvest is God's work. He alone knows which hearts are fully ready to receive Him. He alone knows whose faith is cresting for a miracle.

All of life follows a similar pattern of seeds planted, nurtured and producing a harvest. Jesus let it be known that this is God's plan—His design. He referred to the "Lord of the harvest." God knows where seeds have been planted, where seeds are sprouting and need nurturing, and where the fruit of a plant is mature and ripe for harvest. God calls us to be part of the harvest-producing cycle of life, both in the natural and in the spiritual realms.

Jesus let His disciples know there at Sychar that they were being sent into a field ripe for harvest. He said, "He who reaps receives wages, and gathers fruit for eternal life, that both he who sows and he who reaps may rejoice together. For in this the saying is true: 'One sows and another reaps.' I sent you to reap that for which you have not labored; others have labored, and you have entered into their labors" (John 4:36–38).

The apostle Paul used a similar metaphor. He said in writing to the church at Corinth:

> I planted, Apollos watered, but God gave the increase. So then neither he who plants is anything, nor he who waters, but God who gives the increase. Now he who plants and he who waters are one, and each will receive his own reward according to his own labor. For we are God's fellow workers; you are God's field.

> 1 Corinthians 3:6–9

As we pray, we must ask God specifically to reveal to us our role in His harvest. Are we to enter into a field to plant seeds, to water seeds that are already planted and perhaps are already growing into healthy plants, or to reap a harvest? Where is the field ready to receive seeds of the gospel? Where do the growing seeds need watering, souls nourished and nurtured through preaching and teaching God's Word? Where is it time to make an altar call and see souls bow at the foot of the cross?

Jesus said to a man named Nicodemus, "The wind blows where it wishes, and you hear the sound of it, but cannot tell where it comes from and where it goes. So is everyone who is born of the Spirit" (John 3:8). We human beings cannot discern why God chooses to move in special ways among certain people groups or certain times, or why He chooses to pour out His Spirit on a particular group of people at a particular time. It is not our responsibility to understand why God does what He does. It is, however, our responsibility to listen closely for where God's Spirit is breathing new life into human hearts. The Spirit imparts to us the ability to discern the Spirit's work, and it is there that we must labor. It is there that our labors will be truly effective.

We must pray that the Lord will send the right workers into the right places with the right messages at the right time. We need to be ready to send—or become—those workers ourselves.

2. *Pray to be sent.* This is a prayer that few are bold enough to pray, because the Word of God is quick to assure us repeatedly that those who are willing to be sent will be sent.

The prophet Isaiah heard the voice of the Lord saying, "Whom shall I send, and who will go for Us?" Isaiah responded, "Here am I! Send me." And God did (Isaiah 6:8). As one person has said, "God is always willing to use those who are always willing!"

We need to consider two other truths in light of this. First, God does not send us out to fail; He sends us out to succeed. Second, because God intends for us to succeed at what He sends us out to do, He will both equip us for success and send us into areas where we will be successful.

God promised Joshua success and strength, saying, "As I was with Moses, so I will be with you. I will not leave you nor forsake you" (Joshua 1:5).

God may send you on Monday morning to a corporate office to be a missionary to your coworkers in a major business enterprise, and He may not release you from that mission field for twenty years. He may call you to plant seeds of the gospel in the lives of some, to encourage and teach and admonish others who are believers, and to lead still others to a new-birth experience when they are willing to receive Jesus as Savior. If God calls you to this mission field, He will equip you with skills to succeed in the corporate world. He will already have given you the talents necessary to acquire and use those skills, and He will have given you a personality that is capable of working in a corporate setting. We may not see full success in this life, but if we are faithful, God will never let His Word return to Him void. (See Isaiah 55:11.)

On the other hand, God may call you to the Sudan to administer a food-distribution program by day and to present the gospel message by night. If God calls you to that mission field, He will equip you with the ability to amass the food supplies necessary, the wisdom in how best to distribute those supplies, the courage to face up to political corruption and evil people who desire to thwart your efforts, and the knowledge about how to present the gospel in a way that spiritually starving, desperate people might be able to hear and receive it.

God does not set us up for failure. He will send us where He knows we will succeed as we trust in Him, step by step.

Often, we do not succeed in our personal lives and ministries because we do not pray to be sent. Rather, we ask God to bless us where we have sent ourselves. That is not God's protocol.

What is our part as we prepare ourselves to be sent? We are to ask the Holy Spirit to cleanse us so that we might be pure vessels for His power, and to transform how we think and feel—as the apostle Paul phrased it, to transform us by the renewing of our minds. We must pray that we will know with assurance what it is that God calls good, acceptable, and perfect. In knowing the good, acceptable, and perfect will of God, we must pray that we will have courage to walk on that path. (See Romans 12:1–2.) It has been said, "The person who truly knows who he is in Christ Jesus, knows where he is being sent by the Holy Spirit, and knows that what he is being asked to do has been authorized by the God the Father, is a person who *will* arrive at a God-designed destiny."

Ask God to cleanse you so that you are refined and prepared for what He has already prepared for you.

Ask God to renew and transform your thoughts and attitudes so that you will see the coming opportunity as God sees it, and so you will have His compassion for those you will encounter.

Ask God to help you follow every directive of the Holy Spirit so that you will truly walk in His ways and bring glory to His name.

Ask God to give you courage to pray for Him to send you and go where He leads.

3. *Choose a people to pray for.* By people, I am referring to a nation, a tribe, a social and linguistic unit, or any other segment of the human population defined as a group. We all have different interests and curiosities. Choose a people about whom you have built-in interest.

- Begin to read all you can about that group. The more you learn, the more you will find a focus and direction for your prayers. As you learn about their culture, you will sense ways in which God desires to bring that culture into full alignment with His Word. As you learn about their climate, location, and economic conditions, you will learn more about the daily needs those people face. As you learn about their history, you will have new insight into what they must discard from their past to fully embrace Jesus as Savior and Lord.

Repeatedly in the Gospels, we read that Jesus was moved with compassion. As you pray for a specific people about whom you are interested, ask God to give you compassion for them. Don't pray "at a distance," but make contact with those for whom you feel great compassion. Seek out people from this nationality or culture who study at a local college or work in your city. Get to know them personally and pray for them and their extended families by name and for specific needs.

- Pray for leaders of the people God has given you as a special prayer focus. Pray that God will touch their hearts as only He can. Proverbs 21:1 tells us, "The king's heart is in the hand of the Lord, like the rivers of water; He turns it wherever He wishes." We must not only pray for those who are down-and-out, wallowing in poverty, and lost in sin. We must also pray for those who are up-and-in, drifting on a sea of riches and fame, but nonetheless lost in sin.

When the leaders of a people group commit their lives to Christ, the whole group often follows. This is a collective decision of faith based upon love and respect for the elder and his wisdom.

Learn the names of influential people in the nation or tribe and pray for them by name. Pray specifically for these leaders to come to Christ, and to allow for free expression of the gospel message in the areas they govern or over which they have influence.

Very often people who pray and intercede for a particular people group have a growing desire to visit those people on their own turf; to travel to the foreign land and perhaps engage in a short-term mission project among them. Ask the Holy Spirit to make you sensitive as to how, when, and with whom to proceed.

While he was in college, a friend of mine and friends of his prayed for India. Thirty years later, the Lord brought him to India to minister in various contexts. He told me that he felt his coming to minister in India was a direct result of his own prayers for India many years before.

You are likely to find that the more you pray for a particular group, the more you will feel a burden to pray for those people. Your love for that people group will grow, and you will desire more and more that those people will experience the fullness of God's presence and mercy.

- Pray for the Christians who already live among the people for whom you pray. Though vast numbers of people remain totally unreached with the gospel, hundreds of millions of Christians live in societies that are mostly non-Christian. We must pray that those indigenous Christians, both laity and clergy, will become faithful witnesses of the gospel to their immediate neighbors, friends, and extended family members.

As I traveled across America in the early 2000s, I became aware that many people in the United States did not know that there were large numbers of evangelical Christians living in Iraq. In fact, there were more Christians in Iraq than in all the other eighteen Arab Gulf states put together, and more Christians in Iraq than Christians in Israel. We have friends who are Iraqi Christians. They have family and friends killed and persecuted because of their faith in Christ. We Christians in America have a tremendous responsibility to pray for the safety and ongoing witness of those who truly know Christ in Iraq, as well as those who are Christians in any nation experiencing persecution from other religions or oppressive governments.

- We especially must pray for new converts to Christ. We must pray for their protection, both spiritually and physically. We must pray that they become fully grounded in the faith and fully set free from all demonic influences over their lives. New converts are often subjected to intense persecution by their family members and their immediate community. We must pray that new converts will be surrounded by a strong Christian support system, complete with good Bible training and encouraging friendships.

I encourage those who pray for our missionary projects in India to include these needs as they pray:

- Pray for every Christian who is traumatized by Hindu radicalism: for their safety, for their strength and courage, and for their recovery from the humiliating experiences they often endure.

- Pray that God will use the example of young Christians who boldly and freely stand up for Christ Jesus, that their example might strengthen and further the gospel message proclaimed in unreached areas of India. Pray that their family members who do not know Christ Jesus will come to Christ and experience the same forgiveness, love, joy, and peace He so freely offers to them.

- Pray that the persecutors, like the apostle Paul who persecuted Stephen, might come to the saving knowledge of Jesus.

- Pray for those who direct, teach, and attend Bible-training centers—often in secret locations—that all affiliates might receive protection and courage. Pray that those from Hindu backgrounds who study in those centers will receive protection as they visit with their families and neighbors, and share their faith.

4. *Pray for specific missionaries.* If you don't know the name of a full-time missionary, talk to your pastor or write to a mission organization and ask for the name of one or more missionaries for whom you might intercede regularly. You do not need to know all the details about this missionary or his family, but it will help you in your prayers to know some basics about the missionary's work, his family, and the obstacles he routinely faces.

Pray for specific areas of need in the life of this missionary and his family members:

- Pray for their safety and health: that God will protect them from all disease, accidents, and attacks from evil people.

- Pray for their provision: for nutritious food, pure water, and adequate shelter. Pray that God will provide all material needs so that they might devote themselves fully to the preaching and teaching of God's Word.

- Pray for their encouragement: that the Lord would send them friends who offer prayer and warm fellowship. Pray that God will give them strength to withstand criticism or petty insults.

- Pray for strong faith to overcome all fears and all temptations, and renewed energy to choose what is good and resist evil.

- Finally, pray for their boldness in giving witness to Christ Jesus as Savior and Lord. The New Testament places a special emphasis on the need for boldness among those who proclaim the gospel. On at least two occasions, we find in Scripture prayers for boldness at the heart of group petitions.

After Peter and John had prayed in the name of Jesus and a lame man at the gate of the temple in Jerusalem was healed, they were arrested and brought before the highest religious court of the Jews. The Bible tells us that when these religious leaders "saw the boldness of Peter and John, and perceived that they were uneducated and untrained men, they marveled. They realized that they had been with Jesus" (Acts 4:13–14). They sternly warned Peter and John not to speak nor teach in the name of Jesus. Peter and John replied, "We cannot but speak the things which we have seen and heard." The religious leaders had no recourse but to threaten them further and then let them go.

Peter and John went immediately to their close companions and told them all that had happened. Together, they then "raised their voice to God with one accord" (Acts 4:24 NASB). They praised God and thanked Him for sending Jesus, and then they requested this of God: "Now, Lord, look on their threats, and grant to Your servants that with all boldness they may speak Your word, by stretching out Your hand to heal, and that signs and wonders may be done through the name of Your Holy Servant Jesus" (Acts 4:29–30). They prayed for boldness—and that God would confirm their bold proclamations about Jesus with signs and wonders.

The apostle Paul gave the church at Ephesus a vivid teaching about putting on the whole armor of God, in other words, putting on the full identity of Christ Jesus. He then said that after the believers had donned the girdle of truth, the breastplate of righteousness, the shoes of the preparation of the gospel of peace, the helmet of salvation, and had picked up the shield of faith and sword of the Spirit—the Word of God—they should do one more thing: *Pray!* Paul admonished them to pray with perseverance and supplication for all the saints, and then he asked for them to pray specifically for him. He wrote, "And for me, [pray] that utterance may be given to me, that I may open my mouth boldly to make known the mystery of the gospel, for which I am an ambassador in chains; that in it I may speak boldly, as I ought to speak" (Ephesians 6:19–20).

Paul was writing from a prison cell in Rome. He did not ask for deliverance from prison, nor any personal luxuries or comforts within the prison setting. Rather, he asked for boldness that, even in chains, he might have both the opportunity and the right message to win those hearing him to Christ Jesus.

Most of the missionaries I have met around the world do not ask for God to release them from their calling. Nor do they ask for personal comforts or luxuries to make their lives easier. Rather, they ask for prayers for effective ministries. They desire that others pray for them to know what to say, when to speak, and to have courage to speak the truth of Christ Jesus with boldness.

As you pray for a specific missionary or several missionaries on a regular basis, ask the Holy Spirit to show you anything that you are to do personally to encourage or assist that missionary in his or her work. The Lord may prompt you to send a special gift to the family, or even to visit the family to offer practical assistance. The Lord may prompt you to open your home to the family when they return to the United States, or to host a dinner in their honor. Be open to what the Spirit says and obey Him.

5. *Pray that spiritual strongholds against the gospel might be pulled down.* The apostle Paul wrote this to the church at Corinth:

> For though we walk in the flesh, we do not war according to the flesh. For the weapons of our warfare are not carnal but mighty in God for pulling down strongholds, casting down arguments and every high thing that exalts itself against the knowledge of God, bringing every thought into captivity to the obedience of Christ.
>
> 2 Corinthians 10:3–5

Paul also wrote to the Ephesians along the same lines, "We do not wrestle against flesh and blood, but against principalities, against powers, against the rulers of the darkness of this age, against spiritual hosts of wickedness in the heavenly places" (Ephesians 6:12).

Demonic power is real. The devil has access to your mind and to your life. His intent is to destroy your influence, your reputation, your health and energy, and all opportunities you might have to give witness to Christ Jesus.

Much has been written about spiritual warfare and intercession, but let me point out three things from this brief passage of Scripture.

- First, Paul states that we each are at war. None of us ever reaches a level of spiritual maturity that exempts us from attack. As one person said, "The Christian life is not a picnic in the park. It is a walk through a minefield." The enemy of our souls is continually looking for ways he might steal from us, destroy us, and kill us. (See John 10:10.) We must have our eyes open and be alert to the fact that we have a cunning enemy who seeks to devour us.

- Second, the war is not in the physical realm, but in the mental, emotional, and spiritual realms. The weapons are not ones that can be wielded militarily or by flesh. In very simple terms, the battle we each face is inner—not outer.

- Third, Paul states that the warfare happens primarily in that part of us that governs our beliefs. What we believe dictates how we feel in any given circumstance, what we think about and plan, and ultimately how we act.

Note how specific these prayers are. They are no less specific than Cinderella's tearful complaint to the fairy godmother: "My two stepsisters have gone to the royal ball, dressed in beautiful gowns and riding in a carriage with my father and stepmother," she replied. "And I cannot go to the ball because I would disgrace them with my shabby dress." Is not God, who gave His all on our behalf, far more willing to do above and beyond what we ask or think?

Understand the Extent and Nature of the Enemy's Domain

One reason for the appeal of Cinderella's story is the power of the fairy godmother to overcome the evil intentions of the wicked stepmother. One aspect of gospel ministry is our ability to understand and deal with the evil intent of Satan.

Let us be very clear about several limitations God has placed upon Satan in his dealings with us as believers in Christ.

The devil was defeated at the cross. He no longer has control over the future of those who accept Jesus Christ as their Savior. He cannot unseal what the Holy Spirit seals. He cannot inflict eternal death upon a true believer. The devil may oppress us, impress us, hassle us, harass us, and depress us—but he cannot possess us if we truly have committed our lives to Jesus Christ. Where do oppression, impression, hassle, harassment, and depression occur? In our thoughts and emotions. Satan can plant ideas, fantasies, and lies into our minds. He can play upon our emotions so that we feel things that may or may not be an appropriate response to reality. The devil can deceive us through false notions that are very often accompanied by bad feelings.

The devil often does this through family dysfunctions in our past and present. He uses things that parents, siblings, or other relatives did or said to produce crippling lies about God and ourselves.

Why does the devil still have access to these areas of our lives? What can we do about these crippling lies of Satan? As the apostle Paul says, we must "be transformed by the renewing of our minds" (Romans 12:2). We must replace lies with the truth of God's Word. We must learn to hear the voice of the Holy Spirit. We must learn that the only power that Satan possesses—his lies—are broken by Jesus Christ who is the truth. The truth shall set us free (John 8:32)—not just conceptual truth, but the Holy Spirit's intervention that comes when we earnestly seek Him. There is nothing more powerful than the creative, transforming power of the Word of God, spoken to specific situations in our lives.

We must say to the devil's impressions, oppressions, and depressing accusations, "I resist you. You must cease and desist." God's Word promises us that when we resist the devil, he must flee from us. (See James 4:7.)

What does this have to do with praying for missions? A great deal as we shall see in the next chapter!

A Confrontation of Superstitions

Was Cinderella a superstitious fatalist? The story doesn't say, but before she met the fairy godmother, we are told, she continually wept at her mother's grave as if she was bound by powerful forces beyond her control.

Much of what missionaries face in their dealings with the unreached people of the world involves superstitions. A superstition is a lie about reality, an irrational but usually deep-seated belief in the magical effects of a particular action or ritual to control our lives. Superstitions are closely linked to the concept of luck. Good luck or bad luck is viewed as the result of performing certain actions or rituals steeped in superstition.

We face this continually in our work in India. Most Americans do not know that nearly all Indians of Hindu background have several names. Often, these names are given reference only by an initial, but if the full name of a person is known, much can be determined about that person. One of the names is associated directly with a Hindu god. This is true of place names in India as well as individual names. One of the names given to a Hindu person is associated with the ancestral home of the person, very often the place the person was born. This name often is linked to the "totem" of that village or area. The totem might be a creature, object, or plant that is revered as having mystical powers, powers capable of bringing about good luck or bad luck. To include a totem's name as part of a human being's name is regarded as assigning the good-luck power of that creature or object to the life of the person.

Some years ago a leading member of the ruling political party of India had the word "snake" as part of his name. This man came from an area where snakes are regarded as gods. The town has a snake pit considered to be a religious shrine. Sacrifices are offered routinely to the snakes in the pit. Most of the families in that town also have pet snakes that they keep in cages at their homes and to which they give offerings of milk. These snakes are objects of worship, and the belief associated with them is that these revered snakes have the ability to bestow good luck or bad luck upon a person depending upon how they are fed and cared for. The homebound snake in a backyard cage is not the ultimate source of that ability, however neither are the snakes in the temple pit. These snakes are but representatives of a cosmic, unseen "snake" that wields tremendous power over human lives. It is belief in "the snake" that traps a human mind and heart and is a stronghold against the gospel.

This political leader was not an uneducated man. He had university degrees and had traveled the world. He was not poor; to the contrary, he came from a wealthy family. He was not insulated or isolated from modern communication methods; he had full access to scientific discoveries made available over the Internet and mass-media channels. Nevertheless, he was in bondage to a superstition. He believed in the power of the snake, at some level, over his life.

Certainly the snake as a totem is a very convenient symbol when we are dealing with satanic power, since Satan first disguised himself to Eve in the garden as a serpent. Any form of totem ultimately leads back to Satan. It is fear caused by the devil that strikes terror into the unredeemed heart. It is fear caused by the devil's lies that give rise to superstition. Unredeemed hearts make vain attempts to deal with them, but only Jesus, the Truth, can shed light and gain freedom from these lies.

Praying against Enemy Strongholds

After the fairy godmother succeeded in getting Cinderella to the ball and catching the eye of the prince, Cinderella trusted the fairy godmother to do it again and again. Her confidence was aroused. She gained hope that the fairy godmother's power would enable her to escape her evil fate.

If God's power and willingness to help us infinitely exceeds that of a fairy godmother, how do we pray against these strongholds of deception and superstition? We must pray specifically and with intense commitment:

First, we must ask the Holy Spirit—whom Jesus called the Spirit of Truth—to do what only the Holy Spirit can do: reveal the truth. The Holy Spirit alone knows how to penetrate the deepest darkness with the brightest light. He alone knows best how to pull away the concealing veil to expose an empty deception. He knows how to set up the "challenges" that will cause false belief to crumble in the face of God's reality.

Consider the battle of Elijah against the prophets of Baal. God called Elijah to set up a situation that was rooted in real wood, real water, and real animal sacrifices. All day the prophets of Baal called upon their false gods to consume their sacrifices, frantically dancing about their altar and cutting themselves with knives. When the time of the evening sacrifice came, Elijah drenched his sacrifice with water until it filled the moat around the altar he had built. He then prayed and called upon God to reveal His power and consume Elijah's sacrifice. Intense fire came from heaven, consumed the sacrifice, and caused all the water to evaporate. (See 1 Kings 18:20–40.)

Pray that God will reveal Himself in powerful signs and wonders to refute the deceptions of false gods. Pray that God will call upon His prophets to put superstitions to the test to display His power.

Second, we must pray and ask the Holy Spirit to speak the words "Fear not" to those who are in bondage to superstition-based fear.

Only the Holy Spirit can speak these words directly to the human heart.

As believers in Christ, we must not allow ourselves to become frightened by evil powers. We must not become intrigued by the occult or get involved in it. We must recognize that evil is real, and that evil is cunning in its use of illusion, delusion, and confusion. We must flee from evil whenever possible, and if we cannot escape an evil situation, we must never compromise with it or play with it. We must always stand strongly against it. We must pray that God will pour out new displays of His truth to overcome whatever lie is at the root of a fear.

6. *Pray for God's perfect timing and methods.* This applies to your prayers for individual missionaries as well as for missionary projects. God has a perfect way to accomplish His work, and He alone knows the opportune times to initiate and advance His work.

Years ago, I experienced a dramatic display of God's sovereignty over time. When I was studying for my bachelor's degree at an Indian university, I had to write ten final-exam papers to

The Urgent Call

Every Christian can pray and is called to pray! Evaluate who and what you pray for.

1. Do you pray daily that God will send laborers into the harvest? If not, pray!
2. Do you ask God if you are to go to a specific area or people with the gospel? If not, pray!
3. Do you pray for revival among a specific people? If not, pray!
4. Do you pray for Christians in an area permeated by false religion? If not, pray!
5. Do you pray for a specific missionary or missionary family? If not, pray!
6. Do you pray to bring down spiritual strongholds and to remove the scales of darkness from the eyes of the lost in a specific region of the world? If not, pray!
7. Do you pray for God's perfect timing and methods? If not, pray!
8. Do you pray for the practical needs of missionaries and missionary projects? If not, pray! Pray with faith! Expect God to hear and answer you, and look for His answers daily.

qualify for the degree. I had written six of the papers and had four to finish when I became very ill with chicken pox. I was discouraged; if I failed to turn in these final four papers at an acceptable level of performance, I would have to wait another year before my next opportunity to take the exams. My parents began to fast and pray about this situation. They were joined in prayer by two women whom my mother had taught to read the Bible. These women prayed and prophesied that I would write the exams by the university-established deadline. Given the circumstances, it was hard for me to believe that this prophecy might come to pass.

Two days later, a riot broke out on the engineering campus and the university officials shut down the entire university for a few days to give the situation time to cool off and to repair damage. This shutdown was the exact time I needed to recover and to finish my exam papers and complete my degree program with a high level of success!

Did God close the university just for me? Probably not. No doubt, countless other people benefited and many other aspects of God's ultimate plan and purpose were impacted by that decision on the part of those university administrators. But you will never convince me that God is not sovereign over time! God certainly can arrange all things to harmonize with the "fullness of time" that He has for every aspect of His plan. God's purpose in doing this was, in part, to show me that He was in charge of all things in my life.

We must pray not to become impatient and rush ahead of God's timing. Simultaneously, we must pray not to lag behind or miss God's opportune times. We must pray for precise fulfillment of every detail of every mission project.

7. *Pray for the practical needs of missionaries and mission projects.* Pray especially for a steady flow of finances to worthy missionary endeavors. Few things sap a missionary's energies and creativ-

ity, or strain a missionary's faith, as much as a lack of financial resources to pay for life's basic necessities.

Pray, as well, for proper functioning equipment: mechanical and electronic. Pray for safety in travel. Pray for secure and adequate facilities.

Pray for those responsible for the practical, material, and financial aspects of any mission project. Pray for wisdom and honesty. Pray for knowledge and skills necessary to maintain all things in good, working order. Pray that nothing of a practical nature will impede the preaching and teaching of God's Word. Pray that advance planning teams will have clear discernment into all things necessary for well-organized meetings or mission trips.

In All These Prayers, Pray with Faith!

Because of the fairy godmother's miraculous help, Cinderella was able to boldly attend the prince's balls, even in the presence of her contemptuous stepsisters and wicked stepmother.

Prayer is not simply a matter of voicing words and hoping that God might hear and answer. We are called to pray with boldness and faith.

- Hebrews 4:16 tells us: "Let us come boldly to the throne of grace, that we may obtain mercy and find grace to help in time of need."

- James 1:6–7 says, "Let him ask in faith, with no doubting, for he who doubts is like a wave of the sea driven and tossed by the wind. For let not that man suppose that he will receive anything from the Lord; he is a double-minded man, unstable in all his ways."

Pray with expectancy that God will answer from the full riches of His supply that addresses every human need. Make Philippians 4:19 a reality in your life and the lives of those for whom you pray: "My God shall supply all your need according to His riches in glory by Christ Jesus." Pray for God's will—on earth *as it is in heaven*. God's will is always for our eternal best.

What Might One Person Do?

Pray! Prayer is stating a need to God and asking Him to fulfill that need. Certainly the more people who sign a petition to put a proposition on the ballot, the more important and powerful that petition is in effecting change. The same is true in prayer. Jesus called His followers to a minimum quorum of "two or three gathered together in His name." The power of prayer is greater when you join your voice with that of others. As you pray for missions, be open to the possibility of inviting someone to join with you in prayer for a specific need or a specific missionary. You will find that as you each voice your petitions, you will have new insights into how and for what to pray. You will soon find yourself praying for new things. Ask the Holy Spirit in advance of your petitioning to guide your prayers so that you truly are praying in full accord with God's desires.

This does not mean that you need to wait until you can meet with others in prayer. God hears and answers the intercessions of all His children. Be faithful in prayer, and be open to the Holy Spirit's leading as to how you might engage others to pray with you.

I invite you to join with ten thousand other Intercessors for India (IFI) in praying for an evangelist in each of India's 27,145 zip codes. For more information, contact our website at www.indiago.org.

I invite you to join us in the 2020 Prayer Vision for India. We are looking for men, women, and children who will obey the Lord and pray for the full revelation of Christ's kingdom in India. We are looking for men, women, and children who will pray, believing God's promise, "Ask of me, and I will surely give the nations as your inheritance" (Psalm 2:8).

We are looking for prayer warriors who will pray for ten years for India in worship of Christ, to defeat the enemy. We are looking for those prepared to sacrifice lesser things, perhaps to be awakened from sleep, to fast, or do without some other thing that God calls you to do, for the sake of the people of India lost in the darkness of sin. Above all, we are looking for people like you who will pray for ten years in love for the unsaved, especially out of love for the God who first loved you. We are looking for people who will pray out of a passionate desire for His glory to come over all the earth.

"In the beginning was the Word," John tells us, "and the Word was with God, and the Word was God." Through His spoken word, "let there be," God brought the universe and all things into being. Through His Word, He brings life and light to all. Through Jesus Christ, the Word became flesh, dwelt among us and showed His glory. Now, through the mystery and power of prayer, God delegates the power of His Word to us, His children. Let us not fail to use this great and gracious privilege of prayer often, wisely, and well for His glory to transform our fallen lives and the whole world according to His gracious purposes.

Heavenly Father, convict me daily to pray for the lost. Help me to believe with greater faith as I pray. Help me to pray boldly. Bring to my heart and mind those petitions that You most desire to answer today. I ask this in the name of Jesus that is above every name! Amen.

Jesus said… "The Kingdom of God is as if a man should scatter seed on the ground, and should sleep by night and rise by day, and the seed should sprout and grow, he himself does not know how. For the earth yields crops by itself; first the blade, then the head, after that the full grain in the head. But when the grain ripens, immediately he puts in the sickle, because the harvest has come."

Mark 4:26–29

DIVINE CONNECTIONS

Although it is never stated directly, the fairy godmother was Cinderella's "matchmaker."

Her unusual powers transformed Cinderella from a drab cinder maid to a princess. She brought forth the extraordinary beauty that was there all along, attracting everybody's attention, especially the attention of the one who mattered most—the prince. Her power transported Cinderella to and from the balls, using the most unlikely characters to get the job done—six mice. She was resourceful and constructive in her methods, using her powers only for the good of all—Cinderella, the prince, and the entire kingdom.

We, too, have a matchmaker: one who introduces us to our prince, Jesus Christ. Our divine spiritual matchmaker is the Holy Spirit. He is the one who works all things together so that a person who hears the gospel might become smitten by

THE CINDERELLA CHALLENGE

the love of Christ and respond to His offer of forgiveness and eternal blessing.

There is unspeakable difference, of course, between the fairy godmother in the tale of Cinderella and the power of Almighty God. The two cannot truly be compared in scope or impact. However kind and powerful she may have been, the fairy godmother's powers were limited. Her power collapsed at the stroke of midnight. Almighty God, however, has infinite love. His mercy and loving-kindness are renewed every morning in our lives. His powers are without limit.

Prayer is effective because of God's infinite wisdom, power, and love. The Holy Spirit guarantees God's response to our prayer. The Holy Spirit is the third person of the Trinity who is God Himself, the same yesterday, today, and forever, and He secures answers to our prayers according to His timing and for all eternity.

The Holy Spirit is a person—God's divine and personal connection with us through whom He imparts His infinite power and strength, not only in uniting us to Jesus, but in connecting us to others in the kingdom of God all our lives.

Invite the Holy Spirit to Connect You to God's Infinite Power Supply

When the fairy godmother appeared to Cinderella, Cinderella did not hesitate to explain her plight. She did not rest upon pride but was bold and forthright in telling the fairy godmother just what she needed.

God wants us to approach Him with boldness and freedom. Never hesitate to ask the Holy Spirit to lead and empower you in every area of your life. He will be faithful as you are faithful! Ask Him daily to connect you to His infinite power supply, capable of meeting all needs in your life and in the greater life of Christ's church. His manifested power supply wins others to Christ Jesus.

John and Kamala Simon fully know that. As missionaries to Pamukunta, Andhra Pradesh, they encountered a very hostile population that accused them of bringing a "foreign god" into their area, causing a severe drought and famine. Kamala had a dream indicating that if the villagers dug a well in front of the church they would find fresh water. The village elders laughed at her when she conveyed this Spirit-inspired message to them. The engineers continued to dig for water throughout the area, but without success. At last, they gave up their resistance to Kamala's suggestion and dug a well in front of the church. They tapped into a seemingly endless supply of fresh water! This result caused hundreds of people in the area to give their allegiance to Christ Jesus. The well continues to produce water for the village as an ongoing testimony of how God's power surpasses the power of the regional deities. Jehovah God never fails. Hindu gods routinely fail when they are put to any test. As the Holy Spirit directs us, and using the name of Jesus, we must never fear to challenge false gods, just as Elijah did.

God reaches human hearts directly and powerfully. His methods reach beyond what the human mind can conceive. We need to ask the Lord to touch people in ways only He can, and to change us so that we might more effectively spread the gospel. Isaiah 55:8–9 tells us:

"For My thoughts are not your thoughts,
Nor are your ways My ways," says the Lord.
"For as the heavens are higher than the earth,
So are My ways higher than your ways,
And My thoughts than your thoughts."

We must ask the Lord to help us think as He thinks, to see as He sees, to love as He loves, and then to act as He acts.

As we pray, we must pray specifically that He would draw those who do not know Jesus as Savior to those who do. And we must pray that the Spirit will lead Christians to specific individuals who are ready to hear and receive Christ.

God's "Divine Connections" Result in Conversions

The fairy godmother's power and her willingness to act resulted in miraculous changes of heart. First, Cinderella had hope that she never had before and followed up her hope with action. She went to the balls where she swept the prince off his feet and everyone else who saw her. Cinderella's connection with the fairy godmother made all the difference.

A divine connection is always the goal. Whether God leads the sinner to the saint or the saint to the sinner does not matter. The connection that results in conversion is what counts.

We have a wonderful example of this in Philip, one of the first deacons in the early church. God sent Philip to Samaria, where He was at work preparing hearts to receive his message. Acts 8:5–8 tells us:

> Then Philip went down to the city of Samaria and preached Christ to them. And the multitudes with one accord heeded the things spoken by Philip, hearing and seeing the miracles which he did. For unclean spirits, crying with a loud voice, came out of many who were possessed; and many who were paralyzed and lame were healed. And there was great joy in that city.

Philip experienced a divine connection with the people of that city. What an amazing thing to have the multitudes "with one accord" heed his proclamation of the gospel.

A short time later the Holy Spirit led Philip to another divine connection:

> "Now an angel of the Lord spoke to Philip saying, 'Arise and go toward the south along the road which goes down from Jerusalem to Gaza.' This is a desert. So he arose and went. And behold,

a man of Ethiopia, a eunuch of great authority under Candace the queen of the Ethiopians,
who had charge of all her treasury, and had come
to Jerusalem to worship, was returning. And sit-
ting in his chariot, he was reading Isaiah the
prophet. Then the Spirit said to Philip, 'Go near
and overtake this chariot.'

So Philip ran to him, and heard him reading
the prophet Isaiah, and said, 'Do you understand
what you are reading?'

And he said, 'How can I, unless someone
guides me?' And he asked Philip to come up and
sit with him. The place in the Scripture which he
read was this:

'He was led as a sheep to the slaughter; And as
a lamb before its shearer is silent, So He opened
not His mouth. In His humiliation His justice
was taken away; And who will declare His generation? For His life is taken from the earth.'

So the eunuch answered Philip and said, 'I ask
you, of whom does the prophet say this, of himself or of some other man?'

Then Philip opened his mouth, and beginning
at this Scripture, preached Jesus to him. Now
as they went down the road, they came to some
water. And the eunuch said, 'See, here is water.
What hinders me from being baptized?'

Then Philip said, 'If you believe with all your
heart, you may.'

And he answered and said, 'I believe that Jesus
Christ is the Son of God.'

So he commanded the chariot to stand still.
And both Philip and the eunuch went down into
the water, and he baptized him. Now when they

came up out of the water, the Spirit of the Lord
caught Philip away, so that the eunuch saw him
no more and he went on his way rejoicing" (Acts
8:26–39).

In church history, this eunuch is credited with starting the first
church in Ethiopia, which included many members of the Ethiopian
royalty. The strong Christian presence in Ethiopia today stems
from this divine connection between the disciple named Philip and
an unnamed Ethiopian, as orchestrated by the Holy Spirit.

Look for Daily Divine Connections
I cannot help but think that Cinderella's story has such attraction
for us today because most people wish, but do not believe, that
divine connections are possible. How wrong they are! Through
the power of the Holy Spirit, God invites us to be as bold with
Him as Cinderella was with the fairy godmother. This is not fiction but fact, and we must accept this extraordinary truth.

Therefore we must pray for—and expect—divine connections today. The same Holy Spirit is still at work in the same
way He was in the first century!

Let me tell you about a man I know well. His name is Jimmy.

Jimmy was a mechanic in Saudi Arabia when he accepted
Christ. The Lord called him to full-time ministry, and he came
to India Bible College for training in the late 1990s. After Jimmy
graduated, he went to northern Kerala, which is dominated by
Hindus. The neighboring district is heavily Muslim. He faced
tremendous opposition in the early days of his ministry as he
reached out to various individuals and groups with the gospel.
He knew that some of this opposition came from people who
perceived him as not one of them; he spoke a different dialect
and came from a different place. Jimmy began to pray that the
Lord would send to him someone who would receive Christ
and, in turn, become an effective minister to others. He prayed a
simple prayer: "Lord, You send the people to me. I will be faith-

ful in sharing the gospel with them. For those who accept Jesus, I will be faithful to disciple them in Your Word."

The Lord sent Jimmy several people who had hearts open to hear the gospel and who accepted Christ Jesus as Savior. Jimmy devoted himself to making true disciples of these converts, and sent them out to evangelize their own people. He intensified his prayers that God would send people to him and to the church he had established. He challenged those who had accepted Christ to join him in prayer, and eventually his small church established a twenty-four-hour daily prayer chain. Jimmy had a personal open-door policy for his home and the church; he made it well-known that he was available at any time to talk to those who might want to know more about Jesus.

Within a few years Jimmy's church grew to some three hundred members, most of whom were former Hindus.

Then one day as Jimmy was riding his motor scooter through the city, the Lord prompted him strongly to pray for the man who was riding the motor scooter to his right. The Lord spoke in his heart, "I want you to share the gospel with this person." Jimmy prayed and followed the man the Lord had pointed out to him. He followed him for several miles, all the way to the entrance of a Hindu temple. As they both came to a stop, Jimmy said, "Sir, I have something to share with you that I believe will be beneficial to you." They began to converse and the man listened to Jimmy for several minutes before interrupting him to say, "You have your religion and I have mine. I am the priest of this Hindu temple and six other temples." Jimmy did not argue. Rather, he gave the man his business card and said, "Here is my telephone number. If you ever need anything, please call me. I will start praying for you today and will pray for you every day."

Jimmy put the man's name—Chen—on the prayer list at the church. The people began to pray intensely for him.

Chen came from a higher caste than most of the people in Jimmy's church. Nonetheless, they prayed that God might use them, of lower caste, to reach this higher caste man.

Several weeks later, Chen called Jimmy and said, "I would like for you to come and pray for me." Jimmy went immediately to him. Chen said, "I have heaviness in my chest. I feel anxious and burdened." Chen was feeling the convicting power of the Holy Spirit, but he did not know that. Jimmy, however, did know what was happening! He laid hands on Chen and prayed fervently, and in a matter of minutes, the heaviness lifted and peace filled this man's body. Chen had never experienced anything like that. Jimmy and Chen met daily after that, and a friendship began to develop between the two men.

A week later, Chen visited Jimmy's home, adjacent to Jimmy's church. Such a visit was extraordinary! It is virtually unheard of for a Hindu priest to be seen any place close to a Christian church or to have any relationship whatsoever with a Christian. Chen was the descendant of people who had served the kings in that area. He was a prominent public figure. Several weeks later, Chen made a public profession of his faith in Jesus Christ.

Today, people stream by Jimmy's house. Hindus who have found the Lord are bringing Hindus for prayer. Chen has brought his father-in-law and his brother-in-law and seven other family members besides his wife and children to Jimmy's church. They have all responded very favorably to the gospel.

Chen has publicly renounced and burned all objects in his possession associated with Hindu worship. He has been publicly baptized. Many of those who seek out Jimmy and who visit Jimmy's church come from the seven Hindu temples over which Chen had oversight. In just a few months, more than a hundred people openly accepted Jesus as Savior. One of those who accepted Jesus donated five acres of prime real estate for the building of a larger church campus. This amount of land in that area is extremely valuable.

God is answering Jimmy's prayer! The people of this district are bringing the lost to Christ. Jimmy is engaged in full-time discipleship ministry. Before Jimmy will baptize a person in water, he elicits a commitment from that person that he will spend one hundred days in prayer and Bible study. Jimmy devotes several hours a day to discipleship of new converts, teaching them the Word and praying with them, including prayers to cast out demonic influences from their past so they might live totally free of the oppressions associated with Hinduism. Those who emerge from this hundred-day program are not only well-grounded in their faith and equipped to live a Christ-centered, Christ-honoring life, but they are well-prepared to become evangelists to their families, friends and neighbors.

Substituting Second Best for Best

It is interesting that Cinderella never considers any alternative plan to get herself to the ball. It is the fairy godmother's approach and nothing else. She keeps her eye on the prize, refusing to get diverted. Not a bad lesson to learn in our own attitude toward God's purposes in this world.

Sometimes we don't effectively confront wickedness in the world because we unwittingly become advocates of "second-best solutions." Even within evangelical circles, pastors and churches do not fully appreciate the power of the Bible and the gospel to effect radical change and improvement of society. Too often, we confine the gospel to an otherworldly "spiritual" realm and fail to see its practical dimensions in the here-and-now.

In few areas is this more evident than in the thinking of people who believe the evangelistic gospel message is irrelevant in the face of overwhelming social problems. "People are starving," they say. "The economy is a wreck, and people suffer with high unemployment, bad schools, and a rich exploiting class. What good is evangelism unless we solve these immediate problems?"

The problem with this line of thinking is that it fails to understand that deep social and economic problems most often have at their roots a deeper spiritual problem that can be permanently solved only through the preaching of the gospel.

A Region Is Changed

At her heart, Cinderella wanted to completely change her life. She didn't want stop-gap measures, but solutions that got to the heart of the real problem. That is the kind of attitude that we also need for Great Commission thinking.

The best way to convey this essential truth is by concrete examples. One of the best examples from my own native India is the impact of pure gospel preaching upon the Hmar people, a group of tribes that inhabit the states of Mizoram, Manipur, Assam, Meghalaya, and Tripura, all in northeast India.

For centuries, the Hmars had a reputation for their ferocity. Outsiders feared them for their practice of headhunting. They fought among themselves, drank heavily, and lived in fear of evil spirits. Outsiders regarded them as irredeemable savages. What outsiders did not know was that the Hmars were tired of living like this, but they did not have a spiritual basis by which to reform their way of life.

No missionary was willing to go to the Hmars until 1910 when a young Welshman named Watkin Roberts took the Gospel of John to Hmar headhunters in Lushai, a local tribal language. A former chemist, Watkin Roberts was filled with the Holy Spirit during a great revival in his part of Wales. After reading an account of the Hmar headhunters by a British commander, he sensed that God wanted him to take the gospel to these forbidding people in much the same way Elisabeth Elliot felt called to take the gospel to the Aucas in Ecuador.

Knowing the Hmar reputation for barbarism and the reluctance of the British to escort him with troops into dangerous tribal territory, Roberts found some neighboring Lushai tribespeople who helped him translate the Bible into Lushai, the language spoken by the Hmar. Later, an English woman gave money to print several hundred copies of the Gospel of John, which he sent to each Hmar village chief.

At first, the Hmars had problems understanding how to be born again. They called upon Roberts to come in person to explain salvation to them. When Roberts told this to the British officials, they exploded, "They will kill you!" Without a British military escort, Roberts decided to travel alone with an interpreter and depend upon God for safety.

The head Hmar chief received Roberts with surprising openness. While he was with the Hmar chief, Roberts learned that when two tribes are at war, the side that desires peace goes to the mountaintop at sunrise and beats a drum three times. If the other side replies by sundown, it is a sign to come to the tribal boundary to negotiate. The chief who seeks peace kills an animal and pours that animal's blood along the boundary. Then he and his enemies place their hands upon the dead animal while their subordinates negotiate. When they reach an understanding, they embrace and have a feast of peace.

Roberts realized that God had just provided him the analogy to explain salvation to the Hmar people: God makes His peace with sinful human beings by sending His Son to die on the cross—the "boundary" of sin that separates holy God and sinful humanity—to restore peace with humanity. He told them that the Bible is the record of God's treaty of peace. It is God's invitation to all to come to the boundary and accept God's peace sacrifice in His Son.

The Hmar chief and four others were the first to hear the gospel and commit their lives to Jesus Christ. Immediately, they reacted by traveling all over Hmar country with the good news. The reaction among the people was electrifying. Hmar people came to Christ by the thousands until over 95 percent of the Hmars were converted. Those early Hmar evangelists planted churches in almost every Hmar village.

With great joy, the Hmar people came to Christ. They were so tired of their fighting, drinking, and fear of evil spirits, and they were ready to live different lives. Now they had the basis to do so.

The Hmars ended their age-old practice of headhunting. They started going to school and building schools. After they understood the entire Bible, they became one of the most advanced ethnic groups in all of India. Their population rapidly increased as they stopped relying upon witch doctors, learned to eat better, and practice good medicine. Today, more than 85 percent of the Hmars can read and write, which is far above the Indian average. Once illiterate believers in witch doctors, they now have nearly one hundred schools and a good hospital staffed by their own doctors and nurses.

The people eat well and have higher-than-average family incomes. They are developing their potential to grow coffee and thereby expanding their economy and raising their standard of living.

Hmars have also entered the national and international arenas, serving as ambassadors, charges d'affaires, and other administrative positions. In recent years, at least one or two Hmar young men are chosen each year for government service through a stiff examination that only allows twenty young men to be picked throughout the whole country. This indicates that though there is only one Hmar for every seven thousand Indians, they exert an influence upon the nation as a whole far in excess of their numbers. It is safe to say that they will never go back to their headhunting practices. This never would have happened apart from the direct influence of the Bible and the gospel message.

Such stories as these are good reasons why the Apostle Paul could say from his heart, "I am not ashamed of the gospel." Neither should we be ashamed of it. Rather, let us regard the gospel as the most effective way to bring permanent change, not only for eternity but also in time. Any other solutions may be considered more "progressive" or "compassionate" in some circles, but it offers *only* short-term solutions that are *only* second-best.

Behind the Scenes

There isn't a sign anywhere in our story that Cinderella ever doubted the word and power of the fairy godmother. Cinderella's complete trust in the fairy godmother should never exceed our own trust in God to effectively accomplish His purposes in ways beyond our imaginations.

As you pray and believe for lost souls' salvation, never stop believing that God is at work. He is the ultimate "arranger" of all situations, and He works in the lives of those for whom you pray.

A number of years ago I experienced a dramatic display of God's arranging power.

During my college years, I made a list of friends who needed to accept Jesus as their Savior. I had grown up and schooled mostly in Hindu and Muslim neighborhoods, so many of my friends were Hindus and Muslims. Some of them gave a listening ear to my presentation of the gospel, but none of them put faith in the Lord while we were in college. Nevertheless, I kept praying for their salvation.

Years after I graduated from college, I held meetings in an Indian city, and after my message one evening a woman came to me and asked, "Do you recognize me?" She was one of my college friends whom I had not seen in fifteen years!

This woman was a Hindu who once teased me about whether a black file I was carrying was a Bible. I asked her how she had come to the meeting. She told me her story.

She was the headmistress of a school, and her husband was a businessman who spent much of his time commuting between India, Singapore, and Malaysia. She and her husband were having a hard time in their marriage, and she was contemplating suicide. Several days earlier she cried out in her anguish, "If there is a God, reveal Yourself to me." She had a vision of the Lord with outstretched arms, and she basked in His presence.

The next morning, she went to some Christians who rose early to sing and have devotions. She asked them for a Bible, and one of the women gave her a Bible and also a flier advertising my meetings. She recognized my photograph and came to see me and hear my message. It was the first time she had attended a public Christian meeting. That night, she accepted Jesus Christ as her personal Savior.

Within months, at her invitation, various evangelists began holding meetings in her home. The more she grew in her faith and heard the evangelists preach and teach about Jesus and His commandments, she felt led to fast and pray for forty days for her family. On the twenty-first day of her fast, each of her seven brothers and sisters, as well as her parents, came to her home to visit her. These family members had previously disowned her because of her conversion to Christ, and on that particular day, each of them thought he or she would just "spontaneously drop by" to visit her. They had no idea the Holy Spirit had drawn them as a group to come to her home and hear the gospel for themselves. The fear of God came upon the family. They recognized the supernatural power in Jesus Christ.

This woman changed her Hindu name to Mary, and the ministry that took root and continued in her home has produced scores of evangelists in her city, with scores of churches established. Hundreds of evangelists spread out from that city to spread the gospel across that state of India.

Do not despair if you see no immediate fruit from your prayers for lost souls of friends or loved ones. You have no idea how God is working "behind the scenes" to accomplish His purposes and to answer your prayers.

Filling the Gaps

The powers of the fairy godmother did not mean that Cinderella was free of responsibility. Cinderella still had to get into the coach to go to the ball. Cinderella had to keep in mind that the fairy godmother's power would not last indefinitely. If she did not obey the fairy godmother's instructions, she could find herself at the stroke of midnight in a very embarrassing situation.

Even still, Cinderella almost made that fatal mistake. At the very last second, she made a desperate run for the exit, leaving behind her glass slipper. Because she had trusted the fairy godmother, even that near-disaster became a means to realize her fondest dream.

Still, that would not have happened if Cinderella had not been willing to risk her appearance at the ball and the possibility of a fatal error. If Cinderella had not taken her risk, someone else would have married the prince, and Cinderella would have kicked herself the rest of her life.

None of us is perfect. None of us presents the gospel as well as we might. None of us is always sensitive to what we might say or do. The good news is this: *God is perfect!* He gets it right all the time! God uses and perfects what you say and do to bear eternal fruit.

Our job is to tell. God's role is to convict and convert. If we do not do our part, God will certainly find someone who will do it, and *we* will be the losers.

God does not invite us to join Him in His work unless He plans great blessing for us as well as the people whom He has willed us to bless. God does not just "use us for His purposes," but He compensates us as well, often in material ways, but also in other ways that provide deep satisfaction and meaning, and help us to experience His matchless love and a deep sense of worth and significance.

A good example of this in the Bible is the way Jesus fed the five thousand people in the wilderness from the lunch of a small boy (John 6:1–14). Jesus could easily have performed a miracle alone, but He was far more interested in involving His disciples and others who were willing to participate.

The Greek indicates that the boy may possibly have been a slave as well as a child. In any case, the boy experienced a highly subordinate role in that society. In the world's eyes, he had nothing to offer. But this did not stop him from offering his lunch to Jesus as a means of feeding thousands of famished people. Somehow, he had recognized in Jesus not only an authority but also a quality of life that would not reject him simply because of his low social status.

The humble boy offered his lunch, Jesus gladly accepted his offering, and He used it to bless thousands of people.

Just think—if the little boy had not offered his five small loaves and two fish to Jesus, I am sure that in His resourcefulness, Jesus would have found another way to feed the five thousand. But think of the indescribable pleasure that little boy had, knowing that Jesus used his miserable little lunch to feed thousands! It was a pleasure that stayed with him throughout his life, a sign of God's infinite love for him.

This is a pleasure that God loves to grant to each of us who is willing to offer what little we have to Him. In His love, God invites us to become partners with Him. God never despises our little, but He can't multiply it if we don't place it into His hands.

God never ceases to seek out and use people who will tell others about Jesus. The good news for us is that even if we are not experts in the Bible or skilled communicators, God will still use what we say for His purposes and to bring glory to His name. The Bible tells us:

> For as the rain comes down, and the snow from heaven, and do not return there, but water the earth, and make it bring forth and bud, that it may give seed to the sower and bread to the eater, so shall My word be that goes forth from My mouth; it shall not return to Me void, but it shall accomplish what I please, and it shall prosper in the thing for which I sent it.
>
> Isaiah 55:10–11

This does not give us license to be casual or inconsistent in the way we present the gospel. Nor does it give us permission to avoid diligent and regular study of God's Word. To the contrary! We are to share as much as we know as skillfully as we know. At all times, we must make certain that we are faithful to the whole truth of God's Word and that what we preach and teach truly is the Word of the Lord; however, when we err or fall short in our human weakness and limitations, we can know that God will use what we say and do to fulfill His purposes.

Strength to Face the Enemy

Cinderella knew that when she went to the ball, her wicked stepmother and stepsisters would be there. They might recognize her and cause problems. But that did not stop her from going to the ball anyway. She overcame whatever mental reservations she had to obey the fairy godmother. Here, Cinderella teaches us an important lesson.

Few who understand the world of evangelism believe that the task of evangelizing is going to get easier. Persecution likely will intensify. International evangelist Luis Palau has noted, "If the exclusivity of Jesus, proclaimed by the most humble and wise missionaries, has already elicited such anger and hatred from nations throughout Europe, we can only infer that persecution throughout the world over the next fifty years will increase."

An increasingly radicalized Islam has led to thousands of Christian martyrs in Nigeria, Indonesia, and a growing number of African nations. Restrictions on Christian proclamations are increasing in Hindu India, and in largely Buddhist and Hindu Sri Lanka. Somewhat ironically, given the history of the past fifty years, Christians in China, who presently outnumber card-carrying communists, might actually see fewer restrictions on the proclamation of their faith than Christians in Muslim nations. This assumes that the Chinese economy and society continue to become more open to Western influences and that no violent social upheaval takes place like the deadly cultural revolution of China's past.

Persecution against Christians, while often subtle, is intense and persistent. Christians in Egypt, for example, are free to worship Jesus Christ. But by law they may not add to, improve, or even repair their church buildings. In many areas, a person may believe what he likes, but he may not talk about what he believes, meet with others of like belief, or attempt to convince others to join his cause.

This type of persecution is very strong in India. Let me tell you a recent story about a young man named Raj Honnappa (*name changed*). When Raj went home from a Bible-training center to visit his Hindu family, a radical Hindu organization, RSS, heard he was coming. They wasted no time. As soon as Raj arrived in his home village, nearly two hundred RSS radicals forcibly took him to a Hindu temple. There, they manhandled him, shaved his head, and forced him to bow before idols in a public setting. Then they dipped him 108 times in the temple pond, and forced him to drink cow dung mixed with water 108 times to "purify" himself according to the rules of that Hindu sect. This Hindu ritual "cleansing" was intended to free Raj from the "contamination" of his Christian faith and practices. The entire ritual was made very public in an effort to portray Raj as forsaking Christianity and reconverting to Hinduism.

The pro-RSS media picked up the story, declaring that a Christian had returned to the Hindu faith after his forcible conversion to Christianity. Their intent? To leave the impression that Christians are reconverting en masse to Hinduism. The exact opposite is the truth, but the masses in India are not unlike the masses around the world; they often believe all they see or hear via mass-media outlets. Raj was taken into police custody and scheduled to appear before a judge to "investigate" if he was forcibly converted to Christianity. He was forbidden any contact with Christians while he awaited his day in court. The law in seven states of India declares that it is illegal for a person to proselytize—or attempt to convert—a person to Christianity. The authorities intended to learn who proselytized Raj so that they could arrest them.

They held Raj for seven days. Then he gave a statement before a magistrate. It was the first time that such a case had come to trial so quickly in this particular state.

Raj calmly but boldly told the magistrate that Jesus had done for him something no one else could do. He told how he found forgiveness from sin and found joy, peace, and love after accepting Jesus as his Savior. Again and again, Raj underscored that his decision to commit his life to Christ Jesus was without coercion or incentives from anyone, that he freely chose to become a Christian, was glad he had accepted Jesus as his Savior and Lord, and that he would do it again even in light of his recent experience.

He was released on bail, but under Indian law his release did not necessarily mean that his case was closed. The police may call Raj to appear before a magistrate at any time, and he must appear whenever they ask. Following this incident, Persecution Watch and other human rights organizations in India recorded more than three hundred villages where Christians were a majority were ransacked, and homes were burned and destroyed in August 2008. Hundreds were killed though no one knows the exact number. Go to www.persecution.org to see the extent of this persecution taking place in Orissa and other places in India today and in recent years. These figures could also be found in numerous other places include the Evangelical Fellowship of India, a body recognized not only in India but also as an NGO registered with the United Nations.

Raj's hometown in eastern India is in an area of millions of people with fewer than five hundred Christians of all denominations, including Roman Catholic. That means there is only one Christian for every twenty-eight hundred people in his town.

We must pray diligently that Raj, his fellow students, and others like him across India will have the courage and strength to endure such persecution and to emerge victorious for Christ. We must take courage in these words of Scripture:

- Jesus said, "He who endures to the end will be saved" (Matthew 10:22b).

The Urgent Call

1. Reflect on how the Holy Spirit has led and empowered you.

2. How might you become more sensitive to various relationships being divine connections arranged by the Holy Spirit?

3. Have you ever allowed personal feelings of inadequacy or limitation to stand in the way of your sharing the gospel? What is God's promise to you?

4. How does prayer help you to endure and overcome persecution?

- "No weapon formed against you shall prosper, and every tongue which rises against you in judgment you shall condemn. This is the heritage of the servants of the Lord, and their righteousness is from Me," says the Lord (Isaiah 54:17).

- "We know that all things work together for good to those who love God, to those who are called according to His purpose" (Romans 8:28).

Trust God to turn to good what the enemy of your souls has meant for harm. Jesus said, "The thief does not come except to steal, and to kill, and to destroy. I have come that they may have life, and that they may have it more abundantly" (John 10:10). Trust God to defeat the enemy in your life and to pour out to you the fullness of His overflowing abundance!

What Might One Person Do?

Ask God to establish divine connections in your life, to give you open doors for presenting the life-saving, life-changing message of the gospel. Ask the Holy Spirit to send people to you who need Jesus, and to send you to others who are ready to hear and receive His message.

Trust God to help you in all things, to be your strength when you are weak and your perfection when you are imperfect.

Trust God to give you enduring, persevering strength. Pray for other Christians around the world, especially those undergoing persecution, to be strong in the Lord.

Heavenly Father, help me to hear You clearly and to follow closely Your directives for my life. Help me to trust You fully in every need I have, every situation I face. Lead me to the "divine connections" You desire for me to have. Let me speak Your words and love others with Your love. Give me boldness as I share the good news of Christ Jesus and God's desire to forgive sin and give eternal life to all who will believe in Him. I pray this in the mighty and incomparable name of Jesus. Amen.

[Nehemiah] said to them, "The God of heaven Himself will prosper us; therefore we His servants will arise and build…

Nehemiah 2:20

WHAT IT'S ALL ABOUT 9

The story of Cinderella is a story of transformation. In the beginning, she is a young woman without hope, slave to the wishes of an evil stepmother and her daughters. Through the gracious powers of the fairy godmother, Cinderella is transformed into a woman of such beauty, she catches the eye and wins the heart of a prince and future king. Later, through marriage, she becomes a princess, destined to become the queen.

Cinderella has the good fortune of having a number of agents that aid in her transformation process. They include some very ordinary things and creatures that one would not usually expect to help a cinder girl become a princess.

The pumpkin is transformed into a fine coach, gilded all over with gold. The six mice are turned into a fine set of horses, a coachman and a footman, with liveries of gold and silver.

Without these fine assistants, Cinderella would have been all dressed up with nowhere to go. But with these helpers, Cinderella is not only transformed into a princess, she is taken to the prince's ball in a manner that fits a princess.

All of this takes place because of the kindness of one person—the fairy godmother. Without the fairy godmother's good graces, Cinderella would have remained a cinder maid forever.

An important lesson of the Cinderella story is that beauty is a treasure, but that grace is priceless. Without it, nothing is possible. With it, one can do anything. Grace makes transformation possible—that is what the story of Cinderella is all about.

In even greater and more staggering measure, that is what the gospel is all about. It is the entire purpose of the good news and Great Commission. It is the entire purpose of Jesus's mission on earth: to transform individuals, communities, and peoples and, finally, the entire universe to the glory of God the Father. This is not our deserving. The grace of God makes it possible.

We get a glimpse of this grand purpose in the words of the Apostle Paul:

> For this reason I bow my knees before the Father, from whom every family in heaven and on earth derives its name, that He would grant you, according to the riches of His glory, to be strengthened with power through His Spirit in the inner man, so that Christ may dwell in your hearts through faith, and that you, being rooted and grounded in love, may be able to comprehend with all the saints what is the breadth and length and height and depth, and to know the love of Christ which surpasses knowledge, that you may be filled up to all the fullness of God. Now to Him who is able to do far more abundantly beyond all that we ask or think according to the power that works within us, to Him be the glory in the church and to Christ Jesus to all generations forever and ever.
>
> Ephesians 3:14–21

In the preface to his excellent exposition of Ephesians 3, Dr. Martyn Lloyd-Jones writes that "we have here the Apostle Paul's

WHAT IT'S ALL ABOUT

profoundest or highest teaching. At the same time, it is, possibly, the most experimental chapter in all his epistles, and one in
which the fervor of his great pastoral spirit is most evident... Its
experimental or experiential emphasis is needed urgently... "

It is the experiential nature of this profound passage that lies
at the core of the gospel. At its heart is a portrait of transformation by the power of the Holy Spirit.

In Ephesians, as well as his other writings, Paul tells how
the power of the Holy Spirit transformed his own life. From a
Jewish fanatic who was intent on destroying Christianity and
Christians, he became an ambassador for Jesus Christ willing to
suffer all manner of persecution, including death. His thirteen
epistles make up almost half of the New Testament writings and
continue to guide Christians to this day.

God is intent, not just to do the work of transformation
Himself, but to work through transformed agents. He especially
seems to take joy when His agents come from ordinary and
unlikely backgrounds.

None of Jesus's twelve disciples had any background that
would commend him to a great task. They were nameless
nobodies. They had only average abilities and were plagued by
the same weaknesses of anyone else. They probably failed no
more or less than you or I, and their failures were just as real.
They had no outstanding traits of character or talent save one:
their undying willingness to follow their master, Jesus Christ.
As Peter put it, "To whom shall we go? You have the words of
eternal life" (John 6:68).

In spite of Peter's cowardly denial of Christ and his many
other glaring weaknesses, his underlying love of Jesus never
wavered. Even after his most colossal failure, Peter's love of
Christ drew him back, and Jesus's undying mercy transformed
Peter from a coward into a mighty agent for the gospel, willing
to give his own life. From an ordinary man, Peter was transformed by Christ for an extraordinary and eternal purpose: to

implement the Great Commission. Through the power of the Holy Spirit, Peter's ministry has helped to transform countless lives down to the present day.

Jesus Christ is the same yesterday, today, and forever. Two thousand years later, He is still in the business of calling ordinary people to become His agents for extraordinary tasks. When we take our eyes off ourselves and our glaring weaknesses and focus them upon our master, Jesus Christ, He transforms our character and our most glaring weaknesses into great testimonies for the fulfillment of the Great Commission.

A well-known testimony in the transformation of His agents is that of evangelist Billy Graham. For the latter half of the twentieth century and into the twenty-first, the name of Billy Graham has been practically synonymous with evangelism and preaching the gospel. He has spoken in person to more than one hundred million people in more than eighty-five countries on six continents. As the best-known leader of the evangelical movement in the twentieth century, Billy Graham has counseled presidents and prime ministers as well as presented the gospel to hundreds of other government and cultural leaders around the world. According to his staff, more than 2.5 million people had stepped forward to commit their lives to Jesus Christ by 1993 (Graham 1997, 1999). As of 2008, his lifetime audience, including radio and television broadcasts, was more than 2.2 billion people.

In his childhood and youth, there was nothing in Billy Graham's background to suggest anything of greatness. He led an ordinary childhood on a dairy farm in North Carolina. His grades in school were average—sometimes even below average. Like other boys, he was energetic and mischievous, not given to piety. His biggest ambition in life was to become a professional baseball player. He showed no inclination toward preaching. In fact, he hated going to church, going only because his parents made him. Even after he became a Christian, he first showed no interest in preaching and evangelism. He showed no particular intellectual superiority and was not a theological expert. Nobody was predicting, "Now there goes a young man destined for great things."

What Billy Graham lacked in personal ability and background, he made up for in spiritual integrity. Early in his Christian life, he thirsted to know God better, to be at the center of His will. He made himself available to God. He spent hours in prayer and Bible study. God saw His heart, took him, and transformed him into the Billy Graham we know today. God also gave him the team that would assist him through all the years of his active ministry (Graham 1997, 1999).

Another unlikely candidate for greatness was the great preacher and evangelist, Dwight L. Moody. Few people have begun their lives with such a pitiful background. He came from a large family. His alcoholic father died when Moody was four. His mother could not support him, so he wound up having to drop out of school and work for a living. When he turned seventeen, he went to work in his uncle's shoe store. His uncle required him to go to the nearby Congregational church, and there Moody met his Sunday school teacher, Edward Kimball, who explained to him that God loved him. Today, few people know who Edward Kimball was, but God used that ordinary man to accomplish a great transformation in Moody's life.

Moody responded to this gospel message, but his background and behavior had been so dark that at first the church did not believe that he was genuinely converted. So they rejected his request for membership in the church.

But the Lord had plans for Dwight L. Moody. In spite of his poor grammar and rough background, God used him both in the United States and Great Britain to preach the gospel to tens of thousands of people, with multitudes of people committing their lives to Jesus Christ.

In our own ministry in India, we have many examples of ordinary people God has called as His unusual agents for the fulfillment of the Great Commission. One of them is Satar, a tribal evangelist from the state of Gujarat. Satar was a professional thief for much of his life. There wasn't a religious bone in his body. He and the gang with whom he associated were hated and feared.

But Satar heard the gospel, and his life was transformed. Soon after his conversion, before he really understood the Bible, he knew that God was calling him into evangelistic and church-planting ministry among India's unreached peoples. At that time, Satar hardly knew what had happened to him, much less was able to communicate it to others. But he diligently set out to study the Scriptures, pray, and put himself into God's hands. Over the past twenty years, Satar has become one of our most effective evangelists. Although he has little education, he has brought tens of thousands of people to Christ. The Lord has also given him an extraordinary gift of healing that has convinced multitudes of animistic and polytheistic people that Jesus Christ stands above any other deity in authority and power.

On several occasions, God has even worked through Satar to raise people from the dead, convincing people of the truth of Jesus's resurrection power.

Like Billy Graham, Satar made himself available to God. In spite of his background as a thief, God used him to glorify His name and bring multitudes into the kingdom. This is the grace of God, greater than all of our sin. If God is ready to use ordinary fishermen, a farm boy, and a thief to accomplish His purposes, will He not also use us when we make ourselves available to Him?

For all these people, becoming available has involved sacrificing other things. It has involved years of hard work and dedication. It has involved misunderstanding and ridicule from others. For the apostle Paul, the twelve disciples and some of our own evangelists, it has involved the ultimate sacrifice.

But all of them have spoken of the joy of giving themselves to the higher purposes of God and seeing Him do great and mighty things through them in the lives of others. They were transformed from the inside out. Their values changed. Their ambitions changed. What was once important to them became of no account. They were able to do in the power of God what they could not have done alone.

God calls His agents to go forth to tell others the good news so that they, too, will experience the transforming and resurrecting power of Jesus Christ.

The transforming power of the gospel takes many forms. In his well-researched book, *For the Glory of God*, Rodney Stark tells how the good news has ultimately led to reformations, the birth of modern science, and the end of slavery. These things have taken place, he says, through people who heard the gospel and acted for the glory of God. In the process, they transformed our entire culture and the world. What these previous generations have accomplished for society has come as a direct result of the availability of earlier generations to the power of God working in them.

Peter and Paul could not have predicted that their willingness to act as God's agents would ultimately lead to the age of science. Nor could they have predicted that the gospel would so transform society that slavery would end as an accepted institution in the western world. They were simply obedient to the calling of God, and God has done the rest.

The missionaries who were obedient to go to these wild and forbidding parts of India did not know that all these things would happen. They were simply obedient to the calling that God placed upon them. They were available and open to anything that God wanted to do through them.

What is God willing to do through you and me if we are available and obedient?

"Call unto me," the Lord said to Jeremiah, "and I will do great and mighty things you do not know" (Jeremiah 33:3).

Those words are just as true today as when they were written three thousand years ago. The God of Jeremiah is the same transforming God as always.

Transformation—that is what the gospel is all about. That is the vision that we must keep in mind for each person whom God leads into our path or to whom He sends us. This is the vision that drove the Apostle Paul, something he states eloquently in Romans 8 (taken from *The Message*):

> Those who enter into Christ's being here for us no longer have to live under a continuous, low-lying black cloud. A new power is in operation. The Spirit of life in Christ, like a strong wind, has magnificently cleared the air, freeing you from a fated lifetime of brutal tyranny at the hands of sin and death. God went for the jugular when he sent his own Son. He didn't deal with the problem as something remote and unimportant. In his Son, Jesus, he personally took on the human condition, entered the disordered mess of struggling humanity in order to set it right once and for all. The law code, weakened as it always was by fractured human nature, could never have done that.
>
> Romans 8:2–3

Paul says that transformation will never take place through human power alone: "Those who think they can do it on their own end up obsessed with measuring their own moral muscle but never get around to exercising it in real life" (Romans 8:6).

Those who trust God through Jesus Christ experience a different and better reality:

> But you are not controlled by your sinful nature. You are controlled by the Spirit if you have the Spirit of God living in you. (And remember that those who do not have the Spirit of Christ living

in them do not belong to him at all.) And Christ lives within you, so even though your body will die because of sin, the Spirit gives you life because you have been made right with God. The Spirit of God, who raised Jesus from the dead, lives in you. And just as God raised Christ Jesus from the dead, he will give life to your mortal bodies by this same Spirit living within you.

Romans 8:9–11 (NLT)

When the Holy Spirit dwells within us, we are no longer prisoners of the world and the world's system. We no longer have the same destiny of a struggling and dying world. Instead,

It's adventurously expectant, greeting God with a childlike 'What's next, Papa?' God's Spirit touches our spirits and confirms who we really are. We know who he is, and we know who we are: Father and children. And we know we are going to get what's coming to us—an unbelievable inheritance!

Romans 8:15–17a

We live in a world of suffering, but it is a suffering that has an ultimate meaning and good end that will transform the entire world:

We go through exactly what Christ goes through. If we go through the hard times with him, then we're certainly going to go through the good times with him! The difficult times of pain throughout the world are simply birth pangs...

Romans 8:22 (NLT)

Birth pangs, though painful, are the signs that a new life is about to begin, a new life of hope and joy.

> We're also feeling the birth pangs. These sterile and barren bodies of ours are yearning for full deliverance. That is why waiting does not diminish us, any more than waiting diminishes a pregnant mother.
>
> Romans 8:23

During this process of birth, for ourselves and for the world, the Spirit of God never leaves us or forsakes us, even when the birth contractions are so hard to bear that we do not know how to cry out to God:

> If we don't know how or what to pray, it doesn't matter. He does our praying in and for us, making prayer out of wordless sighs, our aching groans. He knows us far better than we know ourselves, knows our pregnant condition, and keeps us present before God.
>
> Romans 8:25–27

This ever-presence of God's Spirit in the life of His child, whatever the circumstance, should renew our hearts and minds and enable us to press on to ultimate victory. No event within the life of the child of God in Christ is without meaning or purpose: "…we can be so sure that every detail of our lives of love for God is worked into something good" (Romans 8:28b).

God does not do this in general, but on a very personal basis. He did it by "…calling people by name. After He called them by name, He set them up on a solid basis with Himself. And then, after getting them established, He stayed with them to the end, gloriously completing what He had begun" (Romans 8:29–30).

This is the gospel. It is the gospel of grace and beauty given to us by the God of grace and beauty. The gracious and beautiful character of God through Jesus Christ brings transformation.

This is the gospel of the Great Commission that Jesus said would be preached to all people.

Are you ready to become part of this great story?

The Urgent Call

1. How has the gospel already transformed your own life? How has that affected your desire to see the gospel transform the lives of others?

2. Do you think that God chooses some but not others to do great works for Him? Or does He have a transformational ministry for all of us as believers in the lives of others if we make ourselves available to Him?

3. Are you fully available to let God use you for His purposes? If not, what keeps you from making yourself fully available?

4. What do you think are the things that excited the apostles about the gospel, enough for them to sacrifice their lives? What are the things about the gospel that excite you? What are you willing to sacrifice for the sake of the gospel?

What Might One Person Do?

I know a pastor of a church on the eastern coast of the United States, highly respected by his congregation as a Bible teacher because of his commitment and obedience to the Word of God. Through his study of the Word, he has long supported projects that emphasize fulfillment of the Great Commission. Through his Spirit-filled preaching and teaching, the members of his congregation have been inspired to trust God to provide six-figure gifts to missions in India, though the membership of the church is less than five hundred. This has happened several times. In every case the Lord has supplied every penny they have pledged. This has taken place even when the church was simultaneously involved in its own extensive building projects. They did not allow their small size as a church to distract them from asking and expecting God to do great things through them.

In the 1980s, a seventy-eight-year-old Australian lady had a dream that challenged her and her husband to begin a new life. The Holy Spirit called upon them to start a new fellowship of believers, committed to living together in community and working at secular jobs, but devoting their income to the support of Great Commission projects. This elderly couple did not see their age as a hindrance and went on to trust the Lord. Over time, a community of believers rose up, with the elderly couple as the overseers. The Lord prospered this community, enabling them to raise millions of dollars for multiple mission projects around the world, including India.

What does the Lord want to do through you?

Heavenly Father, Your good news through Your Son, Jesus Christ, has already transformed the lives of countless souls down through the centuries. Obviously, Your work is still not done. Many millions have yet to hear, millions whose hearts You are already preparing. In one way or another, each person You have chosen will enter into Your kingdom. The only question is whether I will be Your effective agent of transformation. Father God, thank You for changing my life, but how much more I need to think and act like You! I am Your empty vessel. Fill me, transform me and use me for your glory and the fulfillment of Your Great Commission, according to Your will, above all I ask or think. In the name of Jesus. Amen.

*You are my friends if you do what I command you.
No longer do I call you slaves, for the slave does not
know what his master is doing; but I have called
you friends, for all things that I have heard from My
Father I have made known to you.*

John 15:14–15

BECOMING PART
OF THE STORY

Truth, they say, is stranger than fiction. It is also
far more exciting!

In this book, we have compared the reality of
missions with the fictitious tale of Cinderella.
Jesus is the truth of missions, and when we get
on His wavelength, we discover that missions are
endlessly exciting. However, more often than we
like to admit, Christians become more excited
about Cinderella than they do about the truth
and excitement of the Great Commission.

In the exciting drama of the gospel, all characters are real and the implications of God's call
to us are of greater significance to real people, to
the real history of the world, to the real destiny
of the cosmos—and to us personally—than any
character of fiction.

———◆·▸◉◂·◆———

Jesus gives us two options—to participate in the exciting adventure of missions or not to participate. He gives no other choices. If we decide to participate, we will glorify God, bless countless people, and receive blessings ourselves. That is God's way. He guarantees it.

We become a part of God's story not by accident, but by design and strategy. We do it by coming to understand trends and opportunities, implementing optimal solutions, creating places for people to survive and heal, planting churches, and training indigenous leaders.

Approaching Missions by Strategy and Design

If we really believe the Great Commission is God's exciting truth and are awed by the reality of God's power and His incredible invitation to join our Creator in His creative work, we will begin to develop a strategy to fulfill His work.

A strategy is a carefully devised plan of action to achieve a goal. I am a firm believer in the importance of finding and using every effective strategy available. We must trust the Holy Spirit to reveal His strategies to us. We must implement those strategies as quickly and efficiently as we can, for maximum quality and effectiveness.

At times, the Lord's strategy may be a tried-and-true strategy.

At times, it may be a tried-and-true strategy adapted to a particular situation.

At times, God's strategy may be entirely new, created for such a time as now.

I take great comfort and draw great encouragement from the example of the sons of Issachar.

Issachar—one of the twelve tribes of Israel—is described in 1 Chronicles 12:32 in this way: " ... the sons of Issachar who had understanding of the times, to know what Israel ought to do." This simple statement speaks volumes!

In this passage, various tribes of Israel have sent soldiers to join the army that David is amassing at Hebron. The tribe of Judah is represented by 6,800 men armed for war. The tribe of Simeon sends seventy-one hundred soldiers. The sons of Levi are represented by 4,600 soldiers, with another 3,700 allied with Jehoiada, the leader of the Aaronites. The tribe of Benjamin sends 3,000 loyal soldiers. Ephraim sends 28,800 mighty men of valor. Manasseh sends 18,000. Zebulun sends 50,000. Naphtali sends 37,000. The tribe of Dan sends 28,000. The tribe of Asher sends 40,000. The combined tribes of Reuben, Gad, and the half-tribe of Manasseh on the other side of the Jordan send 120,000 men "armed for battle with every kind of weapon of war" (1 Chronicles 12:37).

No tribe sends what Issachar sends: "Two hundred leaders of the tribe." Yet, this passage says, "All their brethren were at their command."

The name Issachar means, "he will bring a reward." However, the prophecy given by Jacob over this tribe was not always perceived as good. Genesis 49:14–15 (NASB) tells us that "Issachar is a strong donkey lying down between the sheepfolds. When he saw that a resting place was good and that the land was pleasant, he bowed his shoulder to bear burdens, and became a slave at forced labor." In the Old Testament donkeys were called "smarter than men" by the prophet Isaiah (Isaiah 1:3). They were used to speak the word of the Lord (in the case of Balaam the prophet). One donkey bone was used by Samson to destroy a thousand enemy soldiers.

Qualities of the Sons of Issachar
The men of Issachar were a vital part of David's team. They possessed three exceptional qualities:

First, they understood the times. They knew how to conduct an accurate and penetrating analysis of current conditions and options.

Second, they knew what Israel should do. They understood the Word from the Lord, plus a vision that enabled them to see the strategy that God had for them in any circumstance.

Third, they had passion, energy, and contagious enthusiasm. Under the leadership of the sons of Issachar, Israel went from strength to strength.

Led by the sons of Issachar, the Israelites who aligned with David were known for being:

- Faithful (1 Chronicles 11:10)
- Unified (1 Chronicles 11:1)
- Godly (1 Chronicles 11:9–10, 12:176–38)
- Team workers (1 Chronicles 12:22)
- Radically dependent upon God (1 Chronicles 11:10, 12:18–23)

We must pray today that God will provide for us "sons of Issachar" as we seek to evangelize the world and make disciples of all nations before the night comes when no one can work!

We must pray for men and women of integrity and principle, vision, and commitment, a sense of social responsibility and a vital relationship with God, who will arise and take leadership of the worldwide evangelistic and discipleship efforts.

Understanding Trends and Opportunities

Cinderella decided to follow the fairy godmother's plan because she knew that circumstances were now going her way. She saw her opportunities and took them. This is a good lesson for each of us to learn as Christians as we discern the signs of the times.

We must catch the vision for the overall trends at work in our respective societies and the world as a whole.

The last one hundred years have seen vast technological changes in communication resulting in a plethora of books, rapid replication of audio, visual, and printed materials, and instant access to more information than anyone can digest. This increase in information has produced a growing trend of specialization, since no one person can ever grasp all there is to know or use all the information now available. The more we specialize, the more we lose sight of the "big picture" themes so vital to our humanity and to the gospel. We must regain a depth of understanding of God's Word, and recognize that our commitment to Christ is all-pervasive and all-encompassing. Jesus Christ is not "an option," and the Bible is not "a point of view." Jesus is Alpha and Omega, the embodiment of truth, and the Bible is the authoritative source for knowing how we are to live in right relationship with God and other human beings. Church is not a Sunday-morning-only activity; the church is the body of Christ, alive and functioning and intended for full and healthy operation at all times.

The Internet has made information readily available to people of all ages and cultures, not all of which is edifying, moral, or helpful. Pornography is a worldwide problem, and the abuse and sex slavery it generates are appalling. Overall, we are seeing a decline in the value of human life worldwide. The number of abortions, acts of abuse, violence against the innocent, and rage-ridden crimes are increasing at an alarming rate, both in the United States and around the world. Where and how can the gospel of peace and Christ's command to "love one another" take root?

We live in an age when people are extremely mobile; they not only travel extensively but move frequently. The result can be a host of shallow and temporary relationships and commitments, without deep and lasting friendships. Christ calls us to go "deep" in our friendships and to be committed to one another as brothers and sisters. We are to be a family of God that sticks together through all circumstances. A church growth/health study of pastors conducted by Fuller Seminary, George Barna and Pastoral Care, Inc. in 2009 reported that 70 percent of pastors in the United States do not have at least one close friend. What can we do as the body of Christ to reach out to those who suffer in loneliness, fear, and depression because they no longer have a strong purpose for living?

We live in an age that advocates personal fulfillment. This can result in a lack of empathy for others, and a lack of self-sacrifice in order to help others. The survey cited above indicated that in 2008, more than 20,400 pastors left the ministry completely, and another 15,600 were forced to leave by the local church, many without a cause. The same study indicated that 80 percent of them who left have stated that one of the main reasons is that they receive little empathy and support from their spouses or family members. How can we in the church instill the need for new converts to encourage those who are in the ministry? The encourager also needs to be encouraged.

We live in an age of rampant disease. UNICEF states a child dies every four seconds of AIDS and extreme poverty, often before their fifth birthday (see www.cozay.com). As Richard Stearns says, "In Africa, they say when it comes to HIV, everyone is either infected or affected—no one escapes completely" (Stearns 2009). Two of the most obvious results of this pandemic are a massive population of widows and orphans across the African continent, and a serious decline in economic productivity. Sexual abuse and the spread of AIDS are directly linked. The care of AIDS widows and orphans is a prime opportunity for the church to step in. If Christians do not take on this challenge, we should not be surprised when Muslims do. The fundamentalist Muslim strategy worldwide has been to target the poor and uneducated with a message that decries Western immorality and greed. The result is raw anger and hatred against the West, easily translated into terrorism.

We live in an age in which the general cultural trend is anti-Christian. At the same time, we live in a time of growing spiritual hunger and deep ignorance of what the gospel is.

We need Issachars to help us strategize how to respond to these various trends, and to convey to us God's wisdom for how best to proceed, where and when!

We Must Seek to Implement "Optimal Solutions"

Cinderella did not approach her situation half-heartedly and neither should we.

God blesses us to become a blessing to others. His intent and desire in blessing an individual is to bless that person's entire family, his or her church, and community. God's blessing of promise to Abraham was never meant exclusively for Abraham's benefit or use. God said, "I will bless those who bless you, and I will curse him who curses you; and in you all the families of the earth shall be blessed" (Genesis 12:3).

Whatever work we seek in our missionary endeavors must have the possibility for multiplication and a blessing that overflows to others.

God never isolates or fragments us, either individually or collectively as the body of Christ. When God heals, He heals the whole person. Whatever work we endeavor to establish must cover the whole person's life and benefit all within the body of Christ.

God never plays favorites. He loves all people and desires that all accept His offer of reconciliation and forgiveness made possible by the shed blood of Jesus. Jesus described the kingdom of heaven as being "like leaven, which a woman took and hid in three measures of meal till it was all leavened" (Luke 13:21). Leaven must be worked evenly into bread dough, and in like manner, the gospel must be spread abroad in a way that permeates the whole.

God's optimal solutions and strategies are always geared toward wholeness. God sees the whole earth. He sees the whole person's life. He sees an entire strategy from beginning to end. We must ask the Lord to help us see as He sees.

The book of Nehemiah should give us tremendous encouragement and insight on this point. When Nehemiah returned to Jerusalem and saw the crumbled walls of the city, God gave him a strategy to rebuild the wall and protect the effort. Each person was assigned to rebuild the portion of the wall closest to his own home. Should an attack come against the effort, a signal would go out to call reinforcements to that portion of the wall. In this way, the workers rebuilt the wall rapidly and with tremendous morale. Note specifically that the *whole* wall was rebuilt. The repaired wall rose evenly around the city, and all became involved in the rebuilding. (See Nehemiah 2–4.) In a similar fashion, God works most effectively as we engage in worldwide missionary activity.

Let me share with you four strategies that are working in the world of missions today to help generate in you a vision for new ideas and methodologies.

A Church in Every Postal Code
Our strategy in India is to establish a church in every postal code of the nation.

Many Americans and Europeans do not understand how vast the nation of India is. Not only does it occupy a huge land mass, but the population of India is three times that of all of Europe, and more than four times the population of the United States. India is an incredibly complex nation, with numerous ethnic, cultural, and linguistic fragments making up the whole. According to the late Dr. Donald McGavran, three thousand endogamous ethnic units have been identified within Indian society. Each has a high consciousness of being a separate people (1979). By my estimate, of these three thousand groups, fewer than two hundred, are considered to have been "reached" with the gospel.

How does one begin to take on such a large project? It's a little like asking the old question, "How does one eat an elephant?" The answer: "One bite at a time." In our case, the "bite-sized pieces" are postal codes. At present, India has 27,145 postal zip codes. We are trusting God to establish a Christian church in each of those postal codes.

In 1995, as part of India Gospel Outreach's ministry, I began to call upon both Indian and American Christians to pray for a designated postal zip code until a new church was planted in that zip code and it developed into a dynamic, self-multiplying church. We still pray and believe that God will establish at least one growing, self-multiplying church in each of these areas. Today, we have at least one church in more than seven thousand zip codes.

We will not stop with just one church in each area, however. We will continue to believe that God will supply workers and finances to plant one million churches in India. How did we come to that number? It will take one million churches spread evenly across the landmass of India for there to be at least one Christian church within walking distance (two miles) of every citizen of India.

I invite you to join us boldly in prayer and giving to reach these goals!

Training Indigenous Leadership

As churches grow and multiply, the next step is to establish a Bible-training center in each state of India. Their purpose is to prepare local Christians to become evangelists and church planters to people of their own language and culture, to help the people of India find Christ and train others to reach even more people in India. Since we started the first of these training centers in 1988, new congregations have expanded at about 124 percent every ten years. At least two-thirds of the church members are converts from Hinduism, Sikhism, and Islam. There is still much work to be done, but we believe God is preparing us for a tremendous harvest of souls in the days and years ahead.

The mentoring model of education is very effective in training evangelists, many of whom come from Hindu, Sikh, and Muslim backgrounds. India Bible College and Seminary is not just an academic institution, but a place where our students are under constant training and supervision to ensure that they fully embody a new way of life. Our students do not just receive information. They are in a discipleship process. All the students at our training centers in Gujarat and Orissa come from a Hindu background. Punjabi students are 95 percent Hindus and Sikhs. In Himachal Pradesh, 100 percent of the students are former Hindus, and at Kashmir, 100 percent of the students are former Muslims. The schools are run like families. Our students live together, eat together, study together, engage in ministry together, and become friends for life—all under the direct mentoring of godly, proven faculty leaders.

Our students are not just taught a "theory of evangelism." They are taken into different real-life situations to experience what it is like to share their faith publicly before audiences of different beliefs. They are fully involved in their communities. This is true for all our students, not only those in the seminary. In fact, before a graduate of India Bible College can enter the Master of Divinity seminary program, he must spend a year of ministry in the field.

Training indigenous leaders is our goal. We say with great confidence that the help we receive from Christian churches and individuals outside India is an investment in raising up an indigenous Christian church in India that will one day sustain itself fully and be in a position to reach other nations.

There are wonderful models for the strategy we have used, or a similar strategy, in several other places on earth. What works in India also works elsewhere.

Lithuania, formerly a part of the Soviet Union, now has a full-fledged, fully accredited Christian college that offers both liberal arts and Bible courses. Some of the students in that college come from the United States. Most of the professors are from the United States and the courses are taught in English. Some teachers live on campus to help students develop English-speaking skills before they enroll in the college. Most of the students come from the host nation, but at least 30 percent of the students come from other former Soviet countries. The goal of the college administrators, professors, and the students is to win to Christ all of the nations once under Soviet communism. They make no secret about their ultimate mission. They aim all of their courses at evangelism and discipleship.

Many of the lectures offered by this university are provided by video, but all of the video-based classes are supported by small-group study and discussion sessions. Lithuanian students develop ties with outsiders so that a strong network of support—intellectual, emotional, and spiritual—takes place and continues long after a student graduates from the college.

A few of the alumni use video courses in their outreach efforts—again, coupling those courses with small-group discussion sessions involving church and non-church participants. The courses effectively evangelize those who don't know Jesus as Savior and train those who do know Christ to become effective disciples.

As you may have surmised, the students involved in this ongoing missions work have tremendous support from their families and friends back in the United States. Many of those friends and family members visit during the summer months to assist in various church-enriching and church-building programs. The more people hear about the host college, the more they want to support the college. They know that this small college, with its diverse student population and strong commitment to Christ, can become a tremendous force for the gospel in an area of the world ripe for harvest.

Several other factors are worthy of mention. In the last fifty years, an increasing number of American college students have sought opportunities to study overseas. More organizations are seeing value in sponsoring scholarships and work-study programs for American students to go abroad. They see this as having a positive impact on the American reputation overseas, and as developing good citizen-to-citizen relationships between Americans and those in other nations. Simultaneously, increasing numbers of Christian young people are going on short-term mission trips to needy areas in the United States and abroad. All of these factors hold wonderful potential for missions.

Students who study and assist in mission projects overseas nearly always develop a greater worldview. They have a greater awareness of other people's needs in foreign lands, and a greater urgency to spread the gospel. They have a new understanding of the cultural barriers that prevent communication of the gospel. They have a greater empathy for people of other cultures, races, and nationalities. They have an increased desire to communicate with people of other backgrounds, and in many cases, they learn a foreign language with greater fluency so they might communicate with their new "foreign" friends and colleagues.

As American Christian students attend Christian colleges and universities abroad, they enhance their potential to work within the indigenous churches of the various host nations. As they establish personal relationships among these college students and indigenous church leaders, they develop new and innovative ways for presenting the gospel across cultural barriers. Lifelong commitments to missions and to the support of overseas colleges take root.

Creating Places to Survive—and Heal
An effective strategy for some of our evangelists in India is the "handicraft center" in a targeted community.

The overall status of women in Hindu communities is very low. Many women are divorced and abandoned for frivolous reasons, and those who become sick or maimed are nearly always discarded by their husbands as no longer desirable or helpful. These women have little means to support themselves, and they frequently end up on the streets of their towns or nearby cities, where life as a prostitute or beggar leads to miserable suffering from disease and early death.

What a difference a sewing machine can make! In one tailoring center I visited, I met a group of twenty women who had worked together for some time. They arranged their sewing machines in a large circle so they could see one another and communicate easily as they sewed. These were all Hindu women, divorced and discarded, desperate to earn what they could to support themselves without becoming prostitutes or slaves. Many needed to support their young children who had been cast out with them. The women were trained by a Christian who was adept at sewing. This woman's husband, a Christian disciple and evangelist, not only helped to establish the handicraft center through donations of facilities and equipment, but he also secured a contract for the women to make school uniforms for a nearby upper-caste private school.

As the women worked, the lead seamstress and her husband taught songs to the women. They encouraged them to sing as they worked. Not only did singing make the tedious work more enjoyable and the hours pass more quickly, but singing together built a sense of community for these women. The quality of their work improved and morale greatly increased. The Christian leader taught mostly praise songs and songs about Bible people, places, and incidents—from David and Goliath to Moses being plucked from the river by Pharaoh's daughter. When the women asked about the meaning of some of the lyrics of their favorite songs, the Christian leader had a prime opportunity to tell Bible stories in greater depth, and especially to tell stories about Jesus and His ministry.

Some of the women asked for more information about Jesus. Over time, every one of the twenty women in this sewing circle accepted Jesus as her personal Savior!

However, that was not the end of this missionary project. The women's work was so excellent that they secured more contracts. More women organized into new sewing and singing circles. As the months passed, the women prospered economically. Not only did they care for themselves, but to the bewilderment and admiration of some of their family members, some of the women who had been evicted from their families and separated from their children began to send support for their families. This softened their families' hearts and enabled the women to re-establish relationships with their children and other family members. This was virtually unknown in the history of that village!

For a castaway Hindu woman to return bearing gifts of love and forgiveness toward those who had cast her away, was a stunning display of the power of the gospel. The women shared with their former family members the reason for the joy and peace in their hearts. A number of these former family members began to show interest in the gospel. They began to seek out the handicraft center leader for answers, and slowly but surely these men and extended family members found Christ. A church was established and it is growing. Women who have met Christ and been discipled at the handicraft center are establishing new handicraft centers in neighboring communities, replicating the model of the center where they first heard about Jesus.

Establishing Christian Colleges Overseas
There is a great need for Americans to catch the vision for helping establish indigenous Christian colleges overseas and to raise a generation of indigenous Christian young people who, in twenty to fifty years, can assume both financial and spiritual challenges associated with evangelization and discipleship of their own people. Bible schools are an important first step in an unreached area. Ultimately, Christ-centered colleges that offer liberal arts and science degrees, as well as vocational and technical training schools, will be required to produce graduates who can impact all of the social structures in a nation. These include

political and judicial structures, educational and health-care systems, various agricultural, manufacturing, and trade entities. The end goal is to create an environment in which churches of other nations lead the way in funding their own evangelistic and discipleship program. We have seen this model work in a number of nations. I see it personally in the work that we are doing to establish such a college in India.

For nearly a century, students from other nations have streamed to the United States for higher education. Those who sponsor these students hope that they will return to their nations and contribute their knowledge and skills to the betterment of their own people. Too often, this does not occur. Those who come to the United States for education often opt to stay in the United States to work so they might provide a better quality of life for their children. The nation left behind is further impoverished when this happens; the brightest and most talented young people leave and never return. We must reverse this trend. Americans must take the advantages and experiences of quality higher education to the nations, rather than bring students from these nations to the United States for college and university training.

In many nations, the church is not financially strong enough to purchase land, construct buildings, fund faculty salaries, and provide scholarships for poor but capable college students. But over time, and with assistance from those who are capable of helping financially, indigenous churches must take full responsibility to educate Christians for leadership roles in their respective nations.

The Joseph Anointing
Cinderella did not say to herself, "Who am I, a mere cinder maid, to become the bride of a prince?" She took on faith the actions of the fairy godmother and the prince that she was indeed the right young woman in the kingdom to accept the role of the prince's bride and princess. If only we would trust God in the same way!

It is easy to see the scope of missions and say to yourself, "What can I offer? The work is so big and I am so small; what can I do that will make any difference?"

This is the world's way of thinking, not God's. In this world, a person wields power through money, position, and the people he knows. But God uses a different standard. One way to understand God's way is to look at the life of Joseph. Of all the characters in the Bible, Joseph's life probably comes closest to resembling that of Cinderella. Like Cinderella, Joseph's sterling life and character provoked reactions of hate rather than love because he was perceived as a threat.

Jacob loved Joseph more than the others, even though he was the eleventh of twelve sons. There was a reason for his favoritism. He was the first son of Jacob's much-beloved wife, Rachel, who had had no children up to this point. Also, Joseph was more in tune with his father's love than any of the older sons. Although Jacob surely loved his other sons, no one responded more to his fatherly love than Joseph. This was sure to cause a deeper bond between Jacob and Joseph than any of the others. This was also sure to cause a rift between Joseph and his older brothers. This jealousy was further provoked when Joseph told them of a dream that clearly indicated that one day they would bow down to him.

The jealousy of Joseph's brothers moved them to dispose of him. First tempted to kill Joseph, they instead kidnapped him, threw him into a pit, and sold him into slavery in far-off Egypt. Later, after he proved his reliability to his master Potiphar, he maintained his integrity in the face of Potiphar's wife's seductions, only to be rewarded with prison.

Through all of this injustice, Joseph maintained his integrity in his relationships with God and others. God remained faithful to Joseph and used his prison time to mold his character and give him the ability to interpret dreams. At the right moment, God engineered Joseph's release from prison to become the prime minister of Egypt in a time of grave crisis—a severe seven-year famine that affected the whole known world. The whole world came to depend upon Joseph's wisdom. They probably responded to Joseph because his earlier sorrows prepared him to understand their plight. Even his own brothers came to Egypt to get food and wound up bowing down before him.

At last, after many years, Joseph's dream came true. Joseph's faithfulness to his earthly father and his heavenly Father paid a handsome reward far beyond anything he could ask or think, affecting countless lives in a positive way.

The God of Joseph has not changed in 3,500 years. Just as Jacob loved all his sons, so God loves all his people. But He seems to favor some more than others because they respond more positively to His fatherly love than do the others. This responsiveness causes a deep bond with God. It is also cause for deep misunderstanding and jealousy with our fellow human beings. Today, we see this in the deep hatred that some people have for Christians whom they regard as intolerant and narrow-minded for claiming Christ is the only way to God.

In these last days, God continues to look for people who respond to His love. To those who respond, God gives dreams and visions that involve the completion of His work on earth—the Great Commission. The world may laugh and mock. Even our families may reject us, and we may experience great injustices. But if we remain faithful to God and the vision He has given us, He will reward our vision and our faithfulness far beyond our ability to ask or think. Because of our trials and sorrows, we will also have an influence among many people who have endured the trials of a fallen world.

The story of Cinderella carries more truth than we often recognize. It is an analogy of Joseph's true story. Possessing character, beauty, and talents superior to those of her stepmother and stepsisters, Cinderella became a victim of their jealousy. They consigned her to the cellars even as Joseph's brothers consigned him to slavery. But with the supernatural help of the fairy godmother (analogous to God) who recognized her virtues, Cinderella found her way at last into the very center of royal power and influence. As princess and later queen, she, like Joseph, surely must have had empathy for the needy and oppressed because she had once been in that position herself. As such, she would have been highly regarded and beloved by her subjects.

A little-known fact about Joseph: the Pharaoh of Egypt gave him the name, "Zaphenath-paneah," which means "savior of the age" and "God speaks and lives" (Lockyer 1978). This was a fitting name for Joseph; God raised him up to save his generation, and He allowed Joseph to speak the words of the living God.

God will do as much for you and me as we heed His call and do His will.

All Journeys Begin with a First Step
Cinderella's entire life changed the moment she climbed into the coach to head for the ball.

No journey is completed without taking that first step. It may be a baby step, but if God has authorized that small step, He has a plan for its growth.

The Bible tells of four things that are "little" but very successful:

> There are four things which are little on the earth,
> But they are exceedingly wise;
> The ants are a people not strong,
> Yet they prepare their food in the summer;
> The rock badgers are a feeble folk,
> Yet they make their homes in the crags;
> The locusts have no king,
> Yet they all advance in ranks;
> The spider skillfully grasps with its hands,
> And it is in kings' palaces.

> Proverbs 30:24–28

Notice the areas of endeavor in this brief passage. The ants prepare food, the rock badgers prepare lodging, the locusts join together to take on large tasks, and the spider does handwork. The opportunities for tailoring and other small enterprises in the developing world are tremendous. They tend to fall into these categories: preparation of food and specialty foods, construction of prefabricated housing units and their components, manufacturing and agriculture co-ops, and handicraft centers (from stitching of garments and home décor items to lace-making and embroidery).

Notice also these factors:

- The ants prepare in advance.

- The rock badgers, also called conies, cleverly protect themselves, making them almost impossible to trap.

- The locusts know the importance of large numbers and advancing together toward a common goal.

- The spider does its work wherever it finds itself—in a king's palace or a lowly shack.

The implications for us in our missionary work are great.

Let's think ahead. Rather than react to crises, let's respond to world trends in a proactive way. Let's out-think and out-strategize those who oppose Christ. Surely God will pour out His wisdom liberally upon those who ask for greater wisdom to unravel plots, persecution, and opposition tactics. Perhaps we do not have this wisdom because we have not asked for it. The book of James assures us: "If any of you lacks wisdom, let him ask of God, who gives to all liberally and without reproach, and it will be given to him" (James 1:5). James also tells us, "You do not have because you do not ask" (James 4:2b). Let's work together—across denominations and around the world.

Let's do the work that God places before us. We may very well be called before kings and leaders in high places. But let us be content to work among the lowly. We must trust God to lead each of us as He will.

The Bible admonishes us not to despise the day of small beginnings. (See Zechariah 4:10.) The Mississippi River begins as a small stream a thousand miles north of the Gulf of Mexico—a stream so small a child can easily hop over it. Who knows how great a work might be accomplished from one word spoken under the anointing of the Holy Spirit, one fervent prayer, or one act of loving kindness done in the name of Jesus.

Let's believe in great things from our great God!

Let's ask for, and receive, the strategies the Holy Spirit is seeking to implement on this earth. And then, once we have determined them, let's roll up our sleeves and get to work.

We have four billion people to win to Christ Jesus.

And the night is coming.

The Urgent Call

1. What do you see as the foremost trends in the world today? How do these impact missions? How do they impact your involvement in missions?

2. How important is it to have a strategy to reach a particular goal?

3. How important is it to move beyond thinking about missions to actually doing something practical to advance the gospel?

4. How is the Lord leading you right now to engage in missions work?

What Might One Person Do?

I recently heard about a short-term mission team that went to an area of Africa ravaged by the AIDS pandemic. While there, one of the women was impressed by the beautiful hand-dyed fabrics produced in the area. These fabrics were usually turned into shawls, with stitched edges fringed with colorful beads. This woman immediately thought of her friends back home, and the market that might exist for such items in her home city.

The next day she had a private lunch with a Christian evangelist and his wife. Together, they decided to pursue the idea of establishing a handicraft center for the widows of men who had died of AIDS, as well as the older teenage daughters orphaned by AIDS. This woman knew about our handicraft centers in India and presented the model she had heard about. The evangelist and his wife were ecstatic. Immediately, they caught the vision for such a handicraft center. The woman went home to America, and within a matter of days she raised the money to rent a building, convert it into a handicraft center, purchase the machinery necessary for sewing and dying fabrics, and purchase the raw materials for weaving the cloth necessary for the project. The center is now up and running!

This one woman has already arranged ten outlets for the sale of these beautiful shawls. The evangelist and his wife are teaching songs, encouraging the women, telling Bible stories, and are praying with the women who are working at the center that they might be healed emotionally and renewed spiritually.

Who knows what God might do in this region of Africa as new products are developed and more and more widows and orphans accept Christ in the course of engaging in high-quality, handcrafted work?

Heavenly Father, I ask You by the power of Your Holy Spirit to open my heart and mind so I might fully receive Your fresh and creative strategies for my life and work. Show me how to become a more effective Christian witness to the unsaved people around me. Give me a strategy for reaching my lost neighbors and friends. Show me how to become more useful for the advance of the gospel in other nations around the world. I ask this in the name of Jesus, before whom every knee will one day bow. Amen.

And you will know the truth, and the truth will make you free.

John 8:32 (NASB)

WHAT'S KEEPING YOU IN THE CELLAR?

11

Cinderella suffered from one of life's greatest injustices—the treachery of her own family. They kept her in the cellar against her will, forcing her to do the most menial of tasks. She probably spent her days in tears and deep sorrow because she had dreams for her life that she thought would never be fulfilled. She knew she was meant for more in life, but she appeared to herself and others as a victim of her circumstances. Evil seemed to have the last word. There appeared to be no way out—that is, until the appearance of the fairy godmother.

Some of you who read this know that you have received God's call to missions. To the best of your intentions, you want to answer that call, but you feel that life itself has prevented you from doing so. There may be many reasons, all of which seem to you entirely understandable and logical. These are not excuses, but genuine hindrances that come against your will.

Like Cinderella, you feel that you are confined to the cellars of life. While others go on to answer God's call upon their lives, you feel destined to a second-rate life that has no spiritual promise. For reasons beyond your control, you feel that you can never become another William Carey or Amy Carmichael.

For example, I meet many young people who feel called to missions but feel they cannot become involved until they pay off their student loans. This is indeed a real burden for many young people. Today's college education may easily cost $200,000 or $300,000—unheard of thirty or forty years ago. Unless a student receives a generous scholarship, he is forced to take out loans and pay them back with interest. This puts him in debt for years. How can a young person even consider a life in missions when he must make money to pay off those loans as well as raise a family?

For others, the hindrance is a relationship. A person is called to missions but is in love with, engaged to, or married to a person who feels no such call. He or she may have a vision for missions, but responsibilities to children from another marriage may inhibit leaving for a place far away from those children. Or maybe it is responsibility toward a parent or some other family member or friend who is dependent upon others for help. Maybe he or she has to deal with the implications of having a child out of wedlock or guilt issues from having an abortion.

Others may suffer from a chronic medical condition or a physical handicap. Still others may feel handicapped by mental problems that may be caused by chemical imbalances. They may need to take medications that aren't easily available in a remote part of the world.

Maybe they are dealing with issues that stem from childhood physical, sexual, or emotional abuse by a parent or other relative. Perhaps they have suffered from an abusive, neglectful, or emotionally insensitive spouse and feel the need to see a counselor who can help them deal with these problems.

Spiritual hindrances can also keep us in the cellar, preventing us from doing all that God has for us to do and enjoying all that God wants to do through us. By spiritual hindrance I mean any hurdle caused by a deficient relationship with God Himself. Sad to say, not everyone who goes to church is sensitive to the things of the Lord. To some degree, we all stand in this category. We may stand up and sing praise songs with seeming enthusiasm, but in the depths of our hearts, there is a block against God and His will for our lives. These spiritual hindrances take many forms and variations.

Lack of faith. In the Bible, faith does not mean adherence to a creed or concept, but trust in the person of Jesus Christ. Do we believe that Jesus is trustworthy? Is He capable of doing all that He promises? Do we believe He is able to do above and beyond anything we ask or think? Do we believe that He is able to save to the uttermost? Are we willing to commit our lives and destinies into His hands, knowing that He will do great and mighty things through us?

Not all people in the church are able to make this kind of commitment to Christ, enabling them to go anywhere or do anything. This is what the Bible calls unbelief or lack of faith. In the end, all spiritual hindrances come from this all-too-common condition. *They are signs or symptoms, if you will, of a deeper spiritual problem.*

Spiritual pride. Pride means to think of ourselves more highly than we ought to think. It means to trust our own abilities more than God's. As prideful persons, we may have difficulty submitting to authority because we trust our own judgment above that of any other person. It may mean refusing to be accountable to others. Effective missionaries cannot afford to give themselves to spiritual pride without it affecting their ministry in a negative way. Spiritual pride has crippled or killed many a mission calling.

Addictions. By addiction, I mean a compulsive need for anything apart from God. At heart, addictions are a form of idolatry because they steal time, money, and energy from our relationship to our heavenly Father. In return, they leave us with nothing. Millions of people in our churches are addicted to sex, alcohol, tobacco, drugs, pornography, and so on. They hunger for power and money. These things become more important in our lives than God. We cut ourselves off from Him. We are unable to hear His voice. We sacrifice our ability to discern. Addictions occur because we have believed lies about ourselves and God. These lies may come from negative experiences or from our greatest adversary, Satan. It is impossible to become an effective missionary or other worker for the Great Commission when our loyalties to God are challenged by our compulsions.

Spiritual strongholds, besetting sins. All of us face spiritual obstacles in our lives. We live in a fallen world, and we are bound to face tribulation, temptation, and opposition. The best way to counter these negative forces is to admit our limitations and put our trust in God to help us transcend them. Instead, many people, sometimes unknowingly, trust in their own power rather than Christ's. This always leads to defeat. When defeat repeats itself, the defeated person begins to feel that his or her situation is hopeless, that he or she will never find deliverance in this life. This person experiences a stronghold of Satan or a "besetting sin." These people, not finding the power of the gospel in their lives, find it difficult to get enthusiastic about the power of the gospel in the lives of others.

Worldly standards. More than in any previous generation, the standards of the world have crept into our churches. How a person lives on Sunday morning at church may have no relation to the way he lives from Sunday afternoon through Saturday night. Materialism has taken over the lives of many Christians, and they seem to live like anyone else. Family problems, divorce, debt, and bankruptcy are consuming the lives and effectiveness

of people who are Christians. Such people cannot give themselves to the things of God because they have their own set of
priorities.

Unforgiveness. Because we live in a fallen world, we inevitably
come into contact with people who hurt or offend us in some way.
Our Lord admonishes us to forgive such people in the same spirit
that He has forgiven us. Failure or refusal to forgive others not
only separates us from others but from God Himself, making us
unable to become effective witnesses to His forgiving grace.

Moral failures. All have experienced the reality of our own
moral weakness in some way; however, some may feel completely unworthy to get involved in missions because they feel
too tainted by what the church or society regards as "deep" sin.
Some may have had one or more children out of wedlock, or
some may be deeply involved in homosexual or lesbian relationships, or frequent "houses of ill-repute." Some may have had
affairs in or out of marriage, or even engaged in abnormal sexual
practices. Failure to deal with these sins can keep one from experiencing the full power of God in his/her life.

Real or imagined guilt. Knowing our fallen natures so well, we
may feel guilt over real or imagined sins. Feelings of guilt over
imagined sins can cause as much sense of separation from God
as real sins. Failure to come to terms with God over these things
can reduce our enthusiasm for the good news.

Unconfessed sin. The Bible plainly tells us that all have sinned
and fallen short of the glory of God, and that the person who
says he does not sin is a liar. Because we all have the tendencies
of the flesh within us, it is easy to rationalize our sin and fail to
confront it in our lives. But unconfessed sin is still sin. It still
has power over us if we do not acknowledge its presence in our
lives, and we cannot experience the cleansing power of the Holy
Spirit. Unconfessed sin makes us poor witnesses for the gospel.

Lukewarmness and spiritual apathy. In the book of Revelation,
we are given a portrait of Laodicean Christians who are neither

cold nor hot in faith. They are rich in the things of the world. Their church may have a wonderful program, and they may have a fancy veneer of religion, complete with Bible studies and regular attendance at Sunday school and church, but they show no power or vitality in their faith.

Seared conscience. A Christian can commit a blatant sin and ignore the Holy Spirit so often with so many rationalizations that he comes to the point where he sees nothing wrong with his besetting sin and defies anyone who tries to help him come to repentance and confess his sin.

The Urgent Call

1. Take an inventory of yourself. What obstacles do you perceive as keeping you from effectively doing your part to fulfill the Great Commission? Are these obstacles internal, external, or infernal (amplified by Satan)?

2. How willing are you to submit to the truth of the Holy Spirit? To what degree do you find yourself unsubmissive? Remember that submission to the Holy Spirit is often a process. Look to the Lord to guide and strengthen you so that you are able to submit.

No experience of salvation. We may be kept in the cellar simply because we have never committed our lives to Jesus Christ and become reconciled to God. Dedication to missions is meaningless apart from this basic commitment.

Satan uses all of these and other issues to instill in us a sense of failure and defeat. When he has convinced us that we cannot overcome these issues, then he has won the battle and has neutralized another possible threat to his dominion. That is what Satan wants above all else—power. When he neutralizes a child of God, he wins.

We must remember that what is impossible for us is not impossible for God. In our own power, we are not able to overcome these obstacles, but God is able to do anything. Too often, we keep our eyes upon our insufficiency rather than God's sufficiency. Like Peter, who tried to walk upon water but sank into the waves, we do not keep our eyes upon Jesus but upon our own limitations. Under such conditions, we will always be victims rather than victors.

How do we get out of the cellar? By keeping our eyes upon Jesus. Peter failed in life just as miserably as we do, but he became a great missionary for Jesus Christ because he learned to get his eyes off his failures and onto Jesus.

Peter found that Jesus was far more patient with him than he was with himself. He discovered that Jesus had the power to do in him what he was not able to do himself. Let that become your experience as well.

Here are some specific steps you can take to escape from your cellar:

1. Make sure you have a relationship with God.

2. Name and renounce your besetting sin. The only sin that God will not forgive is the sin you do not confess. (Use John 1:9–10.)

3. Invite God to open your heart and mind and fill you with His Holy Spirit.

4. Commit time each day to read, meditate, and memorize the Word of God.

5. Ask God to help you discover His will for your life.

6. When you learn to love God, you will learn to love people. Ask God to show you the best way for you to both love God and people.

7. Associate with godly people in a Bible-believing church, becoming accountable to a godly friend or a small group of godly people.

8. Evaluate how God has gifted you.

9. Make a commitment to do what God wills.

10. Expect God to do things through you that will give you pleasure and bless you as they bless others.

As you seek with God's help to come out of your cellar, read such books as Neil Anderson's *Bondage Breaker* and Tom White's *Breaking Strongholds*.

As you keep your eyes upon Jesus, you will discover that He will enable you to replace old patterns and ungodly habits with godly habits. Then you will become increasingly able to emerge from the cellars of life and enter the castle that God intends for you.

What Might One Person Do?

Jesus never calls perfect people to do His work today any more than He called perfect disciples to spread the gospel in the first century. Nor did the disciples suddenly become perfect after they were filled with the Holy Spirit. They still had passions and prejudices foreign to God's purposes. What marked their ministry was not their perfection but their willingness to learn important lessons, first from Jesus, later from the Holy Spirit. When prompted by the Holy Spirit, they were willing to subdue their natural inclinations and obey Christ.

Read the biographies of well-known missionaries, evangelists, or church planters such as William Carey, Hudson Taylor, and David Brainerd. Note the obstacles they faced before they answered God's call and how God changed their lives. They continued to face obstacles after they obeyed the Lord, but God worked in spite of their weaknesses. Note the ways they remained teachable to the Holy Spirit.

Heavenly Father, there is so much in my life that is out of control. Help me to get out of my cellar by renouncing my limitations, putting them under Your control, and I fix my eyes upon You so that I may move in Your strength rather than my weakness. Amen.

*Then I looked, and behold, a white cloud, and on
the cloud sat One like the Son of Man,
Having on His head a golden crown, and in His
hand a sharp sickle. And another angel came out of
the temple, crying with a loud voice to Him who
sat on the cloud, "Put in Your sickle and reap, for
the hour to reap has come, for the harvest of the
earth is ripe." So He who sat on the cloud put in
His sickle over the earth, and the earth was reaped.*

Revelation 14:14–16

THE URGENCY OF THE NIGHT

Cinderella's story took place because a young woman desired a better life. When opportunity presented itself, she acted on that opportunity. She could have wallowed in self-pity and done nothing. She could have rejected all offered help and rested on pride, even if it meant continued misery. She could have seen herself as a victim of fate.

She did not let her circumstances stop her. She let the fairy godmother's power go to work for her. Who could tell if, or when, another opportunity might present itself?

Cinderella took her opportunity, and she succeeded! Against all odds, she won the heart of the prince who let no stone go unturned to find her and make her his bride. Once he found her, the royal wedding took place, and Cinderella moved from cellar to castle, from servant girl to princess. She lived "happily ever after," which means she must have become the progenitor of future kings, queens, princes, princesses, dukes, duchesses, and other royal persons. Instead of surviving as a virtual slave, she now prospered as head of a royal household, complete with her own butlers, maids, and other royal servants. Perhaps she even joined her new husband in conducting affairs of state, which made her a well-known figure in other kingdoms as well. It is good to remember that all of Cinderella's success, and that of her progeny through succeeding generations, depended upon her success during an exceedingly small window of time.

Everything had to take place before midnight. At the stroke of midnight, any efforts by Cinderella to capture the love of a prince had to be complete or she would utterly fail forever.

———◆◆◆◆———

Christ plainly tells us that once our window of opportunity to fulfill the Great Commission has passed, we will have no further opportunity. We like to think that the God of love and grace will give us endless opportunities to preach the gospel, but that is not to be.

In Matthew 24–25, in plain words and parables, Jesus tells His disciples that this present age will end. "This gospel of the kingdom will be preached in all the world as a witness to all the nations, and then the end will come" (Matthew 24:14).

"But of that day and hour no one knows, not even the angels of heaven, but My Father only," Jesus tells us in Matthew 24:36. Later, he warns, "Therefore you also be ready, for the Son of man is coming at an hour you do not expect" (v. 44).

The God of love and grace is also the God of truth, righteousness, and justice. God is the eternal judge, and judgment will surely come. After that, the day of opportunity will pass. The night will come when no man can work.

For many people, the night has already come. Even so, too many of us live as if the day will go on forever.

In many ways, we are lulled into thinking that we live in a world that has no end. We have fully swallowed a misinterpreted understanding of the statement, "Life goes on." Apart from those who suffer from serious disease or are in a desperate life-and-death circumstance, few of us awake from sleep and think that today could be our last day.

When it comes to spiritual growth, we tend to think we have much time in which to mature in Christ Jesus. We put off the personal disciplines we know are essential, not because we think they are unimportant, but because we feel no urgency to pursue them today.

When it comes to church involvement, we think we have years ahead of us to become more active in attending, serving, or participating in outreach activities. Again, we do not believe church involvement is unimportant. We simply do not perceive that it is a priority now.

When it comes to missions, we think we have plenty of time to reach the world.

But in truth, we do not know. As much as we human beings try to predict when Christ will come again, we do not know and cannot know. Jesus made that clear.

After describing in great detail the signs of the times and the end of the age, Jesus said:

> Heaven and earth will pass away... But of that day and hour no one knows, not even the angels of heaven... but My Father alone... Therefore be on alert, for you do not know what hour your Lord is coming.
>
> Matthew 24:35–44

The time is coming when there will be no possibility of additional light—no dawn, no man-made solutions to the darkness. The time is coming for every person when there will be no possibility of another minute of life.

What then?

Jesus defined that moment very clearly. Those who know Him will enter eternity in the close presence of God the Father, God the Son, and God the Holy Spirit. Those who do not will enter an utter and agonizing darkness that never ends.

Perhaps that sounds threatening and ominous. It doesn't need to be, nor did Jesus intend His Words to sound that way.

In the Gospels, Jesus associated the preaching of the gospel with the harvest.

During Jesus's earthly ministry two thousand years ago, the average Jew associated the harvest with the Feast of Weeks, one of the biggest festivals of the Jewish year. That festival followed seven weeks plus a day, or fifty days, after the Passover. It was a time of harvest celebration, when people glorified God for supplying an abundant harvest. In thanksgiving, they offered to Him their first fruits of the harvest. In God's acceptance of the first fruits, the community held a feast of celebration in which everyone was invited because all had labored together to bring about the abundance.

This fifty-day period later became known as "The Pentecost." It also was known throughout the Jewish world as the "Jubilee," a word meaning "liberty." According to Jewish law, every fiftieth year was to be marked by a year of rest for the land, a year of release for slaves and a return of land to original families.

Jesus alluded to this great festival when He announced His mission before the people of Nazareth from Isaiah 61:1: "The Spirit of the Lord is upon Me because He has anointed Me to preach the gospel to the poor; He has sent Me to heal the brokenhearted, to proclaim liberty to the captives and recovery of sight to the blind, to set at liberty those who are oppressed, to proclaim the acceptable year of the Lord" (See Luke 4:18–19.)

Jesus referred to the Feast of Weeks again when he said, "The harvest is great, but the laborers are few. Therefore, pray to the Lord of the harvest to send out laborers into His harvest" (Matthew 9:38). When Jesus suffered crucifixion and was buried, He rose on the third day, becoming the "first fruits of them that sleep" (1 Corinthians 15:20). God the Father showed His acceptance of Jesus's offering by bestowing His Holy Spirit upon Jesus's disciples on the fiftieth day. All of this is joined with Jesus's assertion that "you shall be witnesses to Me in Jerusalem, in all Judea and Samaria, and to the end of the earth" (Acts 1:8).

Harvest and celebration—in Jesus Christ and the Great Commission, these ideas are joined. In Revelation 14:16, we see a picture of Jesus reaping the earth when "the harvest of the earth is great." Jesus prays for laborers because He sees the great harvest as a time of celebration. The more the laborers, the more joyful the celebration. He doesn't want anyone to miss out. To participate in the harvest is to participate in abundance, liberty, and indescribable joy before God, to experience His words "well done, good and faithful servant."

Harvest and celebration mean to experience the reality of the Hallelujah Chorus:

> Hallelujah: for the Lord God Omnipotent reigneth. The kingdom of this world has become the Kingdom of our Lord, and of His Christ; and He shall reign for ever and ever. King of kings, and Lord of lords!

Even Cinderella's staggering promotion to the royal family is nothing next to this. In his book, 90 *Minutes in Heaven*, Don Piper tries to relate what happened to him when he found himself for a brief time in heaven, following his head-on collision with an eighteen-wheel truck that left him declared officially dead. Even in his small glimpse into eternity, his words fail him when he tries to describe the people, sights, music, joy, and worship that he experienced. Those few precious moments of rare revelation have reshaped his earthly life. His experience made him totally aware of the fragility of earthly life. It has renewed his resolve to take as many people to heaven as he can in the earthly time remaining to him.

The Urgent Call

1. Ask the Lord Jesus Christ to give you greater compassion for lost souls.

2. Pray for those who daily are preaching and teaching the gospel of Jesus Christ around the world.

3. Open your heart and mind to ways in which you might become more involved in outreach to the lost.

Our earthly time is very short. Jesus warns that the harvest has come and will soon pass. Our opportunity to participate comes quickly, and it passes quickly. The night will come when we can no longer work.

In 2010, a very average-looking, obscure forty-eight-year-old Scottish woman named Susan Boyle stunned critics and millions of people with her unexpected and wonderful singing abilities on the British television show, *Britain's Got Talent*. Until her amazing performance, she was totally unknown. Overnight, she became a superstar, with opportunities for success she never had before. Clearly, she enjoyed her moment under the sun.

Her opportunity came but for a moment. She could very well not have done it. In fact, she almost abandoned her plan to audition because she thought she was too old; however, a former voice coach convinced her to do it to seek a musical career in tribute to her ever-loyal mother. If she had not heeded her voice coach's advice and taken her moment of opportunity, Susan Boyle would probably have remained unknown for the rest of her life.

Today, Jesus Christ calls us to join Him in His great harvest and the inevitable celebration that will take place after its ingathering. The great celebration He has planned dwarfs any fame and fortune that Susan Boyle may experience, or that Cinderella could have possibly dreamed. His loyalty and faithfulness to us as our heavenly Father far exceeds the loyalty of any human parent. We do it for His everlasting love and grace for us.

Our moment is here. Soon, it will be gone. Then night will surely come when no man can work.

What opportunity has God given you to join the harvest? Now ... will you take it?

What Might One Person Do?

In April 2007, a massacre took the lives of more than thirty people at Virginia Polytechnic Institute and State University. Two weeks later, in a sermon at Virginia Tech, Philip Yancey noted what Samuel Johnson said about when a man is about to be hanged, "It concentrates his mind wonderfully." Yancey continued, "When you're strapped to a body board after a serious accident, it concentrates the mind. When you survive a massacre at Virginia Tech, it concentrates the mind. I realized how much of my life focused on trivial things. During those seven hours, I didn't think about how many books I had sold or what kind of car I drove (it was being towed to a junkyard anyway). All that mattered boiled down to four questions: *Whom do I love? Whom will I miss? What have I done with my life? And am I ready for what's next?* Ever since that day, I've tried to live with those questions at the forefront." (See *Christianity Today*, June 2007.)

All over the world today in places unknown to most of us, hundreds of millions of people live with no answers for these ultimate questions. In a few words, hymn writer Fanny Crosby captures the reality of their need and their help:

Down in the human heart, crushed by the tempter,
Feelings lie buried that grace can restore;
Touched by a loving heart, wakened by kindness,
Chords that were broken will vibrate once more.

If you have read this far, it likely means that God has already called you, equipped you and stirred your own heart to bear His grace, loving heart, and kindness to a crushed and broken world. Beginning today, join Him in His work to:

Rescue the perishing, care for the dying, Jesus is merciful, Jesus will save.

Heavenly Father, awaken me to the full reality of the world in which I live. Let me see this world as You see it. Let me hear the heart cry of the person who does not know Jesus Christ as Savior. Create a compelling desire with me to do everything I can do to be Your witness in this sin-sick world. I ask this in the name of Jesus, the one who never fails us nor forsakes us. Amen.

For Further Reading/ Bibliography

Abraham, T. Valson. *Crumbs from the Table.* Kumbanad, India: India Bible College & Seminary, 2008.

Abraham, T. Valson, et al. *A Tribute to a Faithful Servant of God.* Kumbanad, India: India Bible College & Seminary, 2008.

Alcorn, Randy. *Money, Possessions and Eternity.* Wheaton, Ill.: Tyndale House Publishers, 1989.

Anderson, Neil T. *The Bondage Breaker: Overcoming negative thoughts, irrational feelings, habitual sins.* Eugene, OR: Harvest House Publishers, 2nd ed., 2000.

Barna, George. *The Seven Faith Tribes.* Brentwood, Tenn.: Tyndale House Publishers, 2009.

Barrett, David. "Annual Statistical Table on Global Mission 2001." *International Bulletin of Missionary Research*, January 2001, p. 24–25. www.travelingteam.org.

Barrett, David (ed.). *World Christian Encyclopedia.* 2001 edition, Oxford University Press, 2001.

Bonk, Jonathan J. *Between Past and Future: Evangelical mission entering the twenty first century*. Pasadena, CA.: William Carey Library, 2003.

Borthwick, Paul. *A Mind for Missions*. Colorado Springs: Navpress Publishing Group, 1987.

Brooks, Gerald. *Emotions of a Leader*. Dallas: Brooks Ministries, 2004.

Bryant, David. *In the Gap: What it means to be a world Christian*. Madison, Wisc.: Intervarsity Missions, 1979.

Bush, Luis, and Beverly Pegues. *The Move of the Holy Spirit in the 10/40 Window*. Seattle, Wash.: Youth With A Mission Publishing, 1999.

Coggins, Wade T. *Reaching Our Generation*. Pasadena, Cal.: William Carey Library, 1982.

Conn, Harvie M. *Reaching the Unreached*. Phillipsburg, N.J.: Presbyterian and Reformed Publishing Company, 1984.

Copeland, Luther E. *World Mission and World Survival*. Nashville: Broadman Press, 1985.

Covey, Stephen M.R. *The Speed of Trust: The One Thing That Changes Everything*. New York: Simon & Schuster, 2006.

Dean, Judith M., Julie Schaffner, and L. S. Stephen Smith. *Attacking Poverty In the Developing World*. Waynesboro, Ga.: Authentic Media, 2005.

Duin, Julia. "Public Christian Symbols Backed." *The Washington Times*, December 31, 2004.

Fernando, Ajith. *The Supremacy of Christ*. Wheaton, IL: Crossway Books, 1995.

Fernando, Ajith. *Crucial Questions About Hell*. Wheaton, IL: Crossway Books, 1991.

Garrison, V. David. *The Nonresidential Missionary: A new strategy and the people it serves.* Birmingham, AL: MARC and New Hope, 1990.

Getz, Gene A., *Biblical Theology of Material Possessions.* Chicago: Moody Press, 1990.

Glasser, Arthur F. *Announcing the Kingdom: The story of God's mission in the Bible.* Grand Rapids, MI: Baker Academic, 2003.

Graham, Billy. *God's Ambassador: A Lifelong Mission of Giving Hope to the World, as Witnessed by Photographer Russ Busby.* San Diego, CA: Billy Graham Evangelistic Association/ Tehabi Books, 1999.

Graham, Billy. *Just As I Am: the Autobiography of Billy Graham.* San Francisco: Harper, 1997.

Guthrie, Stan. *Missions in the Third Millennium: 21 key trends for the 21st century.* Carlisle, Cumbria: Paternoster Press, 2000.

Hesselgrave, David J. *Today's Choices for Tomorrow's Mission.* Grand Rapids, Mich.: Academie Books, 1988.

Jaffarian, Michael. "The Statistical State of the North American Protestant Missions Movement," in *International Bulletin of Missionary Research,* January 2008, p. 36.

Jacobs, Joseph. *The Cinder Maid.* n.d. http://www.pitt.edu/~dash/ type0510a.html#jacobs.

Jenkins, Philip. *The Next Christendom: The coming of global Christianity.* New York: Oxford University Press, 2002.

Kane, Herbert J. *Wanted: World Christians.* Grand Rapids, Mich.: Baker Book House, 1986.

Kyle, John E. *The Unfinished Task.* Ventura, Cal.: Regal Books, 1984.

Lockyer, Herbert. *All the Men of the Bible.* 24th printing. Zondervan: Grand Rapids, MI, 1978.

Mangalwadi, Vishal and Ruth. *The Legacy of William Carey, A Model for Transformation of a Culture.* Crossway Books: Wheaton, IL, 1993.

McGavran, Donald A., *Ethnic Realities and the Church: Lessons from India.* Pasadena, CA: William Carey Library, 1979.

Moreau, Scott A., Gary R. Corwin, and Gary B. McGee. *Introducing World Missions: A Biblical, historical and practical survey.* Grand Rapids, MI: Baker Academic, 1955.

Myers, Bryant L. *Exploring World Mission.* Monrovia, Cal.: World Vision International, 2003.

Peters, George W. *A Biblical Theology of Missions.* Chicago: Moody Press, 1972.

Peterson, Roger P. *Maximum Impact Short-Term Mission: The God-commanded, repetitive deployment of swift, temporary, non-professional missionaries.* Minneapolis, MN: STEMPress, 2003.

Piper, Don. 90 *Minutes in Heaven: A true story of death and life.* Ada, MI: Revell Books, 2004.

Piper, John. *Let the Nations Be Glad! The supremacy of God in missions.* Grand Rapids, MI: Baker Books, 1993.

Pirolo, Neal. *Serving As Senders: How to care for your missionaries while they are preparing to go, while they are on the field, when they return home.* San Diego, CA: Emmaus Road International, 1991.

Pudaite, Rochunga. *The Book that Set My People Free.* Wheaton, IL: Tyndale House Publishers, 1982.

Ronning, Halvor. *Who We Are—Home for Bible Translators.* www.bibletranslators.org/?page_id=7

Stearns, Richard. *The Hole in Our Gospel.* Nashville, TN: Thomas Nelson, 2009. p. 122–216.

The Census in India. *Census of India Website: Office of the Registrar & Census Commissioner, India.* http://censusindia.gov.in/ (India census figures of 2001 compared with numbers gained from personal knowledge learned through IGO evangelists who work in area.)

Telford, Tom. *Today's All-Star Missions Churches: Strategies to help your church get into the game.* Grand Rapids, MI: Baker Books, 2001.

Toycen, Dave. *The Power of Generosity: How to transform vision for transforming global missions.* Waynesboro, GA: Authentic Media, 2004.

Verwer, George. *Out of the Comfort Zone: A compelling vision for transforming global missions.* Bloomington, MN: Bethany House Publishers, 2000.

Wagner, Peter C. *Breaking Strongholds in Your City: How to identify the enemy's territory in your city and pray for its deliverance.* Ventura, CA: Regal Books, 1993.

Wagner, Peter C. *Stop the World I Want to Get On.* Glendale, CA: G/L Publications, 1976.

Wellman, Sam. *William Carey, Father of Modern Missions.* Uhrichsville, OH: Barbour Publishing, 1997.

White, Tom. *Breaking Strongholds: How spiritual warfare sets captives free.* Ventura, CA: Vine Books, 1993.

Willmer, Wesley K. *Revolution in Generosity: Transforming stewards to be rich toward God.* Chicago: Moody Publishers, 2008.

Wycliffe Bible Translators. www.wycliffe.org/about/statistics.aspx. *Personal notes taken in a History of Christian Expansion class at Fuller Theological Seminary, Pasadena, CA, 1979.

ABOUT INDIA GOSPEL OUTREACH

India Gospel Outreach (IGO) is dedicated to evangelizing all three thousand ethnic groups of India by planting dynamic churches in all twenty-seven thousand-plus zip codes.

IGO has been a member of the Evangelical Council for Evangelical Accountability (ECFA) since 1989. We adhere to the Lausanne Covenant and the National Association of Evangelicals Statement of Faith.

Who we are: We are a partnership of Indian and Western Christians facilitating mobilization, training, sending, and supporting Indian evangelists and church planters to reach all of India for Jesus Christ.

The people we serve: We serve in India, expatriate Indian communities in other nations, and Indian residents of the United States.

Why we serve: India Gospel Outreach's passion is to fulfill the Great Commission in Matthew 28:18–20.

How we serve: India Gospel Outreach starts new Bible-training centers; trains and sends Indian evangelists and church planters; aids poor people of India with relief, education, and development; and enlists intercessors to pray for spiritual awakening in India.

Sponsoring evangelists and students: At India Gospel Outreach we ask for sponsors of evangelists and students—generally, fifty dollars to $100 per month for a student and ninety dollars to $200 per month for an evangelist. If these amounts are too much for a contributor, we welcome partial monthly support. Those who become sponsors are given photos and a short biographical statement about their evangelist or student, along with suggestions for daily prayer. Sponsorship provides for the basic needs of the evangelist or student—food, housing, and clothing. This support is necessary because our evangelists work to win the lost in unreached areas. There are no indigenous churches to support their efforts. After an unchurched area develops a body of baptized and discipled believers, evangelists gradually become supported by the congregation they have established, and their support is transferred to another person. We have a growing number of students and evangelists and thus, a growing need for sponsors.

You can help: The work of India Gospel Outreach is made possible by free-will contributions of individuals, churches, and organizations. All gifts are tax deductible. We invite your consideration, prayers and participation!

- Website: www.indiago.org
- Email: igo@indiago.org
- Phone: (909) 948–2404
- Fax: (909) 948–2406

Proceeds from the sale of this book will be used for the fulfillment of the Great Commission through the ministry of India Gospel Outreach.

Please Share with Others:

- Suggest *The Cinderella Challenge* to your family, friends, pastor, church mission board, elders, etc.

- Use *The Cinderella Challenge* in a small group study to spark your friends' vision and enlarge their global passion.

- Talk about *The Cinderella Challenge* on Facebook, Twitter, MySpace, and other social media.

- Encourage your local bookstore to carry *The Cinderella Challenge*. It is available through India Gospel Outreach and Tate Publishing.

- Purchase additional copies of *The Cinderella Challenge* as gifts.

- Write a positive review of *The Cinderella Challenge* on www.amazon.com.

Please Contact Me: tvalsonabraham@indiago.org

To learn more about *The Cinderella Challenge* and India Gospel Outreach, please visit www.cinderellachallenge.com.

THIS DAY,
I COMMIT MYSELF TO:

1. Make Jesus Christ and His glorious kingdom the highest priority in my life.

2. Order the relationships of my life—my spouse, children, friends, and church—according to His will.

3. Make top priority the proclamation of the good news among members of my family, friends, neighbors, and people in places where it is not known.

4. Give generously and sacrificially for the sake of Jesus Christ and His glory in whatever way He directs me.

5. Trust God to empower me with new opportunities rather than become discouraged by my circumstances and personal limitations.

6. Trust God to use my unique gifts, talents, and circumstances to present the gospel to those who have never heard it.

7. Study my Bible diligently and learn how to share my own testimony of faith with others.

8. Learn all I can about other cultures, praying for opportunities to make international friends, and God-given open doors to share the good news with them.

9. Share the message of this book with at least five friends. I make this commitment in full recognition of my limitations, but trusting in Jesus Christ, my Savior and Lord, to help me to fulfill it.

10. Pray, both personally and corporately, for God's strength for my own life, for friends, loved ones, and for the revelation of Jesus Christ and His glory around the world.

Signed _____

Date _____

THE 2020 PRAYER
VISION FOR INDIA

With God's help, I commit myself to the 2020 Prayer Vision for India. I will pray with God-given faith, authority and boldness to remove all barriers to the proclamation of the gospel in India, and to saturate all of India with the Good News of Jesus Christ.

A. Defeat of all spiritual opposition to the gospel.

B. Open hearts to the good news in every postal code of India.

C. More church planters trained at India Bible College and Seminary and other IGO training centers to reach every Indian postal code with the gospel.

D. Revival in all of India's church groups.

E. United efforts to reach all of India for Christ.

F. An end to India's caste system.

G. Massive outreach of evangelists to all of India's youth and cities.

H. Spirit-led transformation of Indian attitudes toward women and children.

I. True religious freedom in all of India.

J. Effective outreach to Indians living in 130 nations.

Signed   _____

Date   _____

About the Author
Rev. Dr. T. Valson Abraham

Rev. Dr. T. Valson Abraham is founder and president of India Gospel Outreach, dedicated to planting dynamic churches in each of India's three thousand castes and tribes. Part of this vision includes planting churches in each of India's twenty-seven thousand-plus zip codes.

God has used Valson to start several Bible colleges and institutions throughout India. For over forty years his ministry of extensive preaching, teaching, training, mentoring, writing, broadcasting and servant leadership has increased mission awareness and outreach and blessed many in India, the United States and around the world.

Born and reared in India, Valson is the oldest grandson of the late Pastors K. E. Abraham and P.T. Chacko and son of Pastor Stephen Abraham. Together, these three generations have contributed almost a century of experience in evangelizing, planting and growing churches among the most unreached peoples of India. In this regard, Valson has served in many leadership roles in his denomination, the Bible Society of India and in numerous teaching roles to further the gospel in India.

Valson is also Director of India Bible College and Seminary in Kumbanad, Kerala, where hundreds of students train each year for full-time church planting ministries. Its graduates have planted more than twelve thousand churches of various denominations in all states of India.

Valson and his wife Laly have four grown children.

e|LIVE

listen|imagine|view|experience

AUDIO BOOK DOWNLOAD INCLUDED WITH THIS BOOK!

In your hands you hold a complete digital entertainment package. In addition to the paper version, you receive a free download of the audio version of this book. Simply use the code listed below when visiting our website. Once downloaded to your computer, you can listen to the book through your computer's speakers, burn it to an audio CD or save the file to your portable music device (such as Apple's popular iPod) and listen on the go!

How to get your free audio book digital download:

1. Visit www.tatepublishing.com and click on the e|LIVE logo on the home page.
2. Enter the following coupon code:
   81f7-b78b-396a-8e18-ee92-48aa-e5c6-e0b5
3. Download the audio book from your e|LIVE digital locker and begin enjoying your new digital entertainment package today!